Integrating Corporate
Risk Management

Integrating Corporate Risk Management

Prakash A. Shimpi, FSA, CFA

Editor

David Durbin, Ph.D.
David S. Laster, Ph.D.
Carolyn P. Helbling
Daniel Helbling

Contributing Editors

TEXERE

New York · London

Photographs:
  Tony Stone, NY
  The Stock Market, NY

This book is printed on acid-free paper.

Copyright © 1999, 2001 Swiss Re New Markets, New York, NY

Published by TEXERE LLC.
Published simultaneously in the United Kingdom.

This publication is designed to provide accurate and authoritative information in regard to the subject matter covered. It is sold with the understanding that the publisher is not engaged in rendering professional services. If the professional advice or other expert assistance is required, the services of a competent professional person should be sought.

Library of Congress Cataloging-in-Publication Data has been applied for.

ISBN: 1-58799-061-X

Printed in the United States of America

10 9 8 7 6 5 4 3 2

Foreword

The business landscape of a corporation is always in a state of change. The increasingly rigorous demands of investors mean that it is less likely that businesses with inadequate rates of return will be able to survive. For corporate managers, therefore, the pressure continues to grow in the search for alternative ways to increase shareholder returns. Capital management and risk management have become centerpieces of corporate governance as companies look to solutions that transcend national boundaries and conventional market constraints.

At the same time, the financial services industry has undergone tremendous change. One development that benefits corporations is the convergence of wholesale financial and risk management services offered by banks and reinsurers. As the distinctions blur between corporate finance, risk management and insurance, corporations have the opportunity to achieve a higher level of capital efficiency by drawing on new ideas that bridge these disciplines.

Swiss Re is pleased to offer this book as a resource to managers who want to learn about these new ideas. Many of the topics raised in this book address not only how an organization views its risks but also how it views itself. The process of integrating risk management is one of self-appraisal—What risks can the company withstand? What activities are fundamental to the core of the company's business? What is an acceptable level of risk for the entire company?

This appraisal touches on the underlying message of this book: Capital and risk are closely interrelated, and an efficient management of one must entail an efficient management of the other. Ultimately, companies find that to answer these questions they have to consider more fundamental structural issues. A constant and close cooperation must develop between those responsible for directing activities, those responsible for raising capital to fund those activities, and those responsible for covering the risks that the activities entail.

It is no longer a matter of managing only capital or risk; it is one of managing capital at risk.

Walter B. Kielholz
Chief Executive Officer
Swiss Reinsurance Company

Contents

If the study of all these sciences which we have enumerated, should ever bring us to their mutual association and relationship, and teach us the nature of the ties which bind them together, I believe that the diligent treatment of them will forward the objects which we have in view, and that the labor, which otherwise would be fruitless, will be well bestowed.

PLATO

Introduction

We used to think that if we knew one, we knew two, because one and one are two. We are finding out that we must learn a great deal more about "and."

Sir Arthur Eddington[1]
(1882–1944)
Professor of Astronomy,
Cambridge University

This is a book about "and":

- Capital management "and" risk management,
- Corporate finance "and" insurance,
- Treasurer "and" risk manager,
- Single risks "and" integrated risks,
- Separate markets "and" converging markets,
- "and" more.

The recent development of new tools and techniques in corporate finance, insurance and risk management requires that we learn a great deal more about the "and" that connects them. This book is our contribution to that effort.

Our starting point is the recognition that risk is the lifeblood of a corporation. It provides the opportunity to turn a profit, but raises the specter of ruin. Managers often tackle risk head-on wherever it appears. The line manager in a manufacturing company minimizes the risk of interruption in the production process by ensuring that the machinery is of the highest quality. The treasurer who receives funds from abroad manages the firm's exposure to foreign exchange risk. The risk manager makes sure that each building owned by the corporation has adequate fire and earthquake insurance. Yet another manager determines the pension liability that the corporation undertakes.

How, then, can the management of this myriad of risks be brought into some common framework for consistency and efficiency? The answer is actually quite simple, but, as always, the devil is in the detail.

It is not necessary for every manager to use the same risk management technique. *What matters most is that they adopt the same framework that embraces a common view of risk.* This framework should allow each manager to express the risks he or she faces and its consequences to the whole firm in a manner that is accessible to other managers. It should allow a bottom-up assessment of risk that results in a corporation-wide risk management perspective. And it should enable top management to dictate the corporate risk appetite and translate that into instructions to line managers.

Risk management has been conducted competently for many years by several different professions. These professionals help corporations manage their insurance risks, financial risks, commodity risks, operational risks and any number of other risks. And there are specialists within each of these categories. Now there is a groundswell of activity in both corporations and their capital providers to understand how all these risks—taken together—affect the corporation. Why the capital providers? Because, as we shall show in this book, the common framework for risk management revolves around the efficient use of capital.

The book is divided into three parts. The first part sets the foundation. It provides an answer to the deceptively simple question "Does risk matter?" It focuses on three players in a corporation: the risk manager who deals with the insurance markets, and the treasurer and the chief financial officer (CFO) who both deal with the financial (or capital) markets. These traditional roles are evolving and becoming more interdependent. The key contribution we make to their evolution is a common risk management framework—the Insurative Model—that can be used by these three parties. We show that risk management is a natural consequence of a firm's need to manage its corporate capital resources.

The second part presents a number of techniques that have emerged recently to meet the challenges of risk management. Each technique can address only a subset of a corporation's risks. But together, they make a formidable addition to the conventional techniques currently employed.

A major objective of this book is to help managers understand these emerging risk management techniques. Examples and case studies are used extensively to do so. Besides describing these techniques individually, we also discuss how they are related to each other. Each technique is classified according to the degree of integration it achieves between the insurance and capital markets.

The third and final part asks us to consider the future. What are the market developments that have led us down this path, where are we now, and what does the future hold for us? What are the prospects and challenges facing the development of this new frontier in risk management? How can corporations and their managers migrate to the new environment?

The chapters that follow are designed to inform and to challenge, but never to overwhelm. We hope that the reader will gain a fuller understanding of what is possible today and will be inspired to achieve the breadth of vision so vital to integrating corporate risk management.

This is not a handbook, it is an "and"-book.

Prakash A. Shimpi

Part I
The Foundations

"Risk and uncertainty are fundamental
to life, both human and corporate."

1

Everyone Is a Risk Manager

DAVID S. LASTER

Risk and uncertainty are fundamental to life, both human and corporate. Businesses spend trillions of dollars each year to address their risk exposures. Among OECD countries, for example, premiums from non-life insurance total 3.5% of GDP.[1] A 1998 survey conducted by the Risk and Insurance Management Society[2] finds that, for a sample of large U.S. corporations, the **cost of risk**—expenditures on risk control and loss prevention, insurance premiums, retained losses, and related administrative tasks—is $5.25 per thousand dollars of sales. For small or mid-sized companies, or firms in industries such as health care and transportation, the cost of risk is several times higher than this. Even these figures vastly understate the true cost of risk, because they exclude the cost of managing business risks, which for many firms are far more significant than insurable risks (Figure 1.1).

The substantial expense that firms incur in managing their risks suggests a basic question: does risk matter enough to justify the resources that firms commit to taming it? Are they getting their money's worth?

DOES RISK MATTER? THE THEORY

There is, at first blush, an economic argument to be made against expending corporate funds to manage risk. On average, for every dollar a company pays in insurance premiums, it receives less than a dollar in claims paid. Insurers incur many expenses other than claims paid—for legal, underwriting, marketing and distribution services, just to name a few. Further, an insurer's shareholders expect and are entitled to receive some measure of profit for the

Figure 1.1   The global risk environment.

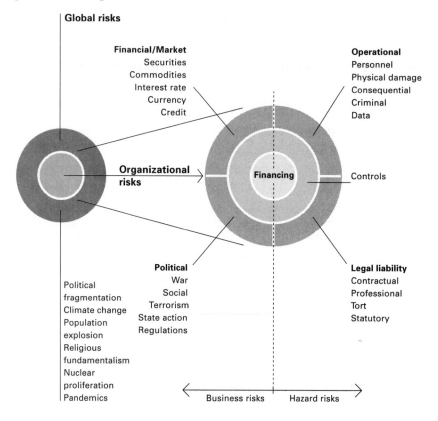

capital they put at risk. Thus, buying insurance would seem on average to be a losing proposition. The same applies to financial risk management—hedging financial risk entails many expenses such as brokerage fees, the bid-asked spread, costs arising from an inability to price derivative securities correctly, and the compensation of professional employees and consultants hired to hedge financial risk.

Basic economic reasoning seems to suggest that, because risk management reduces the expected value of a firm's future cash flows, it destroys rather than creates value for the firm. Why—the argument might go—should an investor forego expected cash flows in exchange for greater certainty with respect to these cash flows? After all, investors can diversify away their business risk exposures at much lower cost by simply purchasing shares in a wide range of companies. So, rather than incurring the heavy expense of managing corporate risk at the operational level, why shouldn't investors manage their risks by purchasing index funds or other similarly diversified portfolios?

The question is disturbing. It suggests that corporate risk management does not add value, but destroys it. After consideration, two reasons emerge, (apart from tax benefits) as to why risk management is both worthwhile and important:

- It reduces the **cost of financial distress**, and
- It reduces the **opportunity cost** of projects forgone.

The costs of financial distress include any added cost of doing business that arises from uncertainty as to whether a firm will continue to operate. Imagine a company that hits the skids, whether due to poor management decisions or a corporate disaster that was nobody's fault. The company starts losing market share and reports losses for a few consecutive quarters. People in the industry begin to wonder whether it will be around a decade from now. This uncertainty will cause the firm to incur any number of additional expenses:

- Banks and other creditors might demand more collateral and charge higher interest rates on loans,
- Suppliers might reduce the size of shipments or require cash on delivery,
- Valued employees might leave the firm,
- Talented prospective employees might require compensation packages above industry norms in order for them to join the company,
- Clients might cancel or decline to renew long-term service contracts, and
- The company's stock price might fall to a level that eliminates or sharply curtails its ability to raise additional funds through equity issuance.

The magnitude of these costs suggests that there is a big payoff for firms that manage their risks in a manner that reduces their chances of experiencing financial distress. In other words, being assured of a strong, secure capital base helps a company maintain credibility, which in the long run saves it money.

Economists have advanced a second argument in favor of risk management, one that concerns the disruption of investment plans. Although publicly traded companies can raise capital by issuing debt or equity, they generally exhibit a strong preference for funding projects with internal cash flows. Issuing securities entails transaction costs, invites unwanted public scrutiny, and might convey a negative signal to investors concerning the company's abilities and prospects. This reluctance to tap into capital markets, known as the **pecking order theory**,[3] makes risk management particularly critical. The more firms depend upon internal cash flows to fund investment projects, the more potentially damaging inconsistent earnings performance might be.

To illustrate, imagine two companies, each of which earns an average return on equity (ROE) of 15%. The first comes within two to three percentage points of this level each year; the second exhibits much greater earnings instability, some years earning a 30% ROE but other years reporting either a negligible profit or a loss. The pecking order theory suggests that the company with unstable earnings might choose to forego, delay or curtail its investment activity because of a temporary setback in operating performance.[4] The opportunity cost to the firm of this earnings irregularity will be especially great if several attractive projects arise at a time when performance is slumping. The company with stable earnings, by contrast, will be better positioned to undertake new projects at all times. A risk management program that steadies a company's performance provides a strategic advantage by enabling it to respond more readily when opportunity knocks.

DOES RISK MATTER? SOME EVIDENCE

The advantage of steady operating performance is not something lost on industry observers. In a recent joint work, economists with the Federal Reserve Bank of New York and Swiss Re examined the characteristics of companies well regarded by industry observers, as reported in an annual *Fortune* magazine survey.[5] Since 1983, the magazine has asked thousands of executives, outside directors and financial analysts to rate their industry's ten largest firms on eight attributes. These are: quality of management; quality of products or services; innovation; value as a long-term investment; financial soundness; ability to attract, develop and keep talented people; community and environmental responsibility; and use of corporate assets. *Fortune* ranks the firms by their overall scores and publishes the results in an article titled "America's Most Admired Companies."

Examining financial data for these companies, the researchers investigated which financial characteristic was the best predictor of corporate reputation. Their answer: **earnings stability**. For each of the thirteen years of survey data, the authors divided the firms into seven categories: the two most admired deciles of firms (Figure 1.2, Q1A, Q1B), the two least-admired deciles of firms (Q5A, Q5B), and the intermediate three quintiles (Q2, Q3, Q4). For each grouping of firms, they asked the following question: Over the past three years, in what fraction of the firms' quarterly earnings announcements was a loss reported? The result was that firms in the bottom decile (Q5B) were fifteen times more likely to report a loss in any given quarter than were those in the top decile (Q1A). Of the firms in the survey, the top ones had reported a loss 2.3% of the time; the bottom ones reported a loss 37.6% of the time.

This finding has interesting implications for the importance of risk management. Companies that exercise control over their operating performance, that are proactive and not reactive, and that earn quarterly profits with great regularity tend to be among the most admired firms in their industries. Companies that are among the least admired, by contrast, tend to have losing quarters with great regularity.

Figure 1.2   Reputation and earnings stability.

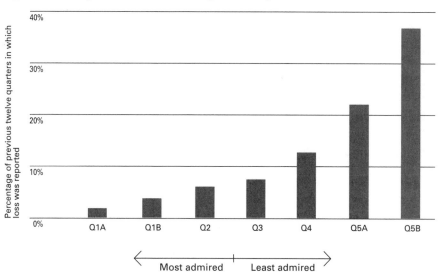

It must immediately be acknowledged that the sources of earnings insta-bility are numerous and varied. Any number of events—natural catastro-phes; sharp movements in exchange rates, interest rates or commodity prices; or changes in regulatory structure—can precipitate a sharp, sudden reversal of corporate fortune. Some industries, moreover, are more prone to cyclical factors than others. Still, with a prudent risk management program in place, a company can gradually stabilize its profitability. Over five to ten years, a company can exit some lines of business, de-emphasize others, and enter still others. It can improve the way it approaches risk by identifying its vulnerabilities and dealing with them in the most appropriate manner. In our experience, the best companies have embraced the concept of integrated risk management and have begun implementing it in some way.

The relationship between successful operations and integrated risk man-agement is further borne out by a recent PricewaterhouseCoopers study of U.K. middle-market companies, defined as firms with annual revenues rang-ing from £5-20 million.[6] The study found that while 80% of these firms think that risk management is "fundamental to success," very few match this conviction with actions that make risk management fully integrated and proactive. Overall, just 16% of the firms surveyed had implemented at least some integrated risk management practices, and even these were usually lim-ited in scope. A different picture emerges, however, when the sample is sorted on the basis of expected earnings growth.

As Figure 1.3 shows, none of the companies anticipating a substantial decline in earnings claimed to have a fully integrated approach to risk man-agement. On the other hand, two-fifths of companies experiencing rapid growth claimed to be following a fully integrated approach to risk manage-ment. In short, faster-growing companies were much more likely to be de-veloping fully integrated approaches to risk. This does not imply that implementing an integrated risk program will kick a company's bottom-line growth into high gear, since growth might be affecting risk management practices rather than vice-versa. We may conclude from the results of this survey that the proactive, innovative, can-do attitude found at rapidly grow-ing companies often goes together with a more holistic approach toward risk management. Middle-market companies that are retrenching tend not to view risk from this holistic perspective.

Figure 1.3   Expected earnings growth and the practice of fully integrated risk management.

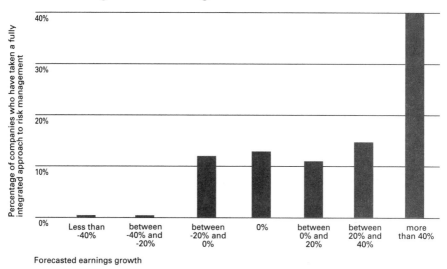

EVERYONE IS A RISK MANAGER

Having established the importance of a good risk management strategy and noting how sound risk management practices are associated with earnings growth and corporate reputation, let us now consider who is responsible for managing a company's risks. Typically, many employees at a firm strive to improve its profitability, but only a handful devote their time to risk management.

The **chief executive officer** (CEO) is responsible for a firm's success in the marketplace and may therefore be deemed its ultimate risk officer. By ensuring that adequate risk management processes are in place at the firm, the CEO can reduce the probability of a major corporate disaster and identify potential roadblocks early on. In determining which initiatives to pursue and which to table, the CEO sets the basic tone for the organization and just how much risk it will bear.

The **chief financial officer** (CFO) has responsibility for managing financial risks, including foreign exchange exposures and interest rate risk. As overseer of the treasury and audit functions, the CFO also must ensure that financial operations are managed in a coordinated, systematic manner.

The **treasurer** is concerned with the acquisition, custody and expenditure of funds. Much of the job involves contending with risk, whether through capital budgeting, credit analysis or charting a strategy for raising funds through the issuance of debt and equity.

Playing a complementary role is the **risk manager**, whose job is to develop and implement strategies that will minimize the adverse effects of accidental and business losses on the firm. The strategies a risk manager uses fall under two broad categories: risk control and risk financing. Risk control minimizes the losses to which a firm is exposed; risk financing ensures that funds are available to cover losses that do occur.

Although the treasurer and the risk manager both concentrate on risk management issues, at many firms they operate independently of one another. The treasurer focuses on financial risk, while the risk manager concentrates on exposure to accidental losses. The two disciplines evolved from different roots: the management of cash flows on the one hand and the purchase of insurance on the other. Yet because the issues they face are analogous and interrelated, there is much to be gained when they coordinate their efforts or, in any event, increase their communication.

A firm's **chief investment officer** (CIO), who oversees the pension fund and other corporate investments, also manages financial risk. However, the CIO's definition of risk management is specialized, pertaining to the task of assembling a portfolio of assets that earns a solid expected return while subject to a low level of risk.

A number of firms have recently begun appointing executives to positions such as **chief risk officer** (CRO) or "vice president, risk management," charging them with the oversight and coordination of all risk management activities. The emergence of this role represents a major step forward for integrated risk management: It vests one person with the authority to rationalize risk management efforts occurring in all parts of the company. An effective CRO promotes cooperation among the various people dealing with risk management issues.

Finally, a variety of line managers, such as the purchasing manager, director of marketing and chief information officer must also factor risk into the various decisions they make. In general, all those responsible for committing a firm's resources to different activities should consider the relevant risks.

RISK IS LIKE AN ELEPHANT

Since the whole idea of a professional risk management is fairly recent, there are many different definitions of just what risk management is. Ironically, the current trend toward integrated or "holistic" risk management has not yet led to convergence or integration of the terms, concepts and models applied to the management of risk. If anything, the approaches used in this fledgling discipline have become more varied and far-flung. A recent address to the American Risk and Insurance Association[7] invoked a familiar metaphor for the current state of risk management. In a well-known poem, six blind men encounter an elephant (page 12). Each describes one part of the elephant in familiar terms. Working separately, they fail to recognize the true attributes of the elephant. In our opinion, the last verse could read instead:

> *So, often with risk management*
> *The experts on the scene*
> *Rail on in utter ignorance*
> *Of what each other mean,*
> *And speak about an elephant*
> *Not one of them has seen!*

This characterization seems far from fanciful, as each specialized group of risk managers focuses on a different set of risks and tools for addressing them. Traditional risk managers use questionnaires, checklists and flowcharts; new-age risk managers use risk matrices and risk grids; financial risk managers use value-at-risk (VAR) models and stress tests; portfolio managers rely on the Markowitz mean-variance framework; and so forth. Nobody has yet gone the extra mile to synthesize or integrate these approaches. In short, risk is like an elephant—large, imposing and tough to get one's arms around.

CONCLUSION

Risk is a basic part of corporate life that, while not avoidable, is nonetheless manageable. Managing risk makes sense because it reduces a firm's chances of experiencing financial distress and shields it against events that might

The Blind Men and the Elephant

by John Godfrey Saxe

It was six men of Indostan
To learning much inclined,
Who went to see the elephant
(Though all of them were blind),
That each by observation
Might satisfy his mind.

The First approached the elephant,
And, happening to fall
Against his broad and sturdy side,
At once began to bawl:
"God bless me! but the elephant
Is nothing but a wall!"

The Second, feeling of the tusk,
Cried: "Ho! what have we here
So very round and smooth
and sharp?
To me 'tis mighty clear
This wonder of an elephant
Is very like a spear!"

The Third approached the animal,
And, happening to take
The squirming trunk within
his hands,
Thus boldly up and spake:
"I see," quoth he, "The elephant
Is very like a snake!"

The Fourth reached out
his eager hand,
And felt about the knee:
"What most this wondrous beast is
like
Is mighty plain," quoth he;
"'Tis clear enough the elephant
Is very like a tree."

The Fifth, who chanced
to touch the ear,
Said: "E'en the blindest man
Can tell what this resembles most;
Deny the fact who can,
This marvel of an elephant
Is very like a fan!"

The Sixth no sooner had begun
About the beast to grope,
Than, seizing on the swinging tail
That fell within his scope,
"I see," quoth he, "The elephant
Is very like a rope!"

And so these men of Indostan
Disputed loud and long,
Each in his own opinion
Exceeding stiff and strong,
Though each was partly in the right,
And all were in the wrong!

thwart or distort its agenda of activities. Progressive, well-managed firms exhibit their quality of leadership in the way they handle risk. At most companies, many different employees are responsible for managing risk. Because they generally work in isolation from one another, with distinct priorities, goals, models and techniques, it would be surprising if some of their efforts were not at cross-purposes.

The motivation for integrated risk management is this: the diverse activities of line managers, the treasurer, the risk manager and others should be coordinated so that, through their joint efforts, the company achieves a maximal reduction of risk at minimum cost.

The key insight that helps rationalize these efforts is that a wide variety of risks—an explosion at a plant, a sharp spike in interest rates, or a contentious strike—all have quantifiable impacts on a firm's profitability and its balance sheet. It therefore follows that they can all be expressed in a common metric and weighed against one another, permitting an assessment of how best to handle each of the risks. If this seems like common sense, it is. As you read the chapters that follow, we ask you to keep an open mind and a desire to improve on existing practices. The process of integrating corporate risk management marks a sea change in the way we think about risk. It will be of great benefit to the companies and individuals who lead the way.

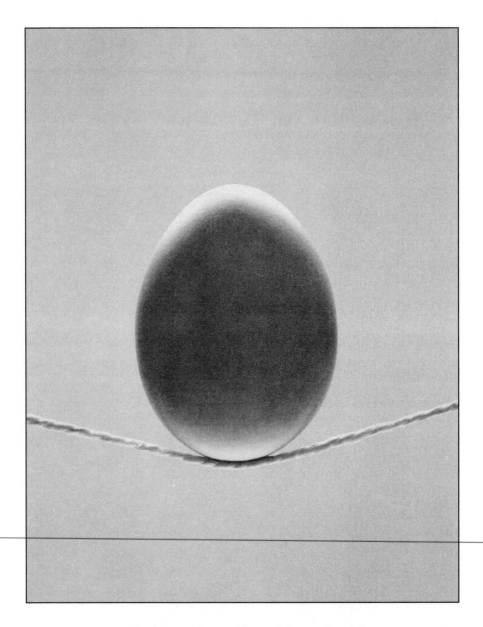

"A risk neglected is a risk retained."

2

The Conventional Approach to Risk Management

DAVID S. LASTER

All too often, risk management at large corporations is compartmentalized. The risk manager deals with pure risks, the treasurer manages financial risks, the chief financial officer strives to achieve an optimal capital structure, and yet other specialists manage pension assets. The professional training of risk managers, treasurers, CFOs and investment managers reflects and reinforces this specialization. Consequently, the various individuals responsible for shielding a firm from risk advance distinct (and sometimes conflicting) agendas, use different techniques and even speak different languages.

Ironically, this lack of coordination is unnecessary. Different risk-related specialties share much in common. Their lack of coordination is not by design, but an accident of history. It reflects the absence of an overarching, unified vision of risk management, whether among practitioners or researchers. With thought and effort, people working in the various risk-related disciplines can chip away at the artificial boundaries separating them.

This chapter takes some modest steps in that direction. It first provides a basic taxonomy of risk management approaches, illustrating how they cut across specialties. It then explores how corporate managers focusing on different aspects of risk management can, by working as a team, devise an approach to managing risk that is coordinated, broad-ranging and cost-effective.

STANDARD APPROACHES TO RISK MANAGEMENT

A dynamic organization is exposed to a staggering array of risks, as rich and diverse as the opportunities it enjoys. This is no coincidence, for risk and opportunity go hand in hand. Regardless of how complex and varied the risks facing it, a firm has only four possible approaches to managing a given risk: it can avoid it, reduce it, transfer it or retain it. The first two approaches—**risk avoidance** and **risk reduction**—minimize a firm's overall exposure to risk. They are sometimes referred to as **risk control**. The latter two approaches—**risk transfer** and **risk retention**—are known as **risk financing**. The goal of risk financing is to fund losses arising from risks that remain after the application of risk control techniques. Let us consider each of these approaches in turn, noting their broad applicability across risk management specialties.

Risk Avoidance

A firm can elect to abstain from investments with payoffs that are too uncertain. Where it draws the line between acceptable and unacceptable risks will depend on a combination of internal and external factors. A firm might reject some initiatives that have a level of uncertainty which exceeds the firm's tolerance for risk. In reaching such decisions, the firm must take industry practices and market realities into account. A leading aircraft manufacturer, for example, may need to "bet the ranch" on radical product redesign every decade or so if it is to stay competitive. Similarly, a firm that is unwilling to tolerate major risks and ambiguities cannot hope for much success in rapidly changing fields like pharmaceuticals, biotechnology or electronic commerce.

Every firm faces certain **core risks** fundamental to its business that it simply has no way of avoiding. One consolation is that risks that cannot be avoided can at least be better understood. Before committing extensive resources, a firm can clarify some of the ambiguities of a project through further investigation—basic scientific research, legal research or market intelligence. Yet even this process of discovery has its limits. In the time it takes a firm to resolve a project's key uncertainties, its competitors might establish themselves as leaders in the field.

Risk avoidance reflects each firm's need to maintain focus and pick its battles. It is not, however, a panacea for the economy as a whole. If society is to progress, individuals and organizations must be prepared to assume the risks of exploring for resources, entering new markets, developing new technologies, and building on previous discoveries. Since risk cannot entirely be avoided it is important to consider how best to reduce it.

Risk Reduction

Risk reduction occurs through **loss prevention**, **loss control** and **diversification**. Loss prevention seeks to reduce the likelihood of a given type of loss occurring. Examples of loss prevention measures include safety devices like smoke detectors and burglar alarms, or the use of security guards. There are a variety of laws mandating loss prevention measures that governments deem socially beneficial. These include building codes, seat belts and airbags. Other loss prevention measures are so cost-effective that insurers either offer discounts for their use or require policyholders to employ them. As with any risk management technique, loss prevention has its limits. Beyond a certain point, its incremental costs exceed its benefits.

Loss control techniques are designed to reduce the severity of a loss, should it occur. Sprinkler systems and firewalls, for example, limit the damage a fire might cause without preventing fires from starting. Equity investors can place stop-loss orders that automatically trigger a sell order once the value of a stock falls below a certain threshold. Firms can limit the downside risk of a project by closely monitoring its progress and regularly evaluating its efficacy. None of these techniques is foolproof. Sprinklers malfunction. Stop-loss orders are ineffective when market liquidity dries up (as in the week of October 19th, 1987) or trading is halted. Projects take surprising twists and turns that often cannot be foreseen.

Diversification provides a third means of reducing risk. Although the idea of not putting all one's eggs in a single basket may be as old as eggs and baskets, it has crystallized over the past half-century with Markowitz's Nobel prize-winning development of portfolio theory. The most exciting thing about portfolio theory is its concrete demonstration that there is such a thing as a free lunch. In particular, an investor whose holdings are concentrated can reduce the risk of these holdings without sacrificing expected return. Portfolio theory offers a new technology for constructing "efficient" portfolios, adding rigor to long-standing rules of thumb.

Diversification pertains as much to insurance as it does to sound investment practice. A company that has a large number of independent **loss units** (for example automobiles, factories or retail outlets) can estimate with reasonable accuracy how much in accidental losses it might expect in a given year. Absent this internal diversification, the firm can purchase coverage from an insurer. The insurer, in turn, achieves the benefits of diversification by providing coverage to a variety of clients. In lines of business or in regions where an insurer cannot attain a desired level of diversification, it can achieve the same effect by reinsuring its risks.

Risk Transfer

A risk can be transferred from one party to another better equipped or more willing to bear it. One common way to transfer risk is through **insurance**. In exchange for an agreed-upon premium the insurer agrees to indemnify its client, up to a specific limit, in the event of loss. (Alternative risk transference arrangements, such as risk retention groups, play a similar role.) Insurance is critical to many types of economic activity. Without it, many businesses—farms, clinics, amusement parks and factories—would be too risky to operate. It is clear that insurance greases the wheels of economic activity.

Legal codes can also effect risk transfer. One of the major developments in commercial risk management in 19th century Germany was the establishment of limited liability. This enabled entrepreneurs to transfer some of their business risks to customers, suppliers and other members of society. The result was a boost in economic activity that facilitated rapid industrialization.

Some speculative risks can be transferred through **hedging**, which is the purchase or sale of goods or services for future delivery. Consider the example of oil. A sudden increase in the price of oil would sharply reduce profitability for airlines, for whom fuel is an important expense. In contrast, petroleum refiners would suffer a decrease in revenues and profits were the price of oil to decline. Airlines and refiners can hedge their commodity price risk by buying and selling oil futures on an organized exchange. Although they might gain nothing in the way of expected profits (one trader's gain will be the other's loss), they stand to gain something even more important: an added measure of certainty in an uncertain world.

In recent years futures and options exchanges have begun trading securities that allow firms to hedge not only commodity price exposures, but other financial risks as well. In particular, large firms now routinely hedge against adverse movements in exchange rates and interest rates. Fueling this increased use of hedging is a growing realization that for many firms, an adverse shift in interest or exchange rates is more likely to cause significant harm than, say, a sudden explosion at an office or factory.

Risk Retention

Companies also retain a variety of risks, whether voluntarily or involuntarily. Voluntary risk retention reflects a conscious decision to absorb certain risk exposures internally, because it is the most cost-effective way of addressing the risk. Thus, a large corporation might choose to retain (or self-insure) the risk of a 25 basis-point change in interest rates. Or it might ask employees not to buy automobile insurance when renting a car for a business trip. Involuntary risk retention occurs when a business fails to identify a given risk exposure and therefore bears the risk unknowingly. A risk neglected is a risk retained.

VARIED RESPONSIBILITIES FOR RISK MANAGEMENT

Large corporations have certain individuals dedicated solely to risk management. Prominent among them are the risk manager, the treasurer and the chief financial officer.

Risk Manager

The corporate risk manager is responsible for dealing with **pure risks**, those risks that can result in either a loss or no loss, but not in a gain. Major categories of pure risk include property, liability and workers' compensation.

It might at first appear that the risk manager is simply the person in charge of insurance-related matters—the "insurance guy," to quote one former risk manager's derisive view of the job. This characterization is inaccurate on at least two counts. First, a capable risk manager tries not merely to get the best deal on insurance, but to minimize the organization's total cost of risk. This requires judicious use of all four of the risk management approaches discussed above, and might even exclude the purchase of insurance altogether. Second, the pure risks for which a risk manager is responsible are not just insurable risks, but uninsurable ones as well. These might include the risk of power outages, computer failures or strikes. By focusing management's attention on key operational risks and devising effective responses to them, a good risk manager can earn his or her salary many times over, notwithstanding the imprecision with which this contribution is measured.

Although risk managers face a variety of challenges, their expertise and authority remain deeply rooted in the insurance market. They work closely with insurers and brokers, focusing on issues like deductibles, the use of captives, and risk financing mechanisms. However, they generally have no say with regard to managing another important class of risks known as **speculative risks**.

Speculative risks involve situations that have a possibility of gain as well as loss. For example, exchange rate exposures are speculative risks because a shift in exchange rates can harm a firm, but might benefit it as well. Other speculative risks for which senior management is responsible include financial risks such as commodity price risk and interest rate risk, and a wide range of other business risks such as competitor risk, reputation risk and regulatory risk.

Treasurer

A treasurer's risk management responsibilities include many speculative financial risks. A major role of the treasurer is to ensure the availability of reliable sources of funds for the firm, whether through bank lines of credit or capital market issuance. At financial service firms, the treasurer often manages interest rate risks. If a firm imports raw materials or sells extensively abroad, the treasurer can hedge the resulting foreign exchange exposures with futures or swaps. If a commodity or basket of commodities is a major input or output for the firm, the treasurer might hedge some of the resulting commodity price exposure. The treasurer might also oversee the management of firm-wide credit risk.

Given the nature of these responsibilities, the treasurer must be familiar with current financial market developments and their potential impact on the firm. Treasurers generally know little about insurance-related issues, which are the specialty of the risk manager.

Chief Financial Officer (CFO)

As one of the most senior members of management, a CFO typically has numerous responsibilities in policymaking, planning and corporate control. One particularly important responsibility of the CFO is to determine the optimal capital structure for the firm. Very often, both the treasurer and the risk manager will report to the CFO. Like the treasurer, the CFO's major concerns typically have much more to do with capital markets than with insurance markets. An effective CFO examines the overall capital needs of the organization and devises the most cost-effective combination of debt and equity for the corporate balance sheet. Off-balance-sheet capital resources such as bank standby credit lines are also considered. Only recently have CFOs begun to include insurance facilities as corporate finance tools.

THE POTENTIAL FOR COORDINATION

Economic theory teaches that when a firm has several different policy instruments at its disposal, the most efficient combination to achieve any given goal is the one for which:

- The incremental benefit of each instrument is the same, and
- The last dollar spent on each instrument provides a dollar of benefits in return.

In other words, if a firm is using its tools optimally, it should have no way of reallocating resources to its benefit; otherwise, improvement is possible. What, one might wonder, has this "marginal" thinking to do with the price of tea in China (or insurance in Hartford)? As it turns out, plenty.

Separately, the treasurer, CFO and risk manager each has a powerful set of skills and techniques for managing risk. Even if they are all masters of their respective specialties, their failure to communicate and coordinate with one another will prevent them from achieving an optimal mix of financing, hedging, and insurance for the entire firm. This is illustrated more concretely in the case study in Chapter 6.

To understand this point, consider how risk is often managed within a firm. The CFO determines the optimal capital structure with respect to debt and equity financing. Taking the structure as a given, the treasurer then devises a strategy for raising capital and hedging financial risks. Meanwhile, in a separate department, the risk manager determines the most expedient way of protecting against accidental and operational risks.

This conventional approach leaves ample room for improvement through coordination. A firm might, for example, be spending hundreds of thousands of dollars to insure its plant and equipment against accidental losses that would be far less devastating than a shift in exchange rates, against which it has little protection. By retaining additional hazard risk and using the savings in premiums to hedge some of its currency exposure, the firm can reduce its overall level of risk. Alternatively, if the insurance market is particularly soft, it might pay for a firm to increase its property/casualty coverage.

To make such decisions in a coherent manner, a firm must have a unified framework with which to view all of its risks. This will enable it to identify and measure its chief risks, or at least get a clear sense of risk management priorities and how much it should be prepared to spend to address them. In keeping with the optimal control criteria set out above, a unified analytic framework permits a side-by-side comparison of disparate risks and how they are managed. Bertolt Brecht declared "A Man's a Man;" effective corporate governance requires management to declare "A Risk's a Risk."

Another important advantage of engaging the CFO, treasurer and risk manager in regular dialogue relates to optimal capital structure. Insurance and alternative risk transfer solutions provide clients with contingent capital that can substitute, at least in part, for debt or equity capital. Through the strategic use of insurance solutions, a firm can reduce its overall cost of capital, allowing it to pursue opportunities that would otherwise have been unattainable. The time has come to begin thinking about capital structure more broadly, not as debt and equity, but as debt, equity and insurance.

"Capital management and risk management are two sides of the same coin."

3

Integrating Risk Management and Capital Management

PRAKASH SHIMPI

Capital management and risk management are two sides of the same coin. Conventional finance theory treats them separately. Capital management focuses on delivering the optimal balance sheet, composed of equity and debt, that minimizes the cost of capital. It is the domain of the CFO. Currently, the term "risk management" refers to the roles of the risk manager and treasurer, working separately in the insurance and capital markets to manage the firm's operational and financial risks.

Simple intuition tells us that capital and risk are related. With a multitude of forms of capital and rapidly developing risk management techniques, it is natural to treat capital management and risk management as two distinct topics. This simplification comes at a price: By considering capital structure and insurance strategies in isolation, we fail to account for important connections between them. To capture this interrelationship requires a framework that incorporates both. Additionally, this framework needs to apply equally to techniques that straddle both the insurance and capital markets.

In this chapter, we develop such a framework—the Insurative Model. We build it by starting with a general discussion of the role of corporate capital and the relationship of capital to risk. Next, we consider two conventional models of corporate capital—one dealing with debt and equity and the other dealing with insurance—and combine them to produce the

Adapted from "Economics of Insuratives: Working Papers," University of London, August, 1999.

Insurative Model. This exercise requires us to delve into finance theory, but we have tried to make the subject accessible to anyone with a basic knowledge of finance. There are, however, several new concepts introduced here that should interest even a seasoned corporate finance specialist. This is the only chapter in this book that discusses finance theory—it is not necessarily light reading, but we hope that we have made it worthwhile reading.

THE ROLE OF CORPORATE CAPITAL

Why does a corporation need capital? A firm can be thought of as a collection of activities that entail risks. To conduct these activities and respond to their risks, the firm needs capital. In other words, it needs capital primarily to fund its operations, to cushion it against adverse financial results, and to assure observers of its financial soundness. A firm's capital can be defined as the sum of three items:

1. **Operational capital**
2. **Risk capital**
3. **Signaling capital**

Operational Capital

This is the capital required to finance corporate activities. If a firm undertakes only risk-free projects, this will be the minimal capital it needs to stay in business. The cost of operational capital for a risk-free project should reflect only the time value of money.

Risk Capital

Corporate activities generate risks. A firm requires capital in addition to its expected operational capital to cover the financial consequences of these risks. The amount of risk capital depends on the risk tolerance of the firm. It is calculated as the capital needed to keep the firm's probability of ruin below some defined level. For example, suppose a statistical analysis of a firm's risk exposure shows that its expected operational capital is $500 million, but there is a 5% chance that it would need $750 million and a 1% chance that it would need $1 billion. In this case, risk capital of $250 million would correspond to a 95% survival probability and $500 million would correspond to a 99% survival probability. The cost of this component of capital should be a combination of both the time value of money and the riskiness of the firm.

The sum of these two items is the **economic capital** of a firm:

$$\text{economic capital} = \text{operational capital} + \text{risk capital}$$

Signaling Capital

Often it is not sufficient that only the managers of a firm be satisfied with the adequacy of the capital they have to cover their risks. Investors, suppliers, regulators, rating agencies and analysts, for example, need to be satisfied as well. They do not have the same risk analysis tools as the firm's managers, and cannot be as familiar with all the risks that the firm has undertaken. Instead, they have their own, more generic risk assessment tools, which are keyed off a short list of items from the firm's financial results. These tools not only measure the adequacy of a firm's capital but also enable a comparison of its financial soundness relative to other firms. Since these tools cannot be as precise as a firm's internal financial model, they tend to be conservative, overstating its capital needs.

Rather than argue the point, managers hold the additional signaling capital to reassure outsiders that the firm is indeed as strong as the managers know it to be. A small amount of this capital is not detrimental. Too much can create a noticeable drag on a firm's financial performance. Managing risks, particularly those that are the focus of external evaluators, can help reduce the amount of signaling capital that a firm needs.

The size of signaling capital for any firm depends on several factors, such as ownership structure, market credibility and industry sector. For highly regulated companies such as banks and insurers, which are subject to risk-based capital requirements, signaling capital may be large. On the other hand, a privately owned manufacturer not subject to the same type of scrutiny may need none.

Capital and Firm Risk

For a firm to operate in the marketplace, it needs sufficient capital to meet the financial obligations arising from its activities (economic capital) and its position in the market (signaling capital). The **capital required** by a firm, therefore, is made up of the following components:

> capital required= economic capital + signaling capital
> = operational capital + risk capital + signaling capital

From the preceding discussion, we recognize that a firm's capital required depends on the firm's risks. Let us define the function $f\{risk\}$ to indicate the amount of capital necessary to cover some given "risk." If we use **firm risk** to denote the risk of the entire firm's activities, so that $f\{firm\ risk\}$ is the amount of capital necessary to cover firm risk, then it is related to the firm's required capital in the following way:

> capital required = $f\{$**firm risk**$\}$
> = **capital needed to cover firm risk**

Figure 3.1 illustrates this relationship for a hypothetical firm.[1] When the firm runs a simulation of its operations, it generates probable future scenarios and determines, in each scenario, the amount of capital it will need to stay in business. The figure shows the capital required on the horizontal axis and the number of scenarios on the vertical axis. It shows that the minimal capital it will need to operate is $500; that amount is considered its operational capital. In only 1% of the scenarios is the capital needed greater than $1500. This means that the economic capital of the firm is $1500, of which $1000 is risk capital.

Although the firm's business itself does not have any other risks, there is a very real risk of not being able to demonstrate capital adequacy to interested third parties. The capital effect of this risk needs to be added on. If this signaling capital amounts to $50, then the capital required is $1550.

CAPITAL RESOURCES

So far we have not discussed the financial instruments that constitute a firm's capital. Let us refer to the capital resources utilized by a firm as **firm**

Figure 3.1   Simulation of a firm's capital required.

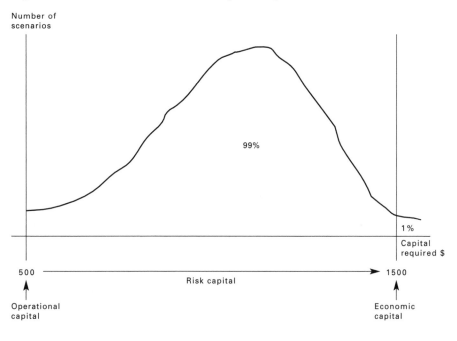

capital. It is easy to think that capital is limited to equity and various classes of corporate debt, i.e. **paid-up capital,** which appear on the firm's balance sheet. Indeed, most of corporate finance literature focuses on these forms of capital. *There are, however, more capital resources available to a firm.*

A firm also has the ability to access **off-balance-sheet capital,** i.e. capital that does not appear on its balance sheet, in order to fulfill the same objectives as it does with paid-up, on-balance-sheet capital. There are two ways to do so. The first is to buy the right to access capital in case it is needed. One example is a bank line of credit. It does not form part of the firm's on-balance-sheet capital, since it is not yet paid to the firm. A fee is paid for the credit line. If the firm utilizes the line and borrows from the bank, the loan at that time is treated as on-balance-sheet capital. This is a cost-effective way for a firm to postpone putting capital on its balance sheet until it needs to. Of course, such a bank facility comes with several terms and conditions that limit its availability and cost.

The second way to access off-balance-sheet capital is to transfer risks to other firms, thereby altering the retained risk profile and the consequent capital structure of the firm. For example, by paying a premium to an insurance company, a firm can eliminate its exposure to property damage at its manufacturing facilities. The firm does not have to keep any paid-up capital to cover this risk, except for some operational capital to pay the on-going insurance premium. All losses arising from that risk are borne by the insurer.

The distinction between these two off-balance-sheet capital resources is fairly straightforward. With the first, the firm still owns the risk, and can raise paid-up capital at some later date if it needs to. With the second, the firm no longer owns the risk, and therefore does not need to raise any paid-up capital to cover it.

Now that we have introduced the concepts of retained risk and transferred risk, we can define them here. **Transferred risk** refers to that subset of firm risk for which losses are borne by another party. The firm pays only the cost of transferring this risk. **Retained risk** refers to those risks for which losses are borne by the firm.

To summarize, once a firm's capital needs have been identified, the capital instruments have to be put in place and, consequently, the firm's risks are either retained or transferred, as the following two relationships show:

firm capital = paid-up capital + off-balance-sheet capital

firm risk   = retained risk + transferred risk

The preceding discussion now allows us to relate the capital resources that a firm has put in place to its required capital, which is a function of its risks, $f\{firm\ risk\}$:

- If firm capital equals required capital, the firm is adequately capitalized.
- If firm capital exceeds required capital, the firm is overcapitalized and is likely not meeting investor expectations.
- If firm capital falls short of required capital, the firm is undercapitalized and taking risks beyond its stated tolerance, exposing itself to insolvency.

Understanding the role of corporate capital, both on- and off-balance-sheet, and its relationship to the riskiness of a firm's activities provides the foundation on which to build a common framework that ties in both the insurance and capital markets.

MODELS OF CAPITAL STRUCTURE

Traditionally, there are two models of a corporation—the Standard Model and the Insurance Model. By combining these two, we develop the common framework, which we call the Insurative Model.

The Standard Model

The Standard Model is the conventional corporate finance approach to developing a firm's capital structure. The firm's risk is not explicitly specified. Instead, the starting point is a statement of the firm's paid-up capital requirement. The objective is to construct a combination of equity, mezzanine (or subordinate) debt and senior debt that an investment or commercial bank can sell to investors or syndicate to lenders. Normally, the distinction between these forms of capital is understood in terms of priority to claims on corporate cash flows while the firm is operating, and on corporate assets if the firm is liquidated.

There is another way to describe this model, one that relates to risk. This model refers only to risks that are retained by the firm. It addresses only on-balance-sheet, paid-up capital. If the firm uses only equity capital, then the shareholders are fully exposed to the firm's retained risks. By introducing senior and subordinate debt, the model distinguishes between the forms of capital by their exposure to the firm's risks. The Standard Model stratifies all the firm's risks and specifies that capital providers share those risks sequentially. The senior debt providers are the least exposed, and the equity investors are the most exposed (Figure 3.2).

In effect, the Standard Model equates the paid-up capital of the firm to the amount necessary to cover its retained risk. It ignores the possibility that other forms of capital may be utilized to cover this risk. Using the function $f\{risk\}$ we introduced earlier, we can write the following relationship:[2]

$$\text{paid-up capital} = f\{\text{retained risk}\}$$
$$= \text{capital needed to cover retained risk}$$

The difference in cost between each form of capital reflects the difference in risk exposure. It is in the firm's interest to introduce debt, since debt can enhance the risk-return profile of the shareholders. Just how much debt the firm should have is a topic discussed at length in most corporate finance texts.[3] It is sufficient for our purposes to highlight, in an abbreviated form, two measures of interest to management. The first is return on equity (ROE) and the second is the weighted-average cost of capital (WACC). We will define and discuss them below.

Before proceeding any further, it is important to recognize two fundamental milestones in corporate finance theory from the seminal work of Modigliani and Miller (MM).[4] MM Proposition I states that, in the absence of taxes, transaction costs and other market imperfections, a firm cannot change the total value of its securities just by splitting its cash flow into different streams. This is because the firm's value is determined by its real assets, and not by the securities it issues. So long as the firm's investment structure—and therefore the cash flows it expects from its operations—is taken as given, the firm's capital structure is irrelevant. In addition, MM Proposition II states that the expected return to shareholders of a firm that has debt will

Figure 3.2   The Standard Model.

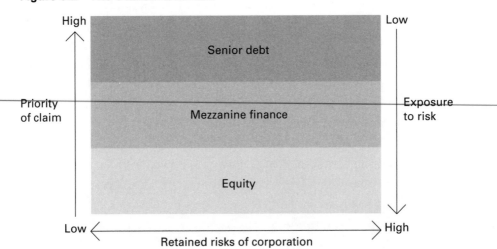

increase in proportion to its ratio of debt to equity. This increase is linear so long as the debt is risk-free. However, if the level of borrowing makes the debt risky, then the debt holders will demand a higher return, leading to a slower increase in the expected return.[5]

The following numerical examples describe the calculation of ROE and WACC, and illustrate the MM Propositions (Box 3.1). Alpha Corporation needs no more than $1500 in capital 99% of the time. It has an expected operational capital need of $500. It is not concerned with holding any additional signaling capital. It purchases insurance at a price (**insurance premium**) of $10 that relieves it of having to raise $500 in paid-up capital.[6] We can refer to this amount of paid-up capital relief as the **insurance capital**. (Note that insurance capital is not the amount of insurance protection purchased—a point we will discuss later.)

Box 3.1   Return on equity for Alpha.

Operating capital	$ 500
Risk capital	$1000
Signaling capital	$ 0
Capital required	$1500
Less capital met by insurance	$ 500
Paid-up capital	$1000 = Book value of assets
Gross income	$ 160 = Earned on assets
Insurance premium	$ 10
Net operating income	$ 150 = Earned by paid-up capital
Debt interest	$ 0
Net operating earnings	$ 150 = Available to shareholders

Return on assets:

$$ROA = \frac{\text{gross income}}{\text{assets}} = \frac{\$\,160}{\$1000} = 16\%$$

Return on paid-up capital:

$$ROP = \frac{\text{net operating income}}{\text{paid-up capital}} = \frac{\$\,150}{\$1000} = 15\%$$

Return on equity:

$$ROE = \frac{\text{net operating earnings}}{\text{equity capital}} = \frac{\$\,150}{\$1000} = 15\%$$

The firm's **gross income**, defined as revenues less operating expenses, excluding debt interest and insurance premium, is $160. Its **net operating income** is $150, which is the gross income less the insurance premium. Its **net operating earnings**, defined as net operating income less the debt interest, is also $150, since Alpha does not have any debt.

With the Standard Model, Alpha's balance sheet relationship does not explicitly reflect the value of its insurance arrangements. It shows only its paid-up capital as $1000, which is assumed to be fully deployed in the firm's productive assets. Although the assets earn a gross income of $160, the paid-up capital earns a net operating income of $150.

Irrespective of its financing sources, the firm's assets earn a gross income of $160. We define the **return on assets** (ROA) as the ratio of gross income to the book value of assets. Alpha's ROA is 16% ($160/$1000). If its financing decisions do not affect the firm's projects, then, in the absence of market imperfections, its return on assets should remain unchanged. Similarly, we define a new measure, the **return on paid-up capital** (ROP), as the ratio of net operating income to the book value of paid-up capital. Alpha's ROP is 15% ($150/$1000).[7]

Alpha does not believe in leverage, the use of debt. Its capital is comprised entirely of $1000 in equity. The entire net operating income of $150 is available as earnings for shareholders. The **return on equity** (ROE), defined as the ratio of net operating earnings to the book value of equity, is 15% ($150/$1000), which is exactly the same as its ROP.

Now consider Beta Corporation. It has exactly the same characteristics as Alpha, except that it is willing to borrow (Box 3.2). Beta's management feels that the operational capital is a stable number, so they therefore raise

---

Box 3.2   Return on equity for Beta.

Paid-up capital	= $1000	Net operating income	= $150
Debt capital	= $ 500	Interest on debt	= $ 50
Equity capital	= $ 500	Net operating earnings	= $100

Return on equity:

$$ROE = \frac{\text{net operating earnings}}{\text{equity capital}} = \frac{\$100}{\$500} = 20\%$$

$500 in debt and $500 in equity. The interest on debt for Beta is 10%, so it takes a charge of $50, assuming no taxes.[8] The income available to shareholders, its net operating earnings, is now only $100 ($150 − $50). However, since there is less equity, the return on equity is higher than Alpha's, at 20% ($100/$500). Beta has reduced its equity and increased the return on that equity by borrowing. This increased return is due to the increased burden of risk that the shareholders take relative to the debt providers.

It should be clear from the preceding discussion that ROE is a profitability measure based on the *book* value of equity. We turn our attention now to measuring a firm's cost of capital, which is based on the *market* value of that capital.[9]

Were corporate debt not risky, it is reasonable to assume that it would be available at the same rate to all firms. In reality, we know that debt is risky and there is a spread over a risk-free interest rate that corporate borrowers have to pay. That spread is a function of the riskiness of the debt. The return that equity holders demand also depends on the risk associated with a firm. The standard measure of the cost of these sources of capital is the weighted-average cost of capital, WACC.

In the Standard Model, which is a model of paid-up capital, the WACC refers only to the average cost of debt and equity. The **cost of debt** (COD) can be determined fairly easily. It is the firm's current borrowing rate on debt; it reflects the expected return of debt holders. One way to compute it is first to project the expected interest expense that the firm expects to pay on its outstanding debt each year. The cost of debt is then the discount rate that equates the present value of this stream of expected interest payments to the **debt value**, the market value of debt. To illustrate, if we assume that the expected interest payment is the same each year in perpetuity, then:

$$\text{Cost of debt} = \frac{\textbf{expected annual interest payment}}{\textbf{debt value}}$$

The cost of equity (COE) requires some thought. Like the cost of debt, it reflects the expected return of shareholders. Unlike the cost of debt, the cost of equity is more difficult to determine precisely, although several methods are available to calculate an approximate value. One method, based on the Capital Asset Pricing Model (CAPM), calculates the cost of equity as the sum of the risk-free rate and the expected risk premium on a firm's shares. The expected risk premium is based on the sensitivity of a share's price to the overall stock market movements. Another method, known as the Gordon Growth Model, is similar to the method used above for the cost of debt. It calculates the cost of equity as the discount rate that equates the present value of future shareholder dividends, assumed to grow at a constant rate, to the **equity value**, the market value of equity.[10]

For our purposes, we use the following simple method to determine the cost of equity. We assume that, in an efficient market, shareholders know what a firm's activities are expected to earn for them over some future period. The cost of equity is the discount rate that equates that stream of earnings to the market value of equity. For example, if this expected net operating earnings is constant each year in perpetuity, then:

$$\text{Cost of equity} = \frac{\text{expected annual net operating earnings}}{\text{equity value}}$$

Once we have determined the cost of debt and the cost of equity, WACC is simply the average of these costs, weighted by the respective market values of debt and equity:

$$\text{WACC} = \quad \text{cost of debt} \quad \times \quad \frac{\text{debt value}}{\text{debt value} + \text{equity value}}$$

$$+ \text{cost of equity} \times \quad \frac{\text{equity value}}{\text{debt value} + \text{equity value}}$$

Let us consider companies Alpha and Beta again. For ease of exposition, assume that market values of debt and equity equal book values, and that the firms will continue to earn the same amounts in perpetuity. The cost of equity is calculated using the formula above (Box 3.3). The cost of equity for Alpha is 15%. Since it has no debt, its WACC is simply the cost of equity of 15%. The cost of equity for Beta is 20%, reflecting the added risk that shareholders of a leveraged firm have to bear. As predicted by MM Proposition I, the WACC for Beta is also 15%, the same as for Alpha.

Of course, we have made several simplifying assumptions here. We made the calculation of cost of equity appear trivial; in reality it is more difficult.

Box 3.3   Weighted-average cost of capital for Alpha and Beta.

$$\text{WACC} = \text{cost of debt} \times \frac{\text{debt value}}{\text{debt value} + \text{equity value}}$$

$$+ \text{cost of equity} \times \frac{\text{equity value}}{\text{debt value} + \text{equity value}}$$

WACC for Alpha:

$$\text{COE} = \frac{\text{expected annual net operating earnings}}{\text{equity value}} = \frac{\$\,150}{\$1000} = 15\%$$

Since debt value = 0, WACC = COE = 15%

WACC for Beta:

$$\text{COD} = \frac{\text{expected annual interest payment}}{\text{debt value}} = \frac{\$\,50}{\$\,500} = 10\%$$

$$\text{COE} = \frac{\text{expected annual net operating earnings}}{\text{equity value}} = \frac{\$\,100}{\$\,500} = 20\%$$

$$\text{WACC} = 10\% \times \frac{\$500}{\$500 + \$500} + 20\% \times \frac{\$500}{\$500 + \$500} = 15\%$$

Furthermore, we made the assumption that when a company borrows, its shareholders are able to demand the appropriate additional return to compensate them for the additional risk. This should be so in efficient markets. However, there is a view that markets are not as efficient as required for the MM propositions to hold. In that case, there is an optimum level of borrowing that does not increase the required ROE as much as predicted by MM, thereby lowering WACC. For example, if the shareholders of Beta feel that the additional risk they take relative to shareholders of the comparable unleveraged firm, Alpha, requires 3% additional return, then Beta's COE would be 18% instead of the predicted 20%, producing a WACC of 14%.

The Insurance Model

It is not common to consider insurance in a corporate finance setting. Nevertheless, doing so provides some insights—we show this in the examples below. In the Insurance Model, risks are specified explicitly. Risks are either transferred through insurance and hedging or retained by the firm. Transferring risks changes the firm's retained risk profile. As a consequence, insurance has a direct impact on corporate capital structure.

It is worth briefly noting the difference between transferring a risk in insurance form and in capital markets (derivatives) form. Risk transfer using insurance indemnifies the firm from losses arising from that risk—the firm can only collect if it actually incurs a loss. Also, before the firm can buy the insurance protection, it has to demonstrate that it has an **insurable interest**, i.e. it is actually exposed to losses from the insured risk. Risk hedges in capital markets are not indemnification contracts. Payments are made irrespective of whether the firm incurs a loss. The firm can purchase the hedge (generally a derivative) whether or not it is exposed to the underlying risk.

For this discussion, the term "insurance" refers to both insurance contracts and capital markets forms of risk transfer. Figure 3.3 shows that insurance is off-balance-sheet capital that covers the risks transferred by the firm. Like debt and equity, different insurance contracts can be constructed to cover separate layers of a risk. Exposure to risk is highest for first loss layers of insurance (or "near-the-money" options), covering losses that occur with a high frequency but have a low severity. Least exposed are excess of loss layers

Figure 3.3 The Insurance Model.

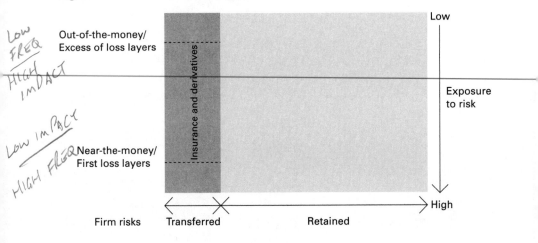

(or "out-of-the-money" options), covering low-frequency events that can have a high severity of losses.

In effect, the Insurance Model equates the off-balance-sheet capital of the firm to the amount necessary to cover its transferred risk. Using the function $f\{risk\}$ again, we can write:

off-balance-sheet capital $= f\{\text{transferred risk}\}$
$$= \text{capital needed to cover transferred risk}$$

The Insurance Model focuses only on the risk being transferred and the cost of doing so. It does not address the capital released by transferring that risk. To do so, we need to develop a corporate finance view of the Insurance Model. This is an important intermediate step on the way to developing the Insurative Model.

In our examples above, the insurance cover would probably be stated as protection for losses up to, say, $1000 (the **insurance limit**) at a **premium rate** of 1%, or an insurance premium of $10. As we stated earlier, such a premium is appropriate for a high-severity, low-probability risk. The premium rate, expressed as a percentage of the insurance limit, does not provide the true cost of insurance as a capital resource, because the insurance limit does not signify the capital relief provided to the firm through insurance. (As mentioned earlier, by buying insurance the firm is relieved from raising some paid-up capital, hence the term "capital relief.") The capital relief is likely to be less than the insurance limit.

The insurance limit defines the maximum loss payable, but it does not reflect the probability of such a loss occurring. The insurance premium of $10 does represent the probability-weighted average of all possible losses, from the first dollar payable to the full insurance limit.[11] It is possible, therefore, that the probability of a full insurance limit loss occurring is less than 1%. In other words, with a probability of 99%, the loss under the insured risk is less than $1000. If a firm defines its probability of ruin threshold to be 1%, then the capital relief provided by the insurance cover is also less than the insurance limit of $1000.

Let us go one step further and assume that the firm has a number of insurance policies in place. Then, the insurance premium of $10 and the limit of $1000 are, respectively, the sums of all the firm's insurance premiums and limits. In this case, it is more than likely that the capital relief is less than $1000, since the probability of full-limit losses occurring simultaneously under all the policies is remote.

After doing a risk mapping analysis (discussed in Chapter 4), the company recognizes that this insurance program releases the need to raise paid-up capital of $500. Without insurance, the firm would have to raise $500 of equity (since equity and not debt is more appropriate to stand behind such risk). In the previous section, we defined this amount of capital need replaced by insurance as the insurance capital. The total of capital resources available to the firm is the sum of debt, equity and insurance capital. The first two are paid-up capital, and the last is off-balance-sheet capital. The following relationships describe the capital resources in the Insurance Model:

$$\begin{aligned} \textbf{firm capital} \ &= \textbf{paid-up capital} + \textbf{off-balance-sheet capital} \\ &= \textbf{debt capital} + \textbf{equity capital} + \textbf{insurance capital} \end{aligned}$$

Conventionally, the Insurance Model makes no statement about the shareholders' return on equity or the corporation's weighted-average cost of capital. Recognizing now that insurance is a component of corporate capital, how would these two measures be affected? We consider first the impact on ROE and then on WACC.

For both companies Alpha and Beta, the mere recognition of insurance has no impact on the ROE, since the earnings and the equity amounts are unchanged. The calculations in Box 3.1 and Box 3.2 remain the same. However, the recognition of insurance as a capital resource could change the amount of insurance that the firms have relative to debt and equity.

Does the ROE remain constant if the ratio of insurance to equity, for instance, is changed? We saw that leverage produced a higher ROE for Beta than Alpha. Therefore, changing the amount of insurance is likely to change ROE. To verify this, consider Alpha's decision to drop its insurance program and replace it with new equity (Box 3.4). First, dropping its insurance program saves $10 in expense. Second, its level of equity capital increases to $1500. The additional $500 is assumed to be deployed fully in the firm's activities and is able to earn the same return on assets, which we know is 16%. The firm earns 16% on assets of $1500, which is $240. This entire amount

Box 3.4   ROE for Alpha and Beta with no insurance if all assets earn 16%.

	Alpha	Beta	
Old paid-up capital =	$1000	$1000	= Old assets
New equity capital =	$ 500	$ 500	= New assets
Return on all assets =	16%	16%	
Net operating income =	$ 240	$ 240	
Interest on debt =	$ 0	$ 50	
Net operating earnings =	$ 240	$ 190	
Total equity capital =	$1500	$1000	
Uninsured ROE =	16%	19%	
Insured ROE =	15%	20%	
Change in ROE=	+1%	-1%	

is available to the shareholders, since there are no other providers of capital. The ROE is therefore 16% as well, an increase from the 15% calculated earlier. This analysis could lead one to believe that the shareholders of the uninsured firm earn an additional 1% return for taking over the risks that would have been otherwise insured. This reasoning is flawed.

To appreciate the flaw, suppose that Beta also decides to drop its insurance program and replace it with $500 of new equity. Like Alpha, the new assets also earn 16%, leading to net operating income of $240 on assets of $1500. Subtracting the interest on debt of $50 leaves net operating earnings of $190 on equity of $1000. Beta's ROE is now 19%, which is 1% less than the 20% calculated earlier. Surely the shareholders of the uninsured Beta are not giving up 1% in return for taking on the additional risks.

To understand the true dynamics, consider the change in return caused by converting $500 of off-balance-sheet capital (insurance) to $500 of paid-up capital (equity). Dropping the insurance program saves a premium expense of $10, or 2% of $500. Raising the new equity increases revenues by $80, or 16% of $500. The net change in return is the sum of these two amounts, which is $90, or 18% of $500. Alpha's ROE with insurance is 15%. The additional $500 equity brings a higher return of 18%. The new ROE is therefore increased to 16%. On the other hand, Beta with insurance has an ROE of 20%. The additional $500 equity brings a lower return of 18%, leading to a lower ROE of 19% (Box 3.5).

Box 3.5   Alternative calculation of uninsured ROE if all assets earn 16% .

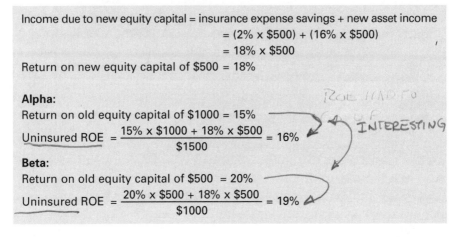

Income due to new equity capital = insurance expense savings + new asset income

$$= (2\% \times \$500) + (16\% \times \$500)$$

$$= 18\% \times \$500$$

Return on new equity capital of $500 = 18%

Alpha:

Return on old equity capital of $1000 = 15%

$$\text{Uninsured ROE} = \frac{15\% \times \$1000 + 18\% \times \$500}{\$1500} = 16\%$$

[handwritten: ROE IN TO BE INTERESTING]

Beta:

Return on old equity capital of $500 = 20%

$$\text{Uninsured ROE} = \frac{20\% \times \$500 + 18\% \times \$500}{\$1000} = 19\%$$

The preceding discussion confirms that insurance does indeed have an impact on the ROE of a firm. We were able to demonstrate this using two simplifying assumptions. These assumptions are embodied in the statement that the new assets can earn the same return on assets (ROA) of 16% as the old assets. Without these assumptions, the impact of insurance on ROE is likely to be even more pronounced. The two assumptions are:

- Availability of investment projects, and
- Efficient markets.

The first states that the firm will be able to deploy fully the additional $500 of equity in new projects to achieve 16% return on assets. In reality, the firm may not have sufficient projects to enable it to do so. More important, though, the firm may have to underinvest this capital to maintain a certain level of liquidity to meet the risky events normally covered by insurance. Instead of earning 16% return on the additional $500 of assets, the firm may only be able to achieve, say, 7%.

The second assumption is one of efficient markets. In contrast to the securities market, where there is a lot of information about the value of the securities traded in an open and transparent manner, the insurance market is one of bilateral negotiations, customized risk portfolios and, at best, opaque pricing. The very existence of the insurance industry indicates that moving

Box 3.6   Uninsured ROE if new assets earn 7%.

Income due to new equity capital = insurance expense savings + new asset income
$$= (2\% \times \$500) + (7\% \times \$500)$$
$$= 9\% \times \$500$$
Return on new equity capital of $500 = 9%

Alpha:
Return on old equity capital of $1000 = 15%

$$\text{Uninsured ROE} = \frac{15\% \times \$1000 + 9\% \times \$500}{\$1500} = 13\%$$

Beta:
Return on old equity capital of $500 = 20%

$$\text{Uninsured ROE} = \frac{20\% \times \$500 + 9\% \times \$500}{\$1000} = 14.5\%$$

(OFF- BALANCE SHEET)

risks from the balance sheet of a corporation to that of an insurance company creates value. Unfortunately, it is difficult to get a fix on that value. However, this value creation does imply that the firm's shareholders would not be able to get that same value by replacing insurance with more equity. Once again, instead of earning 16% return on the additional $500 of assets, the firm may only be able to earn, say, 7%.

Box 3.6 shows that if the new assets are only able to earn 7%, then Alpha's ROE falls from 15% to 13% in the absence of insurance. Similarly, Beta's ROE falls from 20% to 14.5%.

We now turn our attention to the cost of capital. How does one construct the WACC in this case? The Standard Model would look at the cost of debt and equity only. For the companies in our examples, the Standard Model produced a WACC of 15%. That cannot be the true cost, since it ignores insurance. An alternative way to calculate the cost of capital is to develop a true WACC that incorporates both on- and off-balance-sheet capital. We call this the **total average cost of capital** (TACC). The numerator is the sum of the cost of insurance and the costs of debt and equity. The denominator is not just the value of paid-up capital but the total value of firm capital, including insurance.

If we define the total value of firm capital to be **firm value**, then:

$$\text{firm value} = \text{debt value} + \text{equity value} + \text{insurance value}$$
$$= \text{paid-up value} + \text{off-balance-sheet value}$$

and

$$\text{TACC} = \quad \text{cost of debt} \quad \times \frac{\text{debt value}}{\text{firm value}}$$
$$+ \text{cost of equity} \quad \times \frac{\text{equity value}}{\text{firm value}}$$
$$+ \text{cost of insurance} \times \frac{\text{insurance value}}{\text{firm value}}$$

– NEW TERM.

Two terms in the equation have not been defined yet: insurance value and cost of insurance. We address each in turn.

We defined insurance capital earlier as the capital relief provided by insurance. Now we need to determine the value of this capital relief, which we define as **insurance value**. Unlike debt value and equity value, insurance value is not directly observable in the financial markets. We propose that the best estimate of the value of insurance to a firm is the current amount of capital relief that insurance provides. At any point in time, if the firm decides to replace insurance with paid-up capital, it will have to raise new equity. By definition, the amount of new equity will have to equal the capital relief provided by insurance at that instant. At the date of issue, the book value of new equity equals its market value. Hence, the value of the capital relief (book value) is equal to the insurance value (market value).

The **cost of insurance** (COI) is defined as a firm's current insurance rate for its covered risks, measured as a percentage of insurance capital. It is the discount rate that equates the present value of expected insurance premiums to the insurance value. The next step, therefore, is to estimate the future stream of insurance premiums that the firm is likely to pay. When insurance protection is provided in capital markets form (e.g. derivatives), the insurance premium is determined as the current trading price of the cover. When it is provided through an insurance contract, the current insurance premium is not always observable, but it is possible to get indicative quotes. If we assume that the expected insurance premium is the same each year in perpetuity, then:

$$\text{Cost of insurance} = \frac{\text{expected annual insurance premium}}{\text{insurance value}} \; \%$$

For both Alpha and Beta, the insurance value equals the capital relief of $500. If the expected annual insurance premium stays at the current amount of $10, then cost of insurance is 2% ($10/$500).

We now have all the values necessary to calculate the TACC for Alpha and Beta (Box 3.7). The total value of the firm's capital resources, including insurance, is $1500. Both firms pay the same insurance premium ($10) and the same expense on paid-up capital ($150), for a total of $160. This gives a TACC of 10.67% for each firm.

We showed that under the Standard Model, the WACC of the unlever-aged firm, Alpha, equals its cost of equity. In the Insurance Model, it is clear that TACC does not equal cost of equity. This is because insurance is recognized explicitly in the calculations.

If the firm had no insurance as well, would the TACC be equal to cost of equity? Under the idealized assumptions of the MM Propositions, the answer is absolutely yes. In Box 3.4 we showed that the net operating earnings of Alpha without insurance are $240. As before, if the market value of equity is assumed to be its book value of $1500, then cost of equity is 16% ($240/$1500). Substituting into the formula in Box 3.7 gives a TACC for uninsured Alpha of 16%. In Box 3.8, the TACC for uninsured Beta is shown to be 16% as well, as predicted by the MM Propositions.

Box 3.7   Total average cost of capital (TACC) for Insurance Model.

$$\text{TACC} = \text{cost of debt} \times \frac{\text{debt value}}{\text{firm value}}$$

$$+ \text{cost of equity} \times \frac{\text{equity value}}{\text{firm value}}$$

$$+ \text{cost of insurance} \times \frac{\text{insurance value}}{\text{firm value}}$$

Alpha:

$$\text{TACC} = 10\% \times \frac{\$ \ 0}{\$1500} + 15\% \times \frac{\$1000}{\$1500} + 2\% \times \frac{\$ \ 500}{\$1500} = 10.67\%$$

Beta:

$$\text{TACC} = 10\% \times \frac{\$ \ 500}{\$1500} + 20\% \times \frac{\$ \ 500}{\$1500} + 2\% \times \frac{\$ \ 500}{\$1500} = 10.67\%$$

Box 3.8   TACC for uninsured Alpha and Beta.

TACC for uninsured Alpha:

$$\text{Cost of equity} = \frac{\$\ 240}{\$1500} = 16\%$$

Since debt value = 0 and insurance value = 0, TACC = COE = 16%.

TACC for uninsured Beta:

$$\text{Cost of equity} = \frac{\$\ 190}{\$1000} = 19\%$$

$$\text{TACC} = 10\% \times \frac{\$\ 500}{\$1500} + 19\% \times \frac{\$1000}{\$1500} + 2\% \times \frac{\$\ 0}{\$1500} = 16\%$$

If we relax these idealized assumptions and assume, as before, that the new equity for an uninsured firm can only earn 7%, instead of 16%, then it is not reasonable to use the costs of equity of 16% and 19% for uninsured Alpha and Beta. The shareholders would actually earn a lower return, and would adjust their expectations downward. The underutilized equity capital becomes a drag on earnings.

It is notable that the TACC of the insured firm is lower than the TACC of the uninsured firm. Clearly, this need not always be so. A poorly constructed insurance or hedging program may not provide the necessary capital relief to a firm. However, if it is structured appropriately, the reduction in capital costs can be significant. *The conventional focus on WACC in the Standard Model misses this point entirely.*

In summary, the conventional Insurance Model does not consider ROE and WACC explicitly, but it is not too much of a stretch to take a corporate finance view of insurance.

The Insurative Model

The next step is obvious. Combining the effects of the Standard Model and the Insurance Model gives us a simple generalized framework to consider the effects of on- and off-balance-sheet capital, accessing both the insurance and capital markets. We call this the Insurative Model.

In effect, the Insurative Model equates all firm capital to the amount necessary to cover all firm risks, both retained and transferred. Using the function $f\{\text{risk}\}$ as before, we have:

$$\text{firm capital} = f\{\text{firm risk}\}$$
$$= \text{capital needed to cover firm risk}$$

Or:

$$\text{paid-up capital} + \text{off-balance-sheet capital}$$
$$= f\{\text{retained risk}\} + f\{\text{transferred risk}\}$$

STND MODEL   *INSURANCE MODEL*

This is structurally richer than merely combining the Standard Model and the Insurance Model. Recall that in the Standard Model, paid-up capital only referred to retained risk and in the Insurance Model, off-balance-sheet capital only referred to transferred risk. In the Insurative Model, paid-up capital can be used to cover some of both retained and transferred risks. Likewise, off-balance-sheet capital can be used to cover some of both those risks as well (Box 3.9). *This framework captures the economics both of conventional insurance and corporate finance instruments, as well as the new integrated products.*

What implications does this model have for our picture of corporate capital structure? Figure 3.4 shows just how rich the diversity of corporate capital resources can be, and how necessary it is to develop this generalized model of corporate capital and risk.

First, we can identify those resources that provide paid-up capital to the firm. If these cover risks retained by the firm, then they are the familiar varieties of equity and debt as well as some forms of finite risk reinsurance

Box 3.9   Risk related to capital in the Insurative Model.

If paid-up capital (PC) covers the proportions p of retained risk (RR) and q of transferred risk (TR), and off-balance- sheet capital (OC) covers the rest, then:

$$PC = \quad p \times f\{RR\} + \quad q \times f\{TR\}$$
$$OC = \quad (1\text{-}p) \times f\{RR\} + (1\text{-}q) \times f\{TR\}$$

Summing both sides of these equations gives:

$$PC + OC = f\{RR\} + f\{TR\}$$

Or: Firm Capital = Firm Risk

Figure 3.4   The Insurative Model.

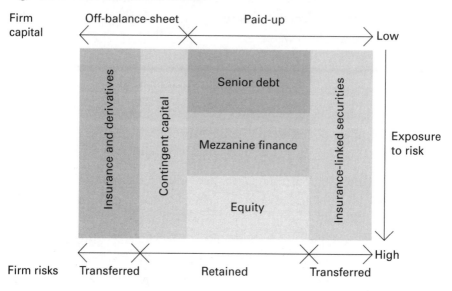

(covered in Chapter 7). If they cover risks that are being transferred away from the firm, then they are the new instruments such as insurance-linked securities which embed insurance risks in corporate bonds (described in Chapter 10).

Second, we can identify those resources that release the firm from raising paid-up capital immediately. If they cover risks that are being transferred away from the firm, then they are insurance or derivative contracts (Chapters 6 and 11). If they cover risks that are retained by the firm, then they are the new instruments such as contingent capital (Chapter 9). In addition, we can consider the effect on corporate capital of transferring risks of discontinued businesses off-balance-sheet using run-off facilities (Chapter 8).

We coined the term Insurative[12] to refer to any corporate capital resource, be it debt, equity, insurance, derivative, contingent capital or any other. The Insurative Model embraces all of these instruments and allows us to evaluate their effectiveness in a consistent framework.

The Standard Model's exclusive focus on debt and equity ignores the range of capital resources available to a corporation. This can distort the view of a firm's capital cost and its return on equity. In particular, minimizing the WACC under the Standard Model may not lead to minimizing the TACC of the corporation.

As we saw in the previous section, if the mix of insurance, debt and equity remains unchanged, there should be no change in the ROE under the expanded model. The generalized framework then states the ROE equation as:

$$ROE = \frac{\text{net operating earnings}}{\text{equity capital}}$$

where net operating earnings is the amount available to shareholders after paying all the costs of other paid-up and off-balance-sheet capital, and equity capital is a book-value measure.

In this model, the TACC considers all sources of capital. The numerator includes the costs of both on- and off-balance-sheet capital. The denominator is not just the value of paid-up capital but the total value of the capital resources of the firm, i.e. firm value. As we stated earlier, the TACC formula is:

$$
\begin{aligned}
TACC = \quad & \text{cost of debt} \quad \times \frac{\text{debt value}}{\text{firm value}} \\
+ \, & \text{cost of equity} \quad \times \frac{\text{equity value}}{\text{firm value}} \\
+ \, & \text{cost of insurance} \times \frac{\text{insurance value}}{\text{firm value}}
\end{aligned}
$$

The sum of the first two terms is the proportion of TACC due to paid-up capital, and the last term is the proportion of TACC due to off-balance-sheet capital. As we show in Box 3.10, WACC, the cost of paid-up capital, is only one component in the true capital cost of the firm.

If we define **paid-up value** to be the value of paid-up capital, then:

$$\textbf{paid-up value} = \textbf{debt value} + \textbf{equity value}$$

This allows us to restate TACC in the following way:

$$
\begin{aligned}
TACC = \quad & \text{WACC} \quad \times \frac{\text{paid-up value}}{\text{firm value}} \\
+ \, & \text{cost of insurance} \times \frac{\text{insurance value}}{\text{firm value}}
\end{aligned}
$$

Although the examples in this chapter have considered debt, equity and insurance (of both insurance risks and capital markets risks) separately,

Box 3.10   Relationship of TACC to WACC.

$$TACC = \text{cost of debt} \quad \times \quad \frac{\text{debt value}}{\text{firm value}}$$

$$+ \text{cost of equity} \quad \times \quad \frac{\text{equity value}}{\text{firm value}}$$

$$+ \text{cost of insurance} \quad \times \quad \frac{\text{insurance value}}{\text{firm value}}$$

Adjust the first two terms:

$$TACC = \text{cost of debt} \quad \times \quad \frac{\text{debt value}}{\text{paid-up value}} \quad \times \quad \frac{\text{paid-up value}}{\text{firm value}}$$

$$+ \text{cost of equity} \quad \times \quad \frac{\text{equity value}}{\text{paid-up value}} \quad \times \quad \frac{\text{paid-up value}}{\text{firm value}}$$

$$+ \text{cost of insurance} \quad \times \quad \frac{\text{insurance value}}{\text{firm value}}$$

Combine the first two terms:

$$TACC = \quad WACC \quad \times \quad \frac{\text{paid-up value}}{\text{firm value}}$$

$$+ \text{cost of insurance} \times \quad \frac{\text{insurance value}}{\text{firm value}}$$

the Insurative framework is general enough to consider risk management techniques that combine facets of all these elements.

This framework shows us that a firm's decisions on insurance and risk retention can be just as important as its decisions on its debt-equity mix. The determination of a firm's optimal debt-equity mix is only the last in a series of capital structure decisions that its management must make. As we show in Box 3.11,

Box 3.11   Steps in determining a firm's debt-equity mix.

1. Identify the firm's risks.
2. Calculate the capital required to cover those risks.
3. Determine the risks to transfer and to retain.
4. Determine the amount of paid-up capital and off-balance-sheet capital needed.
5. Structure the off-balance-sheet capital.
6. Structure the paid-up capital, which includes the decision on debt-equity mix.

the preceding steps include decisions on risk retention, risk transfer, and the amounts and structure of paid-up and off-balance-sheet capital.

It is worthwhile now to highlight a point touched on in the previous section. Financial statements of corporations do not adequately disclose all off-balance-sheet facilities. In particular, insurance protection is not clearly described. Financial managers do try to give an accurate account of their capital costs and return potential. However, being familiar with the Standard Model, they focus on ROE and WACC. The Insurative Model shows that this does not give the true picture: *no distinction is made between companies that are well-insured (or hedged) and those that are not.*

The Insurative Model allows us to compare the impact of derivatives strategies, multi-line insurance covers, contingent capital facilities, finite risk reinsurance, insurance-linked securitization, asset-backed securitization, and various forms of debt and equity in one consistent framework. The prerequisites for making such comparisons appropriately are by no means trivial; they require a thorough understanding of the firm's risks, their interactions and their impact on financial performance. On top of this, the structural features of the insuratives must be modeled and their impact on the firm assessed. Then, the firm must determine the decision criteria for selecting a particular capital structure, and put the appropriate capital resources in place. In the next chapter we discuss some of these elements. For now, we turn our attention to how the interaction between risk and capital management is changing the function of corporate risk management.

THE CHANGING FUNCTION OF RISK MANAGEMENT

This analytical framework was developed to help describe some of the changes that are already taking place in corporate risk management.

We saw in Chapter 1 that the risk manager and treasurer are entrusted with managing operational and financial risks within the framework of a given capital structure, the composition of which is the responsibility of the CFO. Besides avoiding or reducing risk, the risk manager has traditionally had recourse to the insurance markets to transfer risk to third parties, and the treasurer has had recourse to the capital markets to transfer risk and (separately) to obtain financing. The CFO has viewed the capital markets as the primary vehicle for maintaining or transforming capital structure.

As capital and insurance markets converge, progressive organizations have started developing risk management tools that incorporate features of both. For example, one of the new integrated risk management products (described in Chapter 6) provides a single block of insurance capacity that protects against a broad set of risks, both those that are traditionally insured and those that are hedged in the capital markets. It may be inefficient to purchase insurance and financial loss protection separately, because the corporation may be overprotected on the financial side and underprotected on the insurance side, or vice versa. By purchasing an integrated cover that protects both insurance and financial exposures, the corporation is assured that capacity will be available no matter what the source of the loss is. And, of course, no matter what the source of the loss is, the ultimate effect on the bottom line is the same.

Another consequence of the convergence of insurance and capital markets is the development of tools that combine risk transfer and financing. For example, finite risk reinsurance products (Chapter 7) combine financing and risk transfer in a way that allows corporations to achieve in a single transaction the benefits of both insurance and debt financing.

The revolution in risk management techniques has implications for the CFO as well. Any policy regarding capital structure configuration is predicated on an assessment of the risks confronting the corporation. As we saw in the Insurative Model, a company's risk profile may change as a result of the implementation of new risk management instruments, with a consequent change in the corporate capital needs. Instead of simply optimizing the balance of debt and equity, the CFO now has at least three instruments to use: debt, equity and insurance.

In addition, there are techniques that directly address the capital structure issue. Given that equity capital is an expensive source of long-term financing, and that the risk profile of a firm determines its required amount of equity capital, substitutes for paid-up equity capital have the potential to offer significant economies. Contingent capital products (Chapter 9), for example, promise to infuse the company with capital precisely when it is needed—in the event of a catastrophic loss. These products eliminate the need to hold expensive on-balance-sheet equity capital for those rare events that may inflict severe financial harm on a corporation. An off-balance-sheet contingent capital facility (almost insurance, but not quite) can be cost effective.

These examples show that the CFO, treasurer and risk manager need to recognize that integrating corporate risk management can take place at several levels. At its most basic, the integration can occur within the separate worlds of the treasurer and the risk manager. At the next level, integration can occur across the two markets. A further level of integration takes place with the inclusion of the CFO's domain of corporate capital structure. Finally, all these forces can lead to fundamental structural changes in the markets for risk capital.

"It is very much art and not science."

4

Risk Mapping

PRAKASH SHIMPI

Why use a map? Because it gives you the lay of the land, tells you where you are and helps determine the best route to your destination. For the same reasons, it seems like a good idea to have maps for business as well. Managers have run businesses successfully for generations using a variety of business maps, such as 5-year business plans or 3-year projected financial statements. They understand the opportunities they face and the risks they have to manage, but they appear to have done so without resorting to "risk mapping." What is risk mapping, then, and why is it such a necessary part of the process of integrating corporate risk management?

In Chapter 2 we urged that effective corporate governance requires management to declare "A Risk's a Risk." In this chapter, we propose that to do so, corporate managers need to recognize the full spectrum of risks their organizations face and not be colored by their own local experiences and perspectives. **Risk mapping** is the exercise that enables a company to catalog and quantify the impact of the variety of risks it faces. It is very much art and not science. Inevitably, personal judgement weighs heavily in all its phases. There is, as yet, no standard approach to developing a risk map. We present an overview of the key steps, recognizing that there will be significant variations across companies.

Although not labeled as such, risk mapping in some form has always been a part of the management process. Current technology makes feasible a more comprehensive, systematic analysis of a company's risks. The demands of shareholder scrutiny and the desire for earnings stability make it imperative for managers to be better versed in all the risks facing their corporations. In effect, risk mapping centralizes the identification of risks that occur in various parts of a corporation. It is a necessary first step in developing a corporation's risk and capital management strategy.

The exercise of risk mapping sounds like such a daunting task. Where to begin? Which risks should be included? How can you possibly identify all the risks? When do you know you are done? Make no mistake—it is a formidable undertaking. However, the fruits of the labor are well worth it. In our experience, managers value the process of risk mapping as much as they do the risk map itself. It forces them to ask questions, learn more about their organization, and recognize both the opportunities and challenges presented by the risks they face.

THE RISK MAPPING PROCESS

Alice in Wonderland asked, "Would you tell me, please, which way I ought to go from here?" The Cheshire cat replied, "That depends a good deal on where you want to get to." Likewise, to start the risk mapping process, it is important to know what you want to get out of it.

Some of the objectives of risk mapping can be to:

- Articulate the firm's risk appetite in a framework that can be applied across all its operations,
- Develop a catalog of critical risks to the firm and ensure that appropriate processes are in place to manage them, and
- Develop a dynamic financial model of the firm which incorporates all major risks that affect earnings.

From these objectives, some of the tasks emerge rather naturally. First is to develop an idea of what a critical risk is. Management should agree on the measures that will be used to determine the significance of the risk to the firm. Let us call this step **measurement**. Second, in the **classification** step, management should decide how to organize the catalog of risks that will be analyzed. These first two steps establish a framework to develop the risk map.

Box 4.1   Steps in risk mapping.

1. Measurement	Establish parameters to quantify impact of any risk
2. Classification	Organize top-down framework for cataloging risks
3. Identification	Develop bottom-up list of specific risks facing the firm
4. Assessment	Evaluate significance of each identified risk
5. Analysis	Model collective impact of risks on the firm

The third step, **identification**, should list all the risks that the managers deem relevant, using this framework as a guide. Next, in the **assessment** step, each risk is evaluated using the agreed measures to determine how critical it is. Finally, this information is brought together in the **analysis** step. Here, a collective analysis of all the risks generates management reports to satisfy the objectives of the exercise. If the analytical models are built well, they can also be used to test the efficiency of various risk management solutions.

Although our description would imply that these five steps occur sequentially, the reality is that they will often overlap. For example, the process of categorization will be refined during the identification phase, and the measures selected may be modified during the assessment phase. However, if we assume a clean progression from one step to the next, it does make it easier to present each of them in the following sections.

Measurement

A map must have measures that provide qualitative and quantitative information about each location on it. For a corporation, it is natural to think about measures of financial impact on the firm. There are a variety of measures that can be used. Some can reflect the impact on financial statements such as earnings or cash flow volatility. Others can focus on the impact on economic value such as value-at-risk or market capitalization. Perhaps there may be some that capture information such as the degree of reputational damage or percent of market share lost.

There should be one set of measures that can be applied across all types of risk. This requirement is helpful to the extent that it limits the number of choices of measures that are available. On the other hand, it is a hindrance for exactly the same reason! For example, some of the measures that are commonplace in managing financial risks (the "greeks") would not be appropriate for other types of risks. If one of the objectives of risk mapping is to get a better understanding of the risks faced by the firm, it is entirely reasonable to be less precise in measurement and more complete in the list of risks considered.

One measure that has been used in several risk mapping exercises to compare all categories of risk is the **severity of loss**, expressed as a percentage of earnings or profits. This is often combined with a measure of the **frequency** with which the risk occurs.

Within any particular category of risk, additional risk measures can be specified to apply only to those risks. When possible, additional precision within a category is helpful to further rank risks and customize solutions that manage those particular risks.

Classification

This phase of risk mapping takes a top-down perspective on the firm's business risks. It starts with the broadest collections of risks and, at each stage, further sub-divides them into more narrowly defined categories. It is probably easiest to describe this by way of some examples.

For instance, we saw in Figure 1.1 that the corporation first divides risks into two categories: global risks and organizational risks. Global risks are generally beyond the firm's control, although they must be included in the risk map, since responses to those risks have to be developed. Organizational risks arise out of the firm's activities. Even in this simple division, there are risks that occur in both categories. For example, currency risks depend on both the global financial markets and the extent to which the corporation has activities in other countries. Organizational risks are further divided into business risks and hazard risks, which in turn are divided respectively into financial/market risks and political risks, and operational risks and legal liability risks.

If this seems rather abstract, consider the risk categories utilized by a typical telecommunications company (Figure 4.1). The company measures

Figure 4.1   Telecom risk map.

Operational risk

Operational control risk

Errors and omissions
Cost structure
Control procedures
Rebates and withdrawals
Governance and accountability

Information system risk

System synchronization
Unauthorized system changes
Billing accuracy
Disaster recovery
Outsourced services

Employee relations risk

Human resources procedures
Industrial actions
Workers' compensation
Skills and training
Cultural mix

Network risk

Capacity & utilization
Network fraud
Broadband utilization
Network bottlenecks
Unplanned outages

Business risk

Business event risk

Technological advance
Regulatory change
Spectrum auction
Reputation damage
Business interruption

Credit risk

Credit rating
Customer churn
Service provider liquidity
Trade credit
Political risk

Service alliance risk

Service provider concentration
Alliance management
Outsourcing selection
Service quality
Service outages

Legal risk

Professional liability
Directors and officers liability
Contractual liability
Product liability
Third-party liability

Market risk

Equity risk

Shareholder management
Equity base
Dividend policy
Strategic investments
Capital expenditures

Financial risk

Interest rates
Foreign exchange
Credit spreads
Tax expenditures
Cash flow and liquidity

Product risk

Product complexity
Product obsolescence
Product development
Wholesale and retail mix
Packaging and delivery

Competitor Risk

Pricing strategy
Market share
Churn management
Marketing strategy
Product array

its risk in 3 categories: operational, business and market risks. Each of these is further divided into 4 major sub-categories. In the next phase of risk mapping, the firm uses these 12 categories to organize its entire list of risks.

Identification

Once the framework has been established, it can be used to help identify the specific risks faced by the corporation. As management evaluates each of its operations, it will identify the risks inherent in them. Many of the significant risks facing a company are obvious, and management is likely to have an instinctive feel for the nature of those risks. Others may be less obvious, and are identified only through the risk mapping process.

The risk landscape has changed for many companies. The globalization of many markets, coupled with technological advances, has led to the emergence of new industries and new risks. The biggest risks that many companies face at present are not necessarily those that have been covered traditionally by the insurance or capital markets. Some of the most important are negative publicity, warranty obligations, cash flow uncertainty, failed product launches and the departure of managers in key positions. Restructuring and M&A activity are also driving factors. Every corporate restructuring program involves withdrawal from certain lines of business and the elimination of certain liability claims that originated in previous business years.[1]

To illustrate this phase of the process, consider the risks faced by pharmaceutical companies. A survey of CFOs, treasurers and risk managers of 32 leading pharmaceutical companies in the United States and Europe provides insight into the industry's risk landscape (Appendix 4A). The survey explains that both the industry's merger activity and the diversity of businesses owned by these pharmaceutical companies have exposed them to the risks of other industries such as health care, chemicals, medical devices and nutrition (Figure 4A.1 in Appendix 4A). The respondents identified their top 10 risks in descending order as:

1. Product liability
2. Business interruption

3. Environmental pollution
4. Natural disasters
5. Defense of patent infringement
6. Investment in R&D
7. Product recall
8. General liability
9. Changing legal environment
10. Loss of data

It is interesting to note that financial risks such as interest rate risks, currency risks and credit risks did not make the top 10 (Figure 4A.2 in Appendix 4A).

Another illustration shows the risks identified by the managers of the telecommunications company we encountered in the previous section (Figure 4.1). The chart shows only the major risks in each of the categories. What it does not show is the detailed information, developed in this risk mapping exercise, of the characteristics of each risk on the chart—the risk assessment.

Assessment

As the risks are being identified and analyzed, an assessment of the significance of each risk has to be made. This is a combination of both qualitative and quantitative analysis.

A qualitative assessment describes a risk in a way that aids the understanding of how the risk presents itself and how it impacts the firm's operations. An illustration of the type of qualitative information that can be developed is shown in Appendix 4B, an extract from a risk mapping database for the airline industry. It shows that an earthquake can impact an airline in several ways and that there are several standard insurance products that are able to handle many of these exposures. Nevertheless, coverage is still not available for loss of revenues and the higher cost of providing services after an earthquake when there has been no physical damage to an airline's aircraft or infrastructure. For any particular airline, this information will refer to the firm's specific risks and the level of detail will be significantly greater.

Likewise, the information in Appendix 4A is a qualitative assessment of some of the risks that face the pharmaceutical industry. In addition, quantitative analysis using selected measures of risk helps develop a better understanding of the significance of each risk. Figure 4.2 shows the risk map of a pharmaceutical company. The two axes reflect quantitative measures of each

Figure 4.2   Risk profile of a pharmaceutical company.

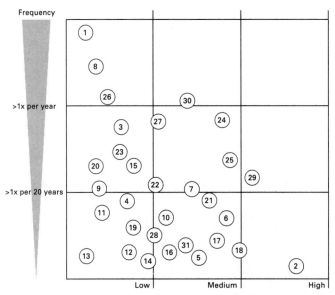

Third party liability
1. Automobile liability/ aircraft
2. Product liability
3. Clinical trials
4. Premises liability
5. Fiduciary
6. Environmental impairment (pollution)
7. Patent infringment

Workforce
8. Workers' compensation
9. Employers liability
10. D&O liability
11. EPL
12. Key person loss
13. Employee theft/ dishonesty

Terrorism
14. Malicious tampering/ extortion
15. Theft/kidnapping/ bombing, etc

First party damage/BI
16. Fire/explosion, etc
17. Natural catastrophes
18. Business interruption
19. Machinery breakdown
20. Marine/cargo
21. Product recall
22. Data loss/inaccuracy

Financial
23. Credit risk
24. Currency exchange rates
25. R&D investments
26. Interest rates
27. Negative publicity
28. Pension fund

Regulatory
29. FDA: mandated recall/interr. in prod.
30. FDA: registration failures/delays

Political
31. Political risk, war

risk. The vertical axis shows the frequency with which a risk occurs. The horizontal axis shows the severity of the risk, using percentage of profits lost as the measure. For the "big picture," it is sufficient to show simply the relative ranking of each risk along each axis. Precision is not the objective. However, some degree of precision is necessary to develop meaningful risk management solutions, and therefore appropriate models have to be built to capture the dynamics of each risk.

Analysis

The analysis phase translates the "big picture" risk map into a more comprehensive corporate model—a more detailed risk map. The financial services industry, particularly banks and insurance companies, has a long history of using corporate models to capture the dynamics of their operations. Their experience can help develop an understanding of the challenges involved in building a corporate model.

In the insurance industry, the **model office** is a term used to describe the asset and liability models that are jointly used to analyze the emergence of profits over the lifetime of the insurance policies sold by a company. These model offices have three elements. First, the underlying models describing each asset or liability are built. Second, a macroeconomic model is overlaid across all the underlying asset and liability models. This ensures that there is consistency of economic drivers across all the asset and liability models.

Finally, the macroeconomic model and the individual asset and liability models feed into a corporate model. The corporate model generates the financial information of the operation such as cash flow reports, pro-forma financial statements and economic value analysis. At this stage, it is common for the model to have the ability to run simulations over a wide variety of scenarios over multiple time horizons, generating a wealth of information on the dynamics of the business.

Although the model office captures the profit dynamics of policies sold by an insurance company, it does not describe its business risks adequately. A significant omission is the organizational risks faced by the firm. The latest evolution of the model office, known as dynamic financial analysis (DFA), promises to be more comprehensive. Analogous to DFA models in the financial markets are value-at-risk (VAR) models. They focus on the dynamics of financial market risks without considering the operational and other non-financial risks of a firm.

A bank's model of a corporation works differently. In order to interest equity investors or to raise debt financing, the bank has to demonstrate the strength of its client's financial performance over some reasonable time period. To do so, the bank builds a corporate model of the client. Generally, the starting point is the client's most recent financial statement. Line items on that statement are then projected over the term of the financing. Sensitivity tests are performed to understand the types of "shocks" that the client is able to withstand and still continue to meet shareholder or debt obligations. These models tend to be less mathematically sophisticated than the insurance model office but they do tend to be more representative of the corporate operations.

Combining the strengths of the bank corporate finance models and the dynamic simulations used by insurers may be the way ahead for corporations with a more sophisticated approach to risk management. Eventually, as is the case with banks and insurance companies, such models will be standard tools for corporate CFOs, treasurers and risk managers. Progressive companies have already begun developing basic models to help evaluate the financial impact of key risks and the relative efficiency of different risk management solutions.

RISK MAPPING IS ONLY THE FIRST STEP

Risk mapping is clearly not a one-time effort. Business and economic environments change, as do their impact on the company. Core business risks may disappear or change in magnitude. Non-core risks may one day become core risks. Subsidiaries are bought and sold. The risk map of the firm is not static. Management should re-evaluate its risk map regularly. Once the risk map has been built, the re-evaluation should be more straightforward. *Risk mapping, if it is to be meaningful, should be as dynamic as the world in which the corporation operates.*

Risk mapping is only the first step in understanding a firm's risks and developing the appropriate capital and risk management responses. We saw in Chapter 3 that an evaluation of the firm's risks is necessary to determine the firm's capital needs. In Part II we examine various tools that can be used to manage those risks.

Appendix 4A

Risk Faced by Pharmaceutical Companies

The Pharmaceutical Industry's Perspective

To gain a clear picture of the risks pharmaceutical companies face, Swiss Re New Markets commissioned an independent market research survey. In the survey, 32 risk managers and 14 chief financial officers or treasurers were asked to outline the biggest risks they confront in their businesses and to explain how they deal with them. The 32 companies surveyed are based in the United States or Europe, and are among the world's leading pharmaceutical businesses.

The survey concluded that pharmaceutical companies are inclined to see themselves as a case apart. They believe that they have a much higher exposure to product liability risks than other industries and they identified three reasons for this. First, the industry's products are used directly on human beings. The products are absorbed by the body with the expectation of producing a beneficial effect. Second, pharmaceutical products are used regularly and by many people. If a problem were to arise, its impact could be enormous compared to what it might cause in other industries. Third, side effects may take a while to appear, sometimes only after several years of continuous use. In the worst-case scenario, such problems may even be passed on to later generations.

Pharmaceutical risks also vary from company to company. According to those interviewed, there is, for example, a distinction between drugs used for shorter and longer terms. If a company's product range leans more toward long-term treatments, it courts a larger product liability risk than if it markets a greater number of short-term treatments. There is also a different level of risk attached to medications used to treat existing illnesses and those used by healthy persons for preventive or even cosmetic reasons.

In addition, according to the survey results, the diversification of many pharmaceutical companies into other industries leaves them exposed to a variety of risks (Figure 4A.1). Those companies active in chemical or

Extracted from Swiss Re New Markets, Risk Handling and Financing in Pharmaceutical Enterprises (Zurich: Swiss Reinsurance Company, 1998).

Figure 4.A1   Business diversification of pharmaceutical enterprises.

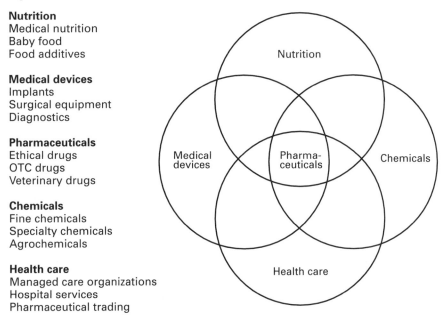

Nutrition
Medical nutrition
Baby food
Food additives

Medical devices
Implants
Surgical equipment
Diagnostics

Pharmaceuticals
Ethical drugs
OTC drugs
Veterinary drugs

Chemicals
Fine chemicals
Specialty chemicals
Agrochemicals

Health care
Managed care organizations
Hospital services
Pharmaceutical trading

agrochemical business showed a perception of risk that was qualitatively different from purely pharmaceutical companies.

Major Perceived Risks

Product Liability

The survey found that the pharmaceutical industry regards product liability as its greatest threat. In addition to liability claims, which can largely be covered by traditional risk transfer methods, companies are particularly concerned about the damage that a major loss could cause to their image. One of the unique problems pharmaceutical companies mentioned in dealing with product liability is the difficulty of building meaningful risk models. The severity and timing of future claims is unpredictable. As a result, risk managers said they had to cope with the possibility that a major liability claim could threaten the solvency of their businesses without their ever knowing just how severe a claim might be.

Those selling into the highly important U.S. market were especially aware of the risk potential of the U.S. legal system. Aside from the direct financial loss incurred through a product liability claim, risk managers also cited a number of less tangible problems, such a loss of market share, that could be equally damaging. They believed that the negative publicity generated by a major claim would likely extend its impact to the company's other products, driving consumers to seek alternatives.

Although pharmaceutical companies go to great lengths to limit their product liability risks using quality assurance techniques—they are legally required to carry out stringent pre-clinical studies and extensive clinical tests—the risk managers surveyed agreed that even the most sophisticated controls cannot entirely prevent occurrences.

Business Interruption

The second most critical concern identified by the survey was the risk of a breakdown in the production process. Those interviewed said the trend toward centralizing production, either in a single unit, or with several units carrying out individual tasks, has increased this risk. In today's fully rationalized business, there is hardly any duplication of production, meaning that a single stoppage could have far-reaching consequences.

At first glance, this may not seem too grave a problem as far as the corporate balance sheet is concerned: the traditional insurance market continues to supply the funds needed to replace damaged infrastructure. While this would be adequate in many other industries, the effects of business interruption are more complicated in pharmaceutical businesses. To begin with, those who depend on certain medications must continue to receive their supplies. If the pharmaceutical company has enough inventory to cover the production shortfall, this may not be problematic. Unfortunately, strict regulations governing the storage of drugs, combined with their often short shelf-life, make this a limited option. Moreover, the survey pointed to the problem that the storage facility itself may have been either lost or contaminated, especially where storage and production occupy nearby units.

According to the survey, risk managers must also consider how to replace intermediate compounds used at different stages in the production process. The later in the chain the interruption occurs, the harder it is to remedy, they agreed. To avoid catastrophic loss, companies must either have the capacity to switch production elsewhere, or be able to procure compounds from other sources.

As a result, intermediaries served by the pharmaceutical industry and its clients are likely to turn to an alternative brand. Once this happens, the risk managers contended, clients may not return to the original product when it becomes available again. A single business interruption incident,

Figure 4.A2 Major risks as percieved by pharmaceutical risk managers.

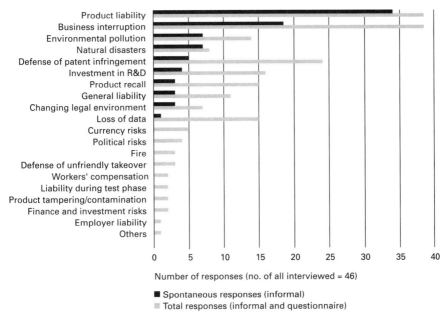

Number of responses (no. of all interviewed = 46)

■ Spontaneous responses (informal)
▓ Total responses (informal and questionnaire)

therefore, can cause both a short- to medium-term decline in turnover and long-term damage to the company's market share and corporate image. Those interviewed said the cost value of this risk is hard to quantify, and insurers are reluctant to cover it. Instead, pharmaceutical companies have to carry this burden alone. In trying to reduce their exposure, risk managers said they have invested considerable amounts in preventive measures, such as technical equipment to protect their manufacturing plants, in attempts to reduce the probability of a loss. Even so, they are aware that no matter how stringent such programs are, the risk of loss is never fully eradicated.

The survey revealed that patent infringement, product recall, R&D and environmental risks, while overshadowed in severity by product liability and business interruption, were nevertheless of significant concern.

Significant Risks

Patent Infringement

Somewhat surprisingly, the survey showed that protecting intellectual property was considered to be a critical risk for pharmaceutical companies. This reflects the increasingly fierce competitive environment for both R&D

and product offerings. Those interviewed in the survey were generally concerned about possible financial losses resulting from the infringement of other companies' patents.

Moreover, the growing number of counterfeit products hitting the market, especially in Eastern Europe and China, represents a considerable threat to established companies, especially when the copy sports the company's brand name. The survey concluded that few risk managers seek protection for this particular hazard. However, they said their attitude may change if the number of violations were to multiply.

Product Recall

The risk involved is less the actual product recall than the subsequent damage to the pharmaceutical business' public image. While having a product recalled and dealing with the fault itself clearly involve heavy costs, risk managers contended that those costs were unlikely to be beyond the company's financial scope. In several ways, recall carries risks similar to those of business interruption. First, a product's image is tarnished by the publicity the product attracts when it is removed from retail shelves. This is aggravated by its unavailability as consumers turn to alternative products. Those interviewed concurred that the fundamental goal of the relaunch must be to restore product image, and that the resources needed would depend on the extent of the bad publicity and the length of the product's absence. Yet the reserves needed to deal with a major recall loss might render any product commercially inviable if factored into its price.

However, few risk managers interviewed have insurance to cover such risks, possibly because the tangible costs associated with recall pose little threat. The survey showed clearly that there is a greater need for some form of risk financing to cover the less tangible problems of recall, given the pharmaceutical industry's growing financial dependency on blockbuster products and centralized manufacturing.

Research and Development

The pharmaceutical industry depends increasingly on R&D to stay competitive and to promote better earnings growth, especially as profit margins are under increased pressure and market competition has intensified. Even so, insurance is not used to transfer R&D risk. Those who responded to the survey said this is because R&D is considered to be an entrepreneurial risk rather than an insurable hazard. Moreover, they said, it would be difficult to define reliably an insurable event, and therefore an adequate price. While events such as fire and natural perils might disrupt or completely destroy an R&D program, wrongly-assessed experimental results or new findings in the later stages of product development could prove detrimental.

Some risk managers mentioned R&D risk in relation to political risk, foreseeing events—particularly in countries where patent piracy is an issue—that would limit access to essential materials and damage an R&D program. Despite the intangible nature of the risks involved, the pharmaceuticals' burgeoning R&D budgets may well increase demand for some form of political risk cover, the survey said.

Environmental Risk

Of the forty-six people interviewed, around one quarter said that environmental risk played a prominent role in their global risk assessment. The most noteworthy finding was that the perception of environmental risk was consistent across all corporate types, regardless of whether they had large chemical or agrochemical units. This growing unease may be rooted in intensified environmental regulation and the host of new laws, or it may be due to fears that new risks, such as those related to genetic engineering, will potentially impact the environment.

Appendix 4B

Example of Airline Risk Landscape

This is an extract from Swiss Re New Markets Airline Risk Landscape Database. This is only one of about 90 separate risks described in this database. In this example, we show an abbreviated description of the losses that arise from an earthquake and describe some of the risk management products available to cover them.

SRNM Airline Risk Landscape

Environment: 1.   Natural & Physical Environment
Category: 1.1   Earthquake
Risk: 1.1.1   Earthquake

Keywords: Outside airline's control
                 Pure risk (downside only)
                 Adequately insured

Description:

An earthquake is a shaking of the earth that is volcanic or tectonic (seismic) in origin.

Manifestation:

Destruction of company owned infrastructure leading to:

- **Physical damage:** Cost of reinvestment in destroyed assets; cost of liability claims.
- **Disruption of services:** Higher cost to reinstate and perform services; loss of revenues; liability claims resulting from non-performance.

Destruction of non-owned infrastructure leading to:

- **Disruption of services:** Airport shut down, fuel delivery, passenger and personnel access to airport, higher cost to perform services, loss of revenue.

A. Existing coverages:

Property insurance

Property insurance is any type of insurance that indemnifies an insured party that suffers a financial loss because property has been damaged or destroyed. Property is considered to be any item that has value. Property can be classified as real property or personal property. Real property is land and the attachments to the land, such as buildings. Personal property is all property that is not real property. The building and personal property coverage form is the form used to insure almost all types of commercial property. The insuring agreement in the building and personal property coverage form promises to pay for direct physical loss or damage to covered property at the premises described in the policy when caused by or resulting from a covered cause of loss. Basic property insurance policies are written to cover the perils of fire, lightning, explosion, windstorm, hail, smoke, aircraft or vehicle damage, riot or civil commotion, vandalism, sprinkler leakage, sinkhole collapse, and volcanic action. Property insurance of an airline excludes aircraft or spare parts.

Business interruption insurance

Covers loss of income as well as expenses if premises have been destroyed by fire or other perils covered under the property policy.

Valued business interruption insurance

Covers loss of earnings for a stated amount for each day that the insured incurs such loss due to interruption of business from a covered peril. Except for the basis of indemnity, insuring conditions are like those of standard business interruption forms.

Contingent business income coverage

Insurance for lost business income caused by a loss at a specific location not owned by the insured, but on which the insured depends for business operations. The loss must be caused by an insured peril. There are two forms for this coverage: broad form, which extends the insured business income limit to include the dependent property, and limited form, which specifies the limit of coverage that is to apply to the dependent property.

Hull all risk insurance

Aircraft are exposed to physical loss or damage on the ground or while in flight.

Key purpose of the hull insurance is the protection of the insured's assets (airframe, engines, spare parts). Insurers undertake at their option to pay for, replace or repair accidental loss or damage to the aircraft described in the schedule arising from the risk covered up to the limit of the amount insured subject to any deductibles. Coverage also includes disappearance if the aircraft is unreported for a certain period after the commencement of the flight.

It covers the aircraft in case of a partial or total loss. The aircraft are insured on a maximum agreed value basis. Under an agreed value policy the insurers are obliged to pay the insured the value agreed upon before the occurrence of a loss. It is used when the insured wishes to secure full monetary payment in the event of a total or constructive total loss, such as where the aircraft are heavily mortgaged. The maximum hull limit usually exceeds the highest aircraft value so that aircraft with a higher value may be attached during the policy period. The hull policy carries a deductible per aircraft type.

Hull insurance

It is designed to protect the insured airline against physical loss or damage to its aircraft, including engines and other components. Hull insurance is one of the most important forms of coverage where aircraft finance companies are concerned. Conventional hull coverage protects the insured with respect to loss of or damage to aircraft caused by such risks as fire, theft and collision, up to the limits of the policy. Operating leases will call for an aircraft to be insured for the "casualty value" or "stipulated loss value" of the aircraft.

Loss of use (consequential loss)

Aircraft owners and operators are exposed to the potential loss of large sums of money as a consequence of the falling-off in earning power that might accompany the laying-up of an aircraft for repair following an accident. Loss of use or consequential loss policies usually relate back to existing hull policies and usually specify that the insurers will only become liable in the event of an accident to the insured aircraft that gives rise to a valid and collectible claim under the existing hull policy. Most loss of use policies will stipulate a maximum amount payable with respect to any one aircraft during the period of insurance.

Spare parts

These are normally covered under the hull policy and limited per location. The main exposure consists of fire, theft and earthquake. The cover
is for engines, spare parts and other equipment yet to be installed on or
to form part of an aircraft that is either the property or under the custody
of the insured.

Aircraft spare parts insurance

Aircraft spare parts leased insurance covers aircraft engines, spare parts
and equipment while the property is on the ground or is being carried as
cargo by air, land or waterborne transit. Once the equipment has been fitted
to or placed onboard the aircraft, it is excluded from coverage. The policy
also does not insure engine loss or damage while the engine is running or
being tested, mechanical or electrical derangement, loss or damage to de-
tached property that will be refitted to the aircraft and not replaced, or property carried on the aircraft as a spare parts kit.

B. Coverage currently not available

Loss of revenues and higher cost of providing services without any physical damage to the insured's infrastructure or other assets such as aircraft.

Part II
The Tools

" 'Market convergence' should not be
misunderstood to mean that everyone
is going to join hands and work together."

5

Converging Markets and Integrated Solutions

PRAKASH SHIMPI

In Part I of this book, we laid the foundations for integrating corporate risk management. The previous chapter on risk mapping described how a company can better understand its risk exposures. Using comprehensive risk identification and various techniques for risk measurement, the volatility of earnings due to individual risk exposures is calculated and then combined to describe the company's overall risk profile. The company's risk profile and management's appetite for risk determine the capital resources necessary to run the business.

In Part II, we introduce some of the new techniques in managing corporate capital and risk. Most corporate managers are familiar with the conventional capital resources such as equity, debt and insurance. Now new techniques are available that can be more responsive to corporate risk and capital management needs. These techniques have emerged not only because of the demand from corporations for better solutions but also from a change in the marketplace of the suppliers of such solutions.

With increasing deregulation in the financial services sector, the activities of banks, insurers and reinsurers are beginning to converge. This has led to a convergence in the types of products and solutions offered by these suppliers of capital. Further, the insurance industry[1] is also expanding the limits of insurability to embrace risks conventionally hedged in the capital markets, and is looking for ways to cover previously uninsurable or difficult-to-insure risks. In this chapter we provide a broad overview of market convergence and the development of integrated solutions.

Market Convergence — Banks, Insurance, and Corporations

The conventional markets for risk capital are fragmented. Certain risks are covered only in the insurance market. Others are covered only in the securities market. Others are neither insurable nor hedgeable and have to be retained by the corporation. Some risks may be covered equally in both markets. For example, credit risk protection can be structured through both the insurance market and the securities market. At the same time, there are elements of credit risk that are uninsurable.

Banks and (re)insurers, intermediaries between a corporation and its sources of capital, may be thought of as "risk consolidators." They provide certain capital-raising and risk management capabilities to a corporation. The conventional markets for risk and the role of the intermediaries are fairly straightforward.

Banks help firms raise equity and debt capital, which ultimately bear all risks retained by the firm. Banks also help corporations manage certain financial risks that are traded in the capital markets, such as interest rate risk, commodity risk and foreign exchange risk. A bank's role is to structure the transaction, and ultimately pass the risk through to the capital markets. Obviously banks have the ability to retain some of the risks on their own balance sheet, and often do. However, the value created by a bank is in providing access to the capital markets at large.

Conventionally, the insurance industry helps a firm manage its risk and capital by transferring risks from the firm to a (re)insurer. Those risks stay on the books of the (re)insurance company, which then has to ensure that it has sufficient capital resources to cover them.

The new market for risk and capital blurs the conventional distinction between banks and (re)insurers. Four central questions emerge:

- Which are the risks being transferred or financed?
- What is the role of the intermediary?

- Where is the capital covering the risks coming from?
- How will the risk transfer or financing be structured?

The risks in any transaction can span the full range of risks facing a corporation. The intermediary, whether it is a bank, (re)insurer or some other entity, serves three functions:

[handwritten: FUNCTION OF CONVERGENCE]

- **Structurer:** designs and implements the transaction.
- **Risk holder:** places the risk on its own books.
- **Distributor:** places the risk with participants in the capital markets.

The capital to manage the risk comes from one of three sources: the intermediary, the capital markets or the corporation itself.

The choices for transaction structure are growing. Beyond the conventional products, banks and (re)insurers have learned from each other and are borrowing techniques to develop more efficient solutions. We consider some of the new techniques commonly referred to as Alternative Risk Transfer (ART) or Integrated Risk Management (IRM) solutions.

[handwritten: PARTICULAR RISK MGT SOLNS]

THE DEVELOPMENT OF ART SOLUTIONS[2]

The development of alternative risk transfer solutions has been closely linked to supply and demand factors, such as capacity bottlenecks and price cycles in the traditional insurance market.

Since ART solutions are developed to answer specific problems in a specific area (e.g. catastrophe risks, environmental liability or workers' compensation) at a specific time, one might expect them to disappear once the conditions that encouraged their emergence (price increases in the traditional market, capacity bottlenecks) no longer apply. Experience shows, however, that the new solutions, once introduced into the market, have proven their value. Captive insurance companies set up by corporations are an example; for almost 20 years their demise has been prophesied with every downturn in the price cycle, yet their numbers continue to grow (Figure 5.1). A short description of captives appears in Appendix 5B.

Figure 5.1   Insurance cycle in the U.S. and formation of captives.

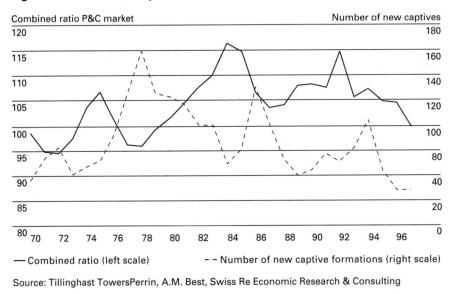

Source: Tillinghast TowersPerrin, A.M. Best, Swiss Re Economic Research & Consulting

It seems that the insurance cycle (i.e. the hardening or softening of prices for insurance coverage) can speed up or slow down the development of new products, but cannot fully explain their existence. The shifting risk land-scape, changes in the competitive environment, the increasing importance of shareholder value, the inefficiencies of traditional insurance solutions, and the emergence of new financial market instruments have all led to changes in client perceptions and needs. To this extent, ART solutions have often devel-oped in response to direct tactical considerations, and subsequently become indispensable for long-term strategic reasons.

The inefficiencies of traditional insurance have also contributed sub-stantially to the development of ART solutions. An analysis of the costs of traditional insurance covers shows that the difference between premiums and expected losses is comparatively high. The reason for this is often to be found in the information differences between (re)insurers and policyhold-ers.[3] In particular, key structural inefficiencies of traditional insurance solu-tions include:

- **Adverse selection:** Traditional insurance prices are determined on the basis of average risks, and are therefore higher than the risk-adjusted premium rates for good risks. As a result, companies with good risks, reluctant to subsidize those with bad risks, turn instead to self-insurance. — NOT GIVEN A REWARD FOR GOOD RESULTS.

- **Moral hazard:** With insurance, the policyholder may have little incentive to prevent or contain a loss. To overcome this "moral hazard," the insurer has to demand a higher average premium. In the case of self-financing, the policyholder has a direct incentive to adopt suitable risk management measures to prevent or minimize losses.

WORKING THE SYSTEM

- **Credit risk:** An insurance contract subjects the policyholder to credit risk—the (re)insurer might lack sufficient funds to honor a claim. The sharp rise in (re)insurer bankruptcies due to the large natural catastrophe losses at the start of the '90s shows just how real this threat is.

RELATIVE TO INSURING COMPANY

- **Limited capacity:** Large companies sometimes find, due to a lack of capacity in the (re)insurance markets, that no cover is available for major risks. Many of the risks that commercial clients face were, for a long time, considered to be uninsurable.

ART solutions have been developed to overcome some or all of these limitations. For example, various ART solutions eliminate the problem of moral hazard by defining the loss event on the basis of an independent index or a physical event. As a consequence, the policyholder's risk is not completely covered—a **basis risk** remains, which is the difference between the policyholder's risk and the coverage provided. As we will see in the chapters to follow, the various ART solutions have to address the trade-off between moral hazard and basis risk.

Concurrent with the developments in the insurance market, there have been tremendous developments in risk management techniques through the capital markets. With increasingly volatile financial markets and new developments in financial analysis theory, a wide range of new financial instruments has come onto the market to hedge **systematic risks** such as interest rates, exchange rates, or risks associated with changes in commodity prices.

[handwritten in left margin: DERIVATIVES ARE BECOMING RISK MANAGEMENT VEHICLES]

The predominant hedge instruments are derivatives such as futures, options and swaps. They have been around for generations, but have seen explosive growth since the '80s. They are now creating a new, challenging environment for the international insurance industry, especially since many innovative risk management concepts can be applied to traditional insurance risks. In addition, insurance concepts can even be formulated for risks that were uninsurable in the past. The object here is to tap into bigger insurance capacities via the capital markets.

INTEGRATED SOLUTIONS

A major objective of this book is to help managers understand the emerging risk management techniques. These techniques borrow features from both the insurance and the capital markets, hence the term "integrated risk management solutions."

We discuss the general characteristics of IRM solutions here before describing specific products in the chapters to follow. As we try to understand their development and relationship to each other, some questions emerge about the meaning of integration:

- How much knowledge do they require of both the insurance and the capital markets techniques?
- How do they affect the firm?
- How involved do the risk manager, treasurer and CFO have to get in the process?

One way to answer these questions is to assess the "degree" of integration. Each solution can be classified as having one of the four following **degrees of integration:**[4]

1. First Degree: Integrate *within* markets, *given* capital structure. These techniques combine risks within one of either the insurance markets or the capital markets, but not across the two markets. The risk manager or treasurer can execute them separately, taking the firm's risk appetite and capital structure as a given. They have been present for several years and most managers are familiar with them by now. Examples in the financial markets are basket options or double-trigger options where two or more capital markets risks such as interest rates, foreign exchange or commodities are combined into one hedge transaction. Likewise, over the last few years, products have been developed in the insurance world that integrate different lines of insurance risk into one multi-line, aggregate insurance policy.[5]

2. Second Degree: Integrate *across* markets, given capital structure. These techniques integrate both insurance and capital markets risks. Their execution requires cooperation between the risk manager and treasurer. They are generally constructed taking the firm's risk appetite and capital structure as given. Although they have been discussed extensively, few transactions have been executed to date.

Currently, significant product development is taking place in the area of multi-line and multi-trigger products, which combine interest rate, foreign exchange and commodity risks with a variety of insurance risks. These solutions can be structured in either insurance form or derivative form. As described in Chapter 6, these transactions generally can take one of two forms:

- Multi-line, multi-year products (MMPs), through which the combined losses from insurance and capital markets risks are covered, and
- Multi-trigger products (MTPs), through which either a capital markets risk cover is triggered by an insurance event or an insurance risk cover is triggered by a capital markets index strike level.

3. Third Degree: Integrate across markets, *changing* capital structure. These techniques are applicable to insurance and capital markets risks, either separately or integrated. They are viewed as alternatives to conventional capital, and can alter both the firm's risk profile and its capital structure. Execution usually involves the CFO as well as other managers.

The motivation for these solutions goes beyond merely hedging a risk and includes corporate capital management considerations. Examples are finite risk reinsurance, run-off solutions and contingent capital, which are discussed in Chapters 7, 8 and 9 respectively.

In contrast to conventional transactions, which spread losses over a large group of policyholders, finite risk reinsurance transactions (often referred to as finite re) spread the losses from risks faced by a single policyholder over a number of years. As such, they involve both underwriting risks and timing risks, and explicitly take into consideration interest income earned during the policy term. In some sense, they are the insurance industry's version of corporate debt.

Run-off solutions are essentially finite risk reinsurance transactions. They merit special attention because they focus on managing risks from prior years or from discontinued operations, and the consequent pressure that such exposure puts on capital and share price. In effect, such transactions seek to move the exposure off the corporate balance sheet for a price, reducing the uncertainty surrounding such liabilities.

Contingent capital facilities are direct substitutes for on-balance-sheet capital. Rather than raising paid-up capital before it is needed, the corporation arranges for some form of either debt or equity capital to be available upon the occurrence of some triggering event.

4. Fourth Degree: Integrate across markets, changing *market* structure. These techniques could be included in the three previous categories, except that they require more than just a firm's unilateral actions. They require changes in the structure of the insurance and capital markets to make the transactions economically viable and executable.

The creation of insurance-linked securities (ILS) through the securitization of insurance risks is one such example. ILSs are structured as bonds whose payment of interest and/or principal depends on the occurrence or severity of an insurance event. In order for ILSs to appear as viable instruments, there had to be sufficient acceptance of the concept by insurers, investors, insurance regulators and securities regulators. Prior to 1995, ILSs existed only in concept—the first transactions with sale of ILSs to qualified investors occurred in 1996. To date, they have been used primarily by the insurance industry to raise risk capital in the capital markets. However, they are just as relevant for non-insurance companies as well, and there is a growing interest in applying the techniques to corporate risks. Chapter 10 describes ILSs in greater detail.

Insurance derivatives are another recent development. They first appeared in 1992 as the catastrophe futures and options offered by the Chicago Board of Trade (CBOT). To date, trading has been modest, even though the instruments and the underlying indices have been adapted and refined to meet client needs several times since they were first introduced. The CBOT instruments have so far not proven to be suitable for managing the risks of non-insurance companies; individual firm loss experience is not likely to be closely related to the indices traded on the CBOT, so that the basis risk is likely to be unreasonably large. Alternatively, the derivative technology can apply very well to other types of risks faced by a corporation. Two such applications are already in use: credit derivatives and weather derivatives. ENRON

Credit derivatives have been traded only since the early '90s, but have experienced explosive growth since then. They began as tools for derivative dealers who needed to generate incremental credit capacity for some counterparties. They have since become standard fare for most financial institutions, and are making strong headway in commercial enterprises as well. Recently, major (re)insurance companies with capital markets subsidiaries have entered the credit derivatives market with significant risk appetite and trading volume.

Why do credit derivatives merit consideration in this fourth degree of integration? Because the development of credit derivatives has forced a fundamental change in the way that both banks and (re)insurers deal with credit risk. Historically, both banks and (re)insurers have been acquirers of credit risk, keeping it on their books. Banks have done so by virtue of their lending businesses. (Re)insurers have been writing credit insurance policies for many years. Until recently, both these industries had very little choice but to keep the credit risk on their books.   ↳ TRADE RISK ON MKT.

The development of the credit derivatives market has changed all that, making credit risk actively tradable. There are still many types of credit risk that are not easily tradable, but for those that are, there is a sizeable liquid market. Today, both banks and (re)insurers are able to evaluate critically their conventional credit risk portfolio and actively alter its risk profile by buying and selling credit derivatives. With this added flexibility, they are able to provide more comprehensive solutions to their corporate clients, who have credit risk concerns of their own. (As this market has been in existence since the '80s, there is a wealth of reference material available to the interested reader. For that reason, we say no more about credit risk management in this book.)

Table 5.1 Comparison of IRM solutions.

	Traditional commercial insurance cover	Captives	Multi-line/ multi-year products	Multi-trigger products	Finite solutions	Contingent capital	Securitization[1]	Derivatives
Risk carrier	(Re)insurer	Policyholder	(Re)insurer	(Re)insurer	Primarily the policyholder	Primarily the policyholder	Capital markets	Capital markets
Diversification mechanism	Portfolio	Portfolio/time, depending on the type of risk	Portfolio/time	Portfolio	Emphasis on time	Time	Portfolio	Portfolio
Duration	1 year	Variable	Multi-year	Variable	Multi-year	Variable	Variable	6-12 months
Credit risk for the insured	Exists	Slight	Exists	Exists	Slight	Exists	None	None
Suitability for protecting individual portfolio (basic risk)	Yes, usual case	Yes, usual case	Yes, usual case	Yes, usual case	Yes, usual case	Yes, usual case	Limited, depends on the definition of the trigger	Limited, depends on the underlying
Moral hazard on the part of insured	Yes	No	Yes	Yes	Limited	Yes	No	No
Increase of insurance capacity	Limited, cyclical	Dependent on policyholder's financial strength	Indirectly through more efficient use of capacity	Indirectly through more efficient use of capacity	Dependent on the policyholder's liquid funds	Good potential, but still in infancy	Good potential, but still in infancy	Good potential, but still in infancy
Additional services[2]	Yes	No	Yes	Yes	Yes	Yes	No	No
Suitability for protecting the balance sheet	Yes	Limited	Yes	Yes	Yes	Yes	Yes	Yes
Suitability for smoothing results	Limited	Yes	Yes	Yes	Yes	No	Limited	Limited

[1] The products treated as securitization solutions which are placed privately and whose trigger is based on an index or physical event.
[2] For example: claims management and settlement, risk assessments and risk management proposals.

Weather derivatives have also developed with the active participation of both the capital markets and the insurance industry. The revenues of many companies are susceptible to weather patterns. Energy producers, food and beverage manufacturers, and companies in the leisure sector are just a sample of the variety of companies exposed to weather risk. Detailed analyses of the degree to which the sales of certain companies are dependent on temperature, rain, snow and sunshine have recently encouraged the emergence of specific products. For the first couple of years, weather derivatives were traded through specialized brokers. Subsequently, insurers and reinsurers stepped into this market and expanded the trading volume by committing significant capital to cover these risks. As we shall see in Chapter 11, weather risk management is an example of using capital markets techniques to expand the limits of insurability.

Table 5.1 lists the integrated risk management solutions introduced above and provides a quick summary of their differences and common features.

EXPANDING THE LIMITS OF INSURABILITY

We mentioned weather derivatives above as an example of expanding the limits of insurability. There are many other opportunities to do so, although it is not always easy to develop a viable solution. With the growth in technology and the Internet, for example, entirely new risks are emerging. The challenges of defining events that are verifiable and measurable, or developing loss estimates where there is little or no historical data make it difficult for a (re)insurer to provide coverage. Even so, as the clipping on page 90 shows, it can be done.

One does not have to look as far as the Internet to find a challenging example. A bank can provide a suitable case in point. The case study in Appendix 5A illustrates the challenge to develop something as seemingly straightforward as coverage for a bank's operational risks.

THE SHAPE OF THINGS TO COME

"Market convergence" should not be misunderstood to mean that everyone is going to join hands and work together. "IRM solutions" should not be

Business Insurance, May 3, 1999 / 3

Policy covers patent risks

By AMANDA MILLIGAN

ZURICH, Switzerland—Swiss Re New Markets has developed a new coverage designed to eliminate some of the risks that deter investors from buying patents.

The coverage was developed specifically for The Patent & License Exchange, a new online patent transaction forum. The company is the policyholder, but each investor is named as an additional insured.

The new coverage protects every patent buyer that closes an online transaction on The Patent & License Exchange from financial loss if the patent is later declared invalid by the court system. said William Hoffman. an associate director of SRNM in Zurich, Switzerland.

The program provides basic property coverage of all patent transactions for the purchase price, which could range from thousands to millions of dollars. In addition, optional protection is available for costs related to producing patented ideas that are later rejected, and is purchased at the buyer's discretion.

The coverage will be sold by a Swiss Re Group unit licensed to do business in the United States, he said.

Coverage would be triggered anytime a court declares a patent invalid.

Availability of the coverage mitigates some investor concerns about patent transactions, said Nir Kossovsky, president and chief executive officer of Pasadena, Calif.-based The Patent & License Exchange.

"The product goes a long way to making buyers and sellers willing to participate in the market, because it transfers one of the major risk elements in the patent sale and licensing," he said.

See **Patents** *on page 10*

Patents

Continued from page 3

"The entity that creates the patent and the knowledge basis behind it is not usually the entity that commercializes it, " he said.

In patent infringement litigation, defendants typically attack the validity of the plaintiff's patent, say legal and insurance sources. The burden of proof in such litigation rests with the defendant, they add.

"If it's litigated, validity will always be an issue," said Joel S. Goldman, a partner with Troutman Sanders L.L.P. in Atlanta, whose specialties include intellectual property and patent litigation. Mr. Goldman noted that patent litigation is expensive.

However, some disagree that all patents traded are risky.

"The name of the game is to get a patent. Once you have the patent, from a litigator's perspective, the risk is minimized," said Michael Aber-

nathy, a partner with law firm Bell Boyd & Lloyd in Chicago.

However, he stressed that an improperly issued patent could be a risk. The key to getting a good patent is to make sure it is carefully drafted, he

---

'Fortune 500 companies are aware that intellectual property is becoming their most important asset,' says William Hoffman.

---

added.

The U.S. Patent and Trademark Office, a division of the Department of Justice, requires three conditions to be met to grant a patent, Mr. Hoffman said. The product must be novel, must have utility and must not be obvious in view of prior innovation, he said.

When a patent is issued, there is a

statutory assumption of validity, said Mr. Hoffman. However, "the PTO doesn't make any promises about a patent, " he added. Patents are sold "as is."

Having insurance coverage becomes important when patents are contested, said Peter Gilster, partner with Blackwell Sanders Peper & Martin L.L.P. in St. Louis. The law firm focuses on intellectual property issues.

Likening patents to property, Mr. Gilster said, "Even in the best of circumstances. . .you don't know what the hidden defects are."

Mr. Hoffman said he expects to see more interest in insuring intellectual property risks.

"Most Fortune 500 companies are aware that intellectual property is becoming their most important asset," said Mr. Hoffman. "And while it's the most important, it's almost completely uninsured."

The Patent & License Exchange will hold its first online patent auction on Sept. 1. **BI**

misunderstood as new jargon for conventional product development. What has emerged, and will continue to do so, is a highly competitive, dynamic environment where innovation combined with sound technical expertise will be necessary to meet the risk and capital management demands of corporations.

In the following chapters, we describe in more detail some of the integrated solutions introduced here. The number of these solutions is increasing and the only limitation seems to be the imagination of the practitioners. It is unlikely that a CFO, treasurer or risk manager will be familiar with all of these techniques. It is our intention here to provide a description of these techniques sufficient to encourage the motivated reader to consider whether any of them may be of value in his or her corporation.

Appendix 5A

A Bank's Operational Risk Management

The risk landscape for banks is broad, but can be grouped roughly into credit risks, market risks and operational risks. It is highly likely that in a few years' time, banks will be in a position to model and manage operational risks similar to the way they currently do for credit and market risks. Presently, however, many banks still under-manage operational risks despite the major crises they have caused in recent years, which include direct financial loss, loss of credibility and even insolvency. It is not surprising that these upsets have originated from a variety of causes, including rogue trading, system failures, lawsuits, customer disputes and fraud.

Estimating the probability and magnitude of operational risks is difficult; events occur infrequently within any single company, and there is currently no standard methodology to quantify expected losses. By transferring their non-core but previously uninsurable risks to the (re)insurance market, banks will be able to free capital that they can deploy more profitably. This should impact positively the bank's return on equity, as it will need less economic capital today and potentially less regulatory capital in the future.

Transferring such business-inherent risks requires close cooperation between banks and (re)insurers. It is predicated on an extensive exchange of information in combination with the sophisticated application of actuarial quantification techniques and know-how.

Concepts for an "operational all-risk" cover have been developed that can answer the banking industry's need for risk protection while utilizing capital more efficiently (Box 5A.1). These concepts involve the transfer of operational risks away from the bank's shareholders to (re)insurers capable of carrying them.

In the past, operational risks were difficult to insure, because moral hazard and adverse selection considerations frequently led to the conclusion that they should be carried by the bank's shareholders. Aside from using equity or reserves to bear such risks directly, virtually the only way to

Guido Fürer and Michael Hammer, "Value Creation Through Convergence," ART 101: The Basics of Alternative Risk Transfer (London: Emap Finance, 1999): 15-24.

Box 5A.1   Operational all-risk coverage.

Physical asset risk	risk that damage to or loss of physical assets will impact the business environment
Technology risk	risk resulting from systems unavailability, poor data quality, system errors or software problems
Relationship risk	risk resulting from relationship issues such as sales practices, customer problems and unsuitable relationships
People risk	risk that business requirements will not be met due to improper personnel policies, motivational issues or fraud
External risk	risk that a contract is or will become unenforceable; risk of change in law or relevant standards

"insure" them up to now has been to use finite risk reinsurance, though tax and accounting considerations usually make this a challenging task.

An "operational all-risk" cover goes beyond a business unit focus to view operating risk in aggregate, by level per business activity. The risk management process consists of the five risk mapping steps described in Chapter 4. The exposure is then assessed using databases containing a history of operating loss events in the financial services sector, with descriptions and cause-and-effect analyses. Predictive modeling is also employed to identify and quantify contributing factors.

This quantification process could go a long way towards defusing moral hazard issues, thus improving the odds of successfully placing such risks in the market. Further risk assessment will help a bank to differentiate between less severe risks and high-severity exposures that could potentially endanger the institution, and to deploy prevention and controlling resources accordingly.

Finally, the application of such new techniques will allow a bank to prepare ahead of time for changes in the regulatory environment—capital allocation requirements for operational risks, for example—thereby putting itself at a competitive advantage.

Appendix 5B

Captives

Until a few years ago, the term "ART," first coined in the United States, was mainly used to describe various forms of self-insurance, including captives, risk-retention groups and purchasing groups.[6] The development of captives has been particularly important worldwide.

Key Features of Captives

A captive is an insurance or reinsurance vehicle that belongs to a company or group of companies, and is not active in the insurance industry itself. It mainly insures the risks of its parent company. Captives perform a number of roles. On the one hand they are a formalized self-insurance vehicle for high-frequency risks that can be carried by the company itself in an efficient way. On the other, they are used as a financing instrument for very specific low-frequency, high-severity risks, for which no cover is available in the traditional insurance market.

Captives are more often conceived as reinsurance companies than as direct insurers. With a reinsurance captive, the risks of the parent company are initially underwritten by a local direct insurer (a "fronter"), and then ceded to the captive in the form of a reinsurance contract (Figure 5B.1). These risks may subsequently be partly retroceded to professional reinsurers. This structure is necessary because direct insurers usually require a national insurance licence in each country where they operate, and are subject to local supervisory controls. Reinsurers, on the other hand, are usually engaged in cross-border activities, and are subject to home country control.

Around 3000 of the 4000 captives worldwide are single-parent captives, i.e. they belong to a single company.[7] With group captives, several companies get together to form a collective captive (similar to a pool). Group captives experienced strong growth during phases of sharp price rises in the United States (mid-'70s and mid-'80s) because the liability problem affected companies across entire sectors (e.g. oil, chemicals or pharmaceuticals).

---

sigma 2 (1999).

Figure 5B.1   How a reinsurance captive works.

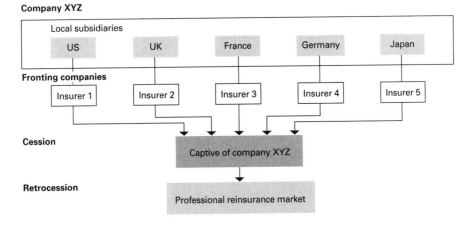

Based on: Wöhrmann, 1998

Recently, "rent-a-captives" have become more popular. Instead of setting up its own captive, a company can rent one. In return for an administration charge, a reinsurer makes an account available to the company, which is used to clear premiums, claims and investment income. The advantage of this arrangement compared with a single-parent captive solution is basically that a company does not have to provide any capital. This makes it especially attractive to medium-sized companies.

One of the latest breed of captives is the "special purpose vehicle," whose main function is to facilitate the transfer of insurance risks to capital markets.

The Advantages of Captives

Captives were originally developed because companies questioned the efficiency of transferring high-frequency risks, since the transfer of what are fairly predictable payment flows (premiums and claims) generates very little benefit and also entails substantial transaction costs. In addition, companies with "good" risks profit directly from their better-than-average claims experience and have a direct interest in trying to improve claims experience through appropriate risk management measures.

At the start of the captive boom, toward the end of the '60s, tax and financial considerations played an important role. Compared with pure

self-financing of risks, captives offer the advantage that premium payments are tax deductible, and underwriting reserves also receive favorable tax treatment in the offshore captive domiciles. Since then, tax
considerations have taken second place. In the U.S., premium payments
are only tax-deductible if the captive writes a substantial quota of third-
party business.[8] In most European countries the company has to prove
that significant risk transfer is involved and that the premium paid is justi-
fied from an underwriting perspective. In some European countries, any
profit made by the captive is also taxed in the home country of the parent
company. The financial advantages also include the explicit recognition of
investment income for claims payments and the ability to influence investment policy, as well as direct access to the reinsurance market.

The number of captives rose sharply in response to the liability crisis in
the United States. This was mainly due to factors such as high prices and
the lack of capacity in the traditional market, as well as the long-term stabilization of insurance costs. There is a close relationship between the insurance cycle in the U.S. and the number of new captives founded in Bermuda.

Captives were originally conceived as an alternative to traditional insurance for individual risks in the property or casualty sector. Increasingly,
a broader spectrum of risks is being ceded to captives, as well as the entire
range of insurance risks such as negative publicity and warranty risks, year
2000 risks and risks from pledged welfare benefits. The captive is increasingly being used as a central conduit for very different risks worldwide and
a platform for alternative reinsurance solutions. Captives are likely to be
used more widely in the future as a holistic risk management instrument.
They allow a business to benefit from the "natural" smoothing and diversification effects of different risks.

Importance of Captives

At present there are around 4000 captives worldwide, generating a premium volume of approximately $18 billion. This is equivalent to a share of
roughly 6% of the global commercial insurance market. Global growth in
the founding of new captives has slowed slightly, but is still very strong,
at 5% (Figure 5B.2). The reason for this slight dip is to be found in signs of
saturation in the U.S. and the U.K., as well as low prices in the traditional
insurance market, which reduces the attraction of captives.

More than half of all captives worldwide belong to U.S. industrial and
service companies. Although the penetration of U.S. captives is high in the
U.S. by international standards, it is not exceptionally so. An international

Figure 5B.2   Uninterrupted growth of captive markets.

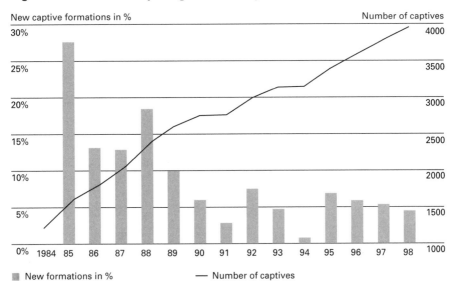

Source: Tillinghast TowersPerrin Captive Insurance Company Directory, various years

Figure 5B.3   Captive domiciles.

No. of captives 1997

Bermuda

Cayman Islands

Guernsey

Vermont

Luxembourg

Barbados

Isle of Man

Ireland

| 200 | 400 | 600 | 800 | 1000 | 1200 | 1400 |

Source: Tillinghast TowersPerrin Captive Insurance Directory, 1998

Table 5B.1 Comparison of captive penetration 1997.

Country	No. of captives 1997		Premium volume Non-life 1997		Captives per billion of premium volume	No. of Fortune 2500 companies		Captives per fortune 2500 company
	Total	% global mkt	$ bn	% global mkt		Total	% global mkt	
USA	2064	56.8%	376.0	42.0%	5.5	819	32.8%	2.5
UK	591	16.2%	56.5	6.3%	10.5	201	8.0%	2.9
Canada	147	4.0%	27.0	3.0%	5.4	85	3.4%	1.7
Sweden	114	3.1%	5.2	0.6%	21.8	49	2.0%	2.3
France	81	2.2%	40.5	4.5%	2.0	117	4.7%	0.7
Japan	66	1.8%	100.8	11.3%	0.7	614	24.6%	0.1
Netherlands	59	1.6%	15.0	1.7%	3.9	49	2.0%	1.2
Belgium	50	1.4%	9.3	1.0%	5.4	25	1.0%	2.0
Switzerland	45	1.2%	9.3	1.0%	4.9	39	1.6%	1.2
Germany	43	1.2%	79.8	8.9%	0.5	156	6.2%	0.3
South Africa	32	0.9%	4.5	0.5%	7.1	34	1.4%	0.9
Norway	29	0.8%	3.5	0.4%	8.2	49	2.0%	0.6
Italy	15	0.4%	26.1	2.9%	0.6	44	1.8%	0.3
Others	301	8.3%	141.3	15.8%	2.1	219	8.8%	1.4
North America	2280	62.7%	402.9	45.0%	5.7	904	36.2%	2.5
Europe	1144	31.1%	295.6	33.0%	3.9	793	31.7%	1.4
Japan	66	1.8%	100.8	11.3%	0.7	614	24.6%	0.1
Rest of world	147	4.4%	95.5	10.7%	1.5	189	7.6%	0.8

Source: Tillinghast TowersPerrin, Disclosure Database, Swiss Re Economic Research & Consulting

comparison shows that the U.K. and Sweden, for example, have a higher proportion of captives, measured either by the size of their insurance markets or their share of the world's biggest 2500 companies (Table 5B.1).

Bermuda is by far the most important domicile for captives in the world. Around a third of all captives are located here. For U.S. parent companies, Bermuda and the Cayman Islands are still the favorite choice. For European countries, the preferred locations are Guernsey and Luxembourg, although Ireland in particular has also recently experienced dynamic growth (Figure 5B.3). Every year new locations are added that attract new captives by offering a favorable regulatory environment and tax regime. One of the new captive domiciles is Lloyd's, through which it has been possible to set up a captive syndicate since the beginning of 1999. The main attraction of Lloyd's is that it has direct insurance licences in more than 60 different countries.

Captives are far from being essential for wide-ranging alternative risk financing solutions. Many of the advantages described for captives can now be achieved through other alternative solutions as well, such as finite risk products or multi-line, multi-year solutions. For many companies, however, captives can prove to be a sensible first step into the alternative risk transfer market.

"The joint exposure is likely to be different
from the exposure of the individual risks."

6

Multi-Line and Multi-Trigger Products

Prakash Shimpi

Traditionally, risk management focused on the measurement and handling of specific and individual risks. Little or no attempt was made to examine the possible interaction between these individual risks and the impact which they, in composite, might have on an organization. Insurance markets reflected this approach accordingly, offering distinct policies for property, casualty and other exposures. Likewise, the most active financial markets offer single-risk hedging, for example interest rate, foreign exchange and commodities.

Yet we know, and can demonstrate on any corporate risk map, that a firm has a variety of risks. Is there value in somehow managing these risks in some combination, or is the conventional, single-risk focus appropriate? We know that diversification is a sound strategy for risks that we retain. Perhaps, then, there is also value in combining risks that are going to be transferred.

Today it is possible to combine risks together in a single integrated risk management (IRM) program. We saw in the previous chapter that there are many ways in which a product can be "integrated." The ones that we will consider in this chapter can be classified as having either the first or second degree of integration. Using the capital structure framework developed in Chapter 3, these products can be executed as insurance policies or derivative contracts to:

- Transfer the risks of a corporation, and
- Provide off-balance-sheet capital to cover those risks.

Generally, these products fall into two categories. In the first, risks are combined into a single multi-line, and possibly multi-year, risk management product. We call these products MMPs—multi-line, multi-year products. In the second, losses are paid when a combination of triggers occurs. We call these products MTPs—multi-trigger products.[1]

We will first describe the general features of MMPs and MTPs. Then we will use some examples to demonstrate how these products work.

Before we proceed, we recognize that many practitioners refer to the products described here as integrated risk management products. We recognize from the preceding chapters and the ones to follow that there are many ways to manage these risks in an integrated manner. Therefore, we use the term integrated risk management (IRM) or alternative risk transfer (ART) to refer to all such tools and techniques, and not just those described in this chapter.

MULTI-LINE, MULTI-YEAR PRODUCTS (MMPS)

An MMP bundles several risks together so that the payment to the buyer reflects the joint losses from these risks. The concept of combining different categories of risk in one product over several years is not new—the first attempts to do so were made back in the '70s.[2] Nevertheless, there is now a high level of activity in this area, with potential for more.

MMPs in the Financial Markets

In the financial markets, a bundle of risks in one product is referred to as a "basket." These basket derivative products have evolved naturally as a response to the demand for customized financial hedging from the more sophisticated clients. Figure 6.1 illustrates how risk is moved from the corporate hedger to the capital markets via a derivatives dealer. Usually, no more than two risks are combined in a single derivative product. The hedger is covered when losses from both risks are greater than a specified amount. The derivatives dealer evaluates the correlations of the underlying financial risks and constructs a basket derivative product that reflects the joint loss exposure of the combined risks. The joint exposure is likely to be different from the exposure of the individual risks. The dealer prices the product based on an estimate of the correlation of the two risks. However, the dealer does not retain all the risks of the basket on its own books. Instead, it seeks to hedge its exposure to

Figure 6.1   Combining risks in a basket option.

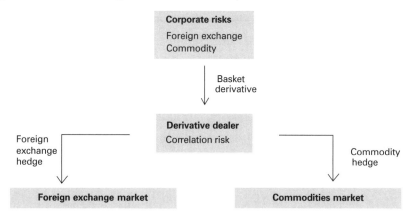

the two underlying risks in the capital markets. Since basket covers are not standard products in the capital markets, the dealer has to separate the risks as best it can and manage its own exposure by trading in the single-risk derivative markets. Inevitably, the dealer has to retain the correlation risk on its own books.

Although these products have been available since the late '80s, they are not as widely used as the single-risk hedges. The reasons for this are twofold. First, single-risk products offer the greatest liquidity and ease of execution, and are therefore likely to be the first choice in any hedging program. Second, the most sophisticated companies today are able to evaluate the interaction of the financial risks that they face, hedge the single risks in the capital markets and keep the correlation risk themselves.

These MMPs are often short-duration contracts, rarely extending beyond one year. One reason for this is that the shorter duration keeps the correlation risk within an acceptable range for the derivatives dealer. Of course, since these are highly customized contracts, multi-year products can also be structured if the corporate hedger insists upon it, and is willing to pay the price.

MMPs in the Insurance Markets

In the insurance markets, MMPs have been around for years, but in different form. First, consider multi-year products. Today, we are used to one-year non-life insurance policies for both personal and corporate risks. In Europe, when the markets were still heavily regulated, most personal lines policies were non-cancellable up to ten years. However, challenged by consumer protectionists, many jurisdictions have held such long-term binding of policyholders to be illegal.[3]

In the corporate insurance arena, three-year policies were fairly standard in the airline insurance market of the '70s. However, some policyholders treated them as shorter-term policies, cancelling them every year during the down cycle and replacing them at reduced rates. When the market hardened, insurers were expected to honor the multi-year policies at the lower rates. Insurers realized that this was a losing proposition and stopped offering multi-year policies altogether.

Multi-line policies under the heading of "global insurance packages" or "Europolicies" achieved their first successes in the early '80s as a response to industrial globalization. However, their packaging consisted of little more than the staples holding different, distinct, single-line standard policies together, though they had a single, unifying cover sheet.

MMPs only became attractive—and successful—after achieving genuine integration of the various insurance lines and sequences of policy years. This was accomplished by defining overall policy limits, especially **aggregate limits**. Under true MMPs, the aggregate maximum amount of loss retained by the policyholder is fixed, irrespective of the sources of loss within the covered risks. The rest, up to an aggregate limit, is passed on to the insurer.

The first of this new generation of MMPs were sometimes referred to as "twinpacks" because they combined property and casualty risks in one program. These programs offered genuine risk transfer for corporations facing potential catastrophe exposure to their balance sheets. They provided tailor-made coverage (often basing attachment points and capacity on industry standards and benchmarks[4]) when and where it was most needed.

MMPs take a "macro" approach to risk transfer rather than a "micro" one (Figure 6.2). They offer balance sheet protection through optimized attachment points that reflect risk category and loss experience. By focusing on risk transfer at true catastrophe levels, and by absorbing less significant risks themselves, corporations can reduce their overall insurance cost while maintaining coverage for the risks that most concern them. They can

Figure 6.2   Macro approach to risk transfer.

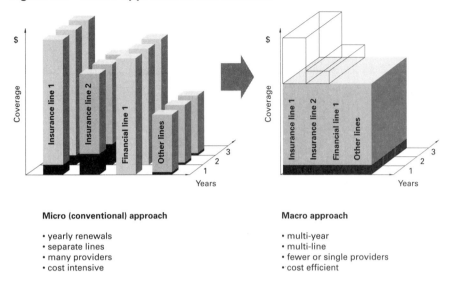

Micro (conventional) approach	Macro approach
• yearly renewals	• multi-year
• separate lines	• multi-line
• many providers	• fewer or single providers
• cost intensive	• cost efficient

also make more effective use of their working capital in their core business activities. Predictable claims can be funded through more efficient mechanisms, thereby avoiding the frustrations of "trading dollars."(**Trading dollars** refers to the effect of paying premiums for highly predictable risks only to get back the same amount as claims payments in the same period.)

MMPs finance risk more effectively because their pricing and structure benefit from the principle of diversification: a portfolio of different risks, spread over time. Corporations are hurt by any hit to their bottom line; the distinction between property and casualty losses is of secondary interest.

Some of the early MMPs provided substantial capacity for both property and casualty catastrophe exposures in a single contract. In most cases, property and casualty covers were offered separately, but the contract included a single limit covering both lines up to several hundred million dollars. Coverage was seldom combined in true risk baskets, because firms were familiar with managing, and insurers with offering, each risk as a single line of insurance. Even so, given the size of the risk capacity offered, such programs quickly became the core of a firm's coverage for low-frequency, high-severity risks. Firms were able to count on one substantial block of capacity over several years in a single contract.

Figure 6.3   MMP for oil and gas company.

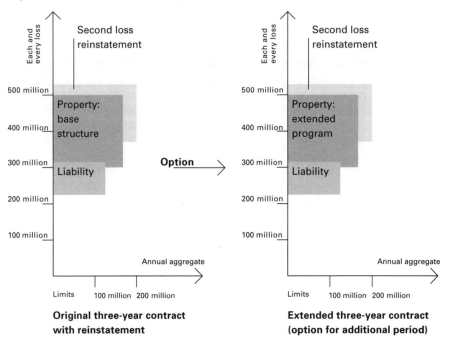

Figure 6.3 shows an MMP designed for an oil and gas company. The MMP is offered as a three-year policy with an automatic option to extend coverage for an additional three years. The program provides loss limits of $300 million, splitting the capacity into $200 million for property and $100 million for liability.

A major consideration for corporations buying such programs was the establishment of a corporate aggregate (annual) retention, set to cover expected losses. The corporate view had to be expressed not just in terms of insurance losses, but also in terms of the actual cost of capital to the company to cover these exposures. Such policies were the first step toward combining an insurance and internal corporate finance view.

Unlike derivatives dealers, (re)insurers have the ability to keep more than just the correlation risks; their tradition is to keep all of the risks transferred to them from the corporation. To this end, some developed multi-disciplinary teams with mathematical, legal and (re)insurance backgrounds to provide industry-specific coverages. These teams had to:

- Compile and code comprehensive databases with historical losses by industry segment,
- Apply state-of-the-art actuarial tools to these data,
- Identify industry trends and fluctuations affecting exposure,
- Establish optimal attachment points based on each industry's exposure profile,
- Assess the risk landscape and translate it into capital requirements,
- Design coverage specifications, and
- Create sophisticated computer tools for underwriters and marketers.

As underwriters and corporations became more comfortable with integration techniques and with the assessment of correlations between different (insurable) risks, programs with single aggregate limits across a number (often up to ten) insurance lines began to emerge—and at considerably lower attachment points.

The current MMPs offer greater variety both in the number and the types of risks covered in a single program. "Traditional" insurance risks such as fire, business interruption and liability can be combined, and premium rates set on an integrated basis. It is also feasible for an MMP to include financial risks currently only covered in the capital markets, such as fluctuations in interest rates, currency exchange rates and commodity prices. The latest generation of MMPs also includes risks traditionally considered to be uninsurable (e.g. political and business risks).

An Example of Managing Individual Risks

Before we show an illustration of some MMPs let us take a short detour. In the introduction, we raised the question of whether there is merit in managing risks in some combination, or whether the conventional focus on managing individual risks is appropriate. In many situations, the single-risk focus is appropriate. However, there are pitfalls. The most important one is that the firm could ignore the interaction of the risks in its portfolio and consequently either over- or under-hedge its risks.

In the next few pages, we work through an example of how this can occur. Those of you who do not need to be persuaded can jump to the next section.

In our experience, though, there is a merit in working through a real illustration to highlight the major issues. We consider the case of Oilcat Corporation.

Oilcat has two major risks that can have a significant effect on its earnings. The first is the price of oil, and the second is the occurrence of a major natural catastrophe, such as an earthquake or hurricane, that can severely damage its physical assets.

If the price of oil is high, Oilcat's revenues are excellent. If it is low, they are not. It calculates that although its average earnings are $1250, it can earn $1500 in a good year and $1000 in a bad one. Oilcat's senior managers find this volatility in earnings to be too high and have asked their treasurer to reduce it. Management believes that it can absorb earnings volatility of $150, and would like to hedge the rest.

The Treasurer.   The treasurer does some quick calculations to assess the risk exposure and develop an oil price hedge. These are summarized in Box 6.1. Assuming that one of the two scenarios (price rise or fall) will occur with equal probability, he verifies that the average revenue is indeed $1250. Oilcat quantifies its risk in terms of **earnings volatility**, which is the standard

Box 6.1   Oilcat oil price hedge.

(all figures in $)
Before hedge

	Price rises	Price falls	Average	Volatility
Probability	50%	50%		
Unhedged earnings	1500	1000	1250	250

Average earnings $= 0.5 \times 1500 + 0.5 \times 1000 = 1250$
Earnings volatility $= \{0.5 \times (1500 - 1250)^2 + 0.5 \times (1000 - 1250)^2\}^{\frac{1}{2}} = 250$

After hedge on $100 of earnings volatility

	Price rises	Price falls	Average	Volatility
Probability	50%	50%		
Unhedged earnings	1500	1000	1250	250
Futures payments	−100	100	0	100
Hedged earnings	1400	1100	1250	150

Average earnings $= 0.5 \times 1400 + 0.5 \times 1100 = 1250$
Earnings volatility $= \{0.5 \times (1400 - 1250)^2 + 0.5 \times (1100 - 1250)^2\}^{\frac{1}{2}} = 150$

deviation of earnings. He calculates this to be $250. His task is to reduce volatility to $150. He does so by entering into a futures contract. Ignoring all frictional expenses, the futures contract he enters into pays up to $100 when the oil price falls, and requires Oilcat to pay up to $100 if it rises. The resulting earnings volatility is the targeted $150.

The Risk Manager.   Meanwhile, in a separate part of the organization, the risk manager (RM) has been doing her homework. An analysis of Oilcat's physical assets shows that the catastrophe (cat) damage could be as much as $1000, severely reducing earnings. Fortunately, the probability of such an event is low at 10%, i.e. there is a 90% chance that there will be no hit whatsoever. The RM is not familiar with the oil price market, so she concentrates on developing an insurance program to hedge average earnings. From a conversation with the CFO, she knows that average earnings are $1250 and that management wants to reduce earnings volatility to $150. She uses that as a starting point for her analysis. Her calculations and the insurance program she develops are shown in Box 6.2.

If no cat occurs, average earnings stay at $1250. If there is a cat, the average earnings fall to $250. The average of these earnings is $1150, and the cat-related earnings volatility is $300. Having heard the call to reduce earnings volatility to $150, she calculates that to do so would require her to insure half of the cat exposure, retaining the remaining risk. Since the probability of a cat is 10%, with a hit of $1000, the premium to cover the full risk, ignoring any frictional costs and premium loadings, is $100. To cover 50% of the risk, the premium is $50. If there is a cat, Oilcat will get paid $500, so that its net revenues after insurance premium are $450. This insurance program reduces earnings volatility by 50% to $150.

In this rather simplified illustration, two key points emerge:

1. Although senior management stated earnings volatility of $150 as an objective, the treasurer and RM started from different points, and therefore had different views on the earnings volatility of the firm as a whole.
2. Although both the treasurer and the RM competently fulfilled their responsibilities, the single-risk hedging did not take into account the

Box 6.2   Oilcat catastrophe (cat) risk insurance.

(all figures in $)
Before insurance

	No cat	Cat	Average	Volatility
Probability	90%	10%		
Uninsured average earnings	1250	250	1150	300

Average earnings = 0.9 x 1250 + 0.1 x 250 = 1150
Earnings volatility = $\{0.9 \times (1250 - 1150)^2 + 0.1 \times (250 - 1150)^2\}^{\frac{1}{2}} = 300$

After insurance on $150 of earnings volatility

	No cat	Cat	Average	Volatility
Probability	90%	10%		
Uninsured average earnings	1250	250	1150	300
Insurance payments	−50	450	0	150
Insured average earnings	1200	700	1150	150

Insured average earnings = 0.9 x 1200 + 0.1 x 700 = 1150
Earnings volatility = $\{0.9 \times (1200 - 1150)^2 + 0.1 \times (700 - 1150)^2\}^{\frac{1}{2}} = 150$

Note that the insurance premium is deducted from the insurance payments in the cat scenario.

overall earnings profile of the firm, i.e. the impact of the interaction of both oil price risk and cat risk on corporate earnings.

The Chief Financial Officer.   Continuing with this illustration, the CFO receives both the oil hedging and the cat insurance proposals. Having just read a book on Integrating Corporate Risk Management, he recognizes that there may be some benefit to bringing the two risk management programs together into one program. But first he wants to see whether these two programs separately achieve the corporate goal. He puts together a simple worksheet, shown in Box 6.3.

When all four scenarios (two oil price scenarios times two cat scenarios) are considered, the average earnings are not $1250 as previously calculated by the treasurer, but $1150 as calculated by the risk manager. The treasurer's number is wrong because he ignored the cat risk in his calculations. He only considered the volatility due to the oil price. The RM happened to arrive at the correct number. She, too, only considered the risk within her

Box 6.3 Oilcat effect of separate covers.

(all figures in $)

Cat event	No cat	No cat	Cat	Cat		
Oil price	Rise	Fall	Rise	Fall	Average	Volatility
Probability	45%	45%	5%	5%		
Earnings before	1500	1000	500	0	1150	390.5
Futures payments	−100	100	−100	100	0	−100
Insurance payments	−50	−50	450	450	0	−150
Earnings after	1350	1050	850	550	1150	212.1

Before risk covers

Average earnings $= 0.45 \times (1500 + 1000) + 0.05 \times (500 + 0) = 1150$

Earnings volatility $= \{0.45 \times (1500 - 1150)^2 + 0.45 \times (1000 - 1150)^2$
$+ 0.05 \times (500 - 1150)^2 + 0.05 \times (0 - 1150)^2\}^{\frac{1}{2}} = 390.5$

After risk covers

Average earnings $= 0.45 \times (1350 + 1050) + 0.05 \times (850 + 550) = 1150$

Earnings volatility $= \{0.45 \times (1350 - 1150)^2 + 0.45 \times (1050 - 1150)^2$
$+ 0.05 \times (850 - 1150)^2 + 0.05 \times (550 - 1150)^2\}^{\frac{1}{2}} = 212.1$

responsibility, the cat risk, and did not explicitly consider the oil price risk. However, because she used the pre-cat average earnings of $1250 as her starting point *she did in fact consider both risks.*

It is no surprise now that the earnings volatility is different from that calculated by either the treasurer or RM. It turns out to be higher than either of them had expected, $390.5. The CFO's analysis shows that putting the two separate programs together would only reduce earnings volatility to $212.5, which does not meet the corporate objective of $150.

How can the CFO fix this situation? He can do so by recognizing that he has two tools to achieve the corporate objective—he can adjust both the oil hedge and the cat insurance to fix the situation. There are many combinations that will reduce earnings volatility to $150. Box 6.4 shows two possible adjustments. In the first case, the oil hedge is increased to $250, holding the insurance program constant. This hedge amount reflects the single-risk earnings volatility due to oil price (Box 6.1). It is therefore not surprising that Oilcat's earnings under this program vary only with the occurrence of a cat, i.e. they are $1200, unless a cat reduces them to $700.

Box 6.4   Oilcat CFO's possible adjustments.

(all figures in $)

Strategy 1 Fully hedge oil price risk

| Cat event | No cat | No cat | Cat | Cat | | |
Oil price	Rise	Fall	Rise	Fall	Average	Volatility
Probability	45%	45%	5%	5%		
Earnings before	1500	1000	500	0	1150	390.5
Futures payments	−250	250	−250	250	0	−250
Insurance payments	−50	−50	450	450	0	−150
Earnings after	1200	1200	700	700	1150	150

Earnings volatility = $\{0.45 \times (1200 - 1150)^2 + 0.45 \times (1200 - 1150)^2$
$$+ 0.05 \times (700 - 1150)^2 + 0.05 \times (700 - 1150)^2\}^{1/2} = 150$$

Strategy 2 Fully insure cat risk

| Cat event | No cat | No cat | Cat | Cat | | |
Oil price	Rise	Fall	Rise	Fall	Average	Volatility
Probability	45%	45%	5%	5%		
Earnings before	1500	1000	500	0	1150	390.5
Futures payments	−100	100	−100	100	0	−100
Insurance payments	−100	−100	900	900	0	−300
Earnings after	1300	1000	1300	1000	1150	150

Earnings volatility = $\{0.45 \times (1300 - 1150)^2 + 0.45 \times (1000 - 1150)^2$
$$+ 0.05 \times (1300 - 1150)^2 + 0.05 \times (1000 - 1150)^2\}^{1/2} = 150$$

In the second strategy, the cat insurance is purchased to cover the full $1000 possible loss, thereby reducing the cat retention to nil. This situation is parallel to the preceding one. Now Oilcat's earnings are unaffected by a cat, i.e. they are $1300 when oil prices are high, and $1000 when oil prices are low.

As the CFO does his analysis, he starts to put the numbers on a spreadsheet. In doing so, he finds that he is able to develop a general formula for the effect of the risk management program. This formula has two drivers: the proportion of oil price risk hedged and the proportion of cat risk covered.[5]

This analysis gives the CFO yet another insight. It is possible to keep the average earnings at some target level ($1150) and adjust the hedge and insurance to meet the earnings volatility goal ($150). There are many possible combinations! However, he also notices that the pattern of earnings that can emerge across the possible scenarios can vary widely, depending on the risk management program developed.

The CFO, together with the treasurer and RM, makes a few other observations:

- The current separate programs can be brought together into a single risk management exercise to develop consistent earnings and volatility measures, but the execution of the two parts can be kept in the separate domains of the treasurer and RM. This approach can work so long as the risk management program keeps a clear separation between the two risks and does not get more ambitious in integrating them.

- The cost of this program is the cost of the insurance policy, since the futures contract is costless at inception. The up-front cost of the joint program is greatest at $100, when the full amount of cat insurance is purchased. It is minimized by limiting the amount of insurance purchased—but that increases the range of earnings in the scenarios ($700 to $1200 in CFO's Strategy 1), even though the calculated earnings volatility can be made stable.

- If, instead of a futures contract, Oilcat hedges the risk with options, then it will have to pay an option premium. In that case the cost of the program is the sum of the option premium and the insurance premium. There may be cost savings in combining these two risks and purchasing an MMP from an insurer or reinsurer.

- The scenario that causes the most concern is the one where a cat event occurs when oil prices are low. Perhaps Oilcat can benefit from a hedge that pays off only when those two events occur—a multi-trigger product.

The Value of MMPs

MMPs allow a corporation to manage the amount of risk it retains and the amount of overall protection that it gets. As the following example shows, MMPs can deliver more than simply the addition of two separate risk programs.

Twinline Corporation is exposed to property insurance risk through its physical assets and to financial market risk through its investment portfolio.

Its risk management operation is state of the art. Twinline calculates that it is willing and able to retain $50 of property losses and $50 of interest-rate-related investment losses. It hedges or insures losses above those amounts in the appropriate markets. The worst case loss for Twinline is $100 if both risks develop high losses. In effect, this amount defines Twinline's maximum loss threshold.

The property insurance program pays up to a limit of $150 in losses over the $50 retained by Twinline. Likewise, the interest rate hedge pays up to$150 in losses over the $50 strike. Figure 6.4 illustrates the two separate programs. It shows:

- The maximum loss that Twinline can face is $100, which is the sum of the retention on the two risks, and
- The maximum loss that will be covered by the two programs together is $400, which can occur only when both risks have losses of $200 each.

Twinline now recognizes that there is a better way to cover the two risks. It can purchase an MMP that has the following terms:

- The retention is set at $100 for aggregate losses. Here, aggregate losses refer to the sum of both property losses and investment losses. The retention is a function of both the risks.

Figure 6.4   Twinline's conventional risk management program.

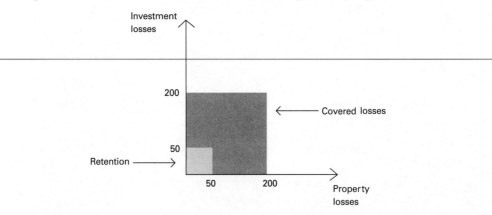

- The policy limit is $300 over the retention of $100. This means that aggregate losses up to $400 resulting from *any combination* of losses from the two risks will result in a payment to the policyholder of $300.

Figure 6.5 illustrates this MMP. In comparison with the conventional approach, the MMP has increased coverage by fully responding to large combined losses, irrespective of their composition—area A in the figure. It also eliminates cover for low losses in one line if losses in the other line are also relatively small—area B in the figure.

Clearly the two programs are different. With the MMP, Twinline retains more risk. However, these are the relatively predictable, low-severity, high-frequency risks. The sum of those claim payments should approximate the sum of the related insurance premiums. The MMP adds some high-severity, low-frequency risks to the program. At this level, the probability of a loss event is low. As we saw in Chapter 3, keeping capital on the balance sheet against such risks is inefficient; it is better to transfer the risk. The premium for that layer should be far less than any potential claims payment.

Structuring the program as a multi-year cover can achieve cost savings in administration. The real benefit, however, is in the added diversification of the risk over time.

Whether the premium of the MMP is greater or less than the conventional program does depend on the particular features of the risks being

Figure 6.5 Twinline's MMP provides superior coverage.

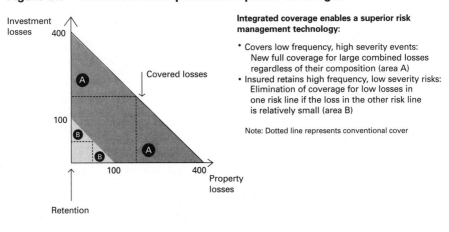

Integrated coverage enables a superior risk management technology:

- Covers low frequency, high severity events: New full coverage for large combined losses regardless of their composition (area A)
- Insured retains high frequency, low severity risks: Elimination of coverage for low losses in one risk line if the loss in the other risk line is relatively small (area B)

Note: Dotted line represents conventional cover

covered. It is possible to achieve real cost savings when the probability of losses in area A is considerably less than that of area B.

The Benefits of MMPs[6]

The benefits of MMPs for policyholders can be summarized as follows:

- **Efficiency gains:** The volatility of the loss experience in the deductible for this type of integrated risk portfolio is less than the sum of the volatilities of individual risk categories. Ultimately, the cost advantages of MMPs lie in the exploitation of business-specific diversification potential for the deductibles, reducing any overinsurance.
- **Stabilization of risk costs:** Since premium payments are fixed over several years, the policyholder benefits from more stable risk costs. These include not only the insurance premiums, but also the losses in the deductible and the uninsured losses.
- **Administrative efficiency:** Although MMPs are usually more complex than traditional products, they allow the policyholder to achieve substantial efficiency gains in administration. The negotiation and coordination costs decrease as the number of participating insurers shrinks. The same applies for the multi-year term, which obviates the need for the usual contract renewal procedures at the end of each policy year. The upfront cost will be greater, but the overall program cost is likely to be lower than that for traditional products.
- **Flexibility:** MMPs are usually tailored specifically to client needs. Their formulation requires a detailed analysis of the client's risk portfolio and risk tolerance. The aim of this customized approach is to avoid overinsurance, caused for example by many different uncoordinated insurance policies, and to fill any gaps in cover.

It is only fair to state here that MMPs are not very common in current business practice. We examine some of the prospects and challenges for such products in Chapter 13. To summarize, the main reasons for the slow growth of these instruments, which look very attractive in theory, are as follows:

- High initial setup and transaction costs, even though the multi-year average cost may be acceptable,
- High credit risk, since there are just a few MMP providers today,
- Capacity available in current MMP programs is not sufficient to cover the full insurance amount of existing risks,
- Traditional risk management focus on managing single risks, and
- Lack of accounting and regulatory clarity on some issues.

The development of an MMP structure can be fairly straightforward when only two or three risks are being considered, and some such structures are being executed in the marketplace. The level of complexity increases with the number of risks in the program. Appendix 6A discusses a case study based on an actual assignment for a multinational corporation and indicates the challenge of including a large number of risks.

MULTI-TRIGGER PRODUCTS (MTPS)

In an MTP, the payments due to losses on one risk are only made to the buyer if triggered by an event on some other risk. Although this is a relatively new product for the insurance market, it has been around for some time in the financial markets.

MTPs in the Financial Markets

In the financial markets, multi-trigger derivative products are commonly known as "knock-in" products. The idea behind the name is that an option, for example, is made effective, or knocked in, if a triggering condition is met.

In the simplest illustration, a conventional option on a stock is a knock-in, since the option can be exercised only when the stock price has crossed the option's strike price level. In the spirit of the multi-line risk products described earlier, a knock-in option has a triggering event based on some risk other than the one underlying the derivative contract. For example, an option on a stock is knocked in if the 5-year interest rate increases by 100 basis points (i.e. 1%). In this case, if interest rates do not increase by 100 basis points, the option purchaser will not be able to exercise the stock option, regardless of the movements in the underlying stock. Only once the 5-year interest rate has moved beyond 100 basis points will the option purchaser truly have the right (not obligation) to exercise the option. In some cases, the amount paid to the purchaser on the stock option will also depend on the interest rate trigger.

Clearly, such features limit the circumstances under which the option will make a payment to the purchaser. Consequently, its price should be cheaper than a comparable conventional option.

We have shown only the simplest example of an MTP in the financial markets. There are many more, with a variety of features that limit both the availability of an option, and the amount payable when available.

MTPs in the Insurance Markets

In the insurance markets, MTPs experienced a sharp rise in popularity in the first quarter of 1994, initially as reinsurance products for direct insurers. The 1994 Northridge, California, earthquake resulted in insured losses of approximately $10 billion. In the same quarter a massive fall in the U.S. bond market led to (unrealized) capital losses for U.S. non-life insurers estimated at $20 billion.[7] This double whammy led insurers to consider purchasing MTPs.

Since then, many more non-insurers have become interested in MTP covers. This is especially true of companies whose earnings power is heavily affected by fluctuations in commodity prices, exchange rates and interest rates.

The most important feature of these covers is that claims are paid only if all trigger events occur. From the insurer's viewpoint this reduces the number of circumstances under which a claim is paid, which in turn allows cover to be offered at a cheaper rate. To illustrate, let us assume that the probability of a full insurance claim under the first trigger (e.g. fire damage) is 10%. The probability of occurrence of the second trigger (e.g. a specific increase in the yield on government bonds) is also 10%. Excluding transaction costs, profit margins and so on, the premium rate on the line of cover provided works out to be the product of both probabilities, i.e. 1%, assuming the events are not correlated.

The difficulty is to find two triggers that work well together to manage a firm's risk exposure. The correlation between the two risks underlying the triggers needs to be well understood so that protection is there only when necessary and the expected cost efficiencies are actually achieved. To avoid moral hazard, one of the triggers should be related to an observable index outside the influence of the policyholder. On the other hand, from the policyholder's perspective, basis risk is minimized if the other trigger refers to the company's own losses.

The Value of MTPs

The possible combinations of triggers provide an endless variety of MTPs. Consider just the following few examples:

- The deductible applicable under a property insurance policy may fall in the event that a specific loss, such as may be caused by an increase in the price of raw materials, arises from the firm's normal business.
- Stop-loss cover for a captive insurer is provided so that the claims ratio is revised upwards as soon as the prices of government bonds fall below a certain level.
- Catastrophe cover is provided to Oilcat Corporation only if oil prices fall below a certain trigger level; only 50% of cat losses are covered if oil prices fall by 10%, and 100% of losses are covered if they fall by 20%.
- Twinline's MMP insurance program is available only if both a financial trigger (investment losses greater than, say, $25 million) and an insurance trigger (property losses greater than, say, $25 million) occur.

In all these cases, the corporation is able to customize an MTP to suit its own needs. It is not much of a stretch to recognize that MTPs, by their very construction, are multi-line products and therefore share many of the features of MMPs discussed earlier.

As earlier, we illustrate how an MTP works by way of an example. Littlesub Insurance Company is a captive insurance entity of a major manufacturer. It covers a number of conventionally insurable risks of its parent and does some third-party business as well. Littlesub has in place traditional reinsurance stop loss programs that protect it if its loss ratio exceeds a certain level. Littlesub also has an investment portfolio of bonds and equities. Littlesub is able to afford higher losses only when the investment portfolio is performing well. It needs additional protection for such losses if the invest-ment portfolio is underperforming. It works with its reinsurer to customize an MTP that is triggered off the performance of the investment portfolio.

Box 6.5 shows how Littlesub's MTP (I) works. The pure insurance loss ratio is adjusted upward or downward, depending on the performance of the investment portfolio. This increases Littlesub's effective retention when in-vestment performance is good, and decreases it when it is bad. We show two scenarios. In the first, investment performance is good as the market value grows by $100. The insurance loss ratio of 70% is adjusted downward to re-flect this investment performance. Consequently, the contract's loss ratio is calculated to be 60%, which is within Littlesub's retention. Therefore, it does not receive any payment from the reinsurance policy. In the second sce-nario, the investment performance is not good, and Littlesub shows a fall in its portfolio value of $50. This raises the loss ratio to 75%, which is 10%

Box 6.5   MTP(I) for Littlesub Insurance Company.

(all figures in $)

Period of cover is 12 months commencing January 1

Retention   = 65% loss ratio of net earned premiums

Limit   = 150

Loss ratio formula:

MTP loss ratio = Insurance loss ratio + Financial loss ratio

where Insurance loss ratio $= \dfrac{\text{Net incurred insurance losses}}{\text{Net earned premium income}}$

and Financial loss ratio $= \dfrac{\text{Decrease in market value of investments}}{\text{Net earned premium income}}$

Sample outcomes	Scenario 1	Scenario 2
Net earned premium income	1000	1000
Net incurred insured losses	700	700
Change in investment value	100	–50
Insurance loss ratio	70%	70%
Financial loss ratio	–10%	5%
MTP loss ratio	60%	75%
Retention	65%	65%
Payment on MTP	0%	10% ($100)

Note that a negative financial loss ratio indicates an increase in the market value of the portfolio.

more than the retention. The payout from the MTP is therefore $100 (10% of $1000), which is within the maximum limit of $150.

MTP(I) can be considered a single-trigger product, since the coverage is available only if the single trigger condition (i.e. the retention) is met during the contract period. Littlesub can also consider an extension of this concept, MTP(II), by using two triggers where coverage is activated only if both trigger events occur. Such a structure would be useful for companies that are worried about simultaneous catastrophic losses.

Littlesub has two major concerns. The first is that the insurance loss ratio may be above 65%. The second is that the investment portfolio value may fall by 40% during the year. In this case, MTP(II), shown in Box 6.6, may provide the appropriate protection.

In this example, even though Littlesub has an insurance loss ratio of 70% in both scenarios, the second condition (the investment value trigger) is only met in Scenario 2. Since the conditions have not been met in Scenario 1, the

Box 6.6   MTP(II) for Littlesub Insurance Company.

(all figures in $)
Period of cover is 12 months commencing January 1
Retention   = 65% loss ratio of net earned premiums
Limit   = 150

First trigger   Insurance loss ratio is greater than 65%
Second trigger Market value of investment portfolio on December 31 is
                40% less than value on January 1.
MTP loss ratio = Insurance loss ratio if both triggers met

Sample outcomes	Scenario 1	Scenario 2
Net earned premium income	1000	1000
Net incurred insured losses	700	700
Change in investment value	100	−50
Insurance loss ratio	70%	70%
Investment value increase	10%	−50%
Both triggers met?	No	Yes
MTP loss ratio	0%	70%
Retention	65%	65%
Payment on MTP	0%	5% ($50)

MTP loss ratio is 0, and Littlesub does not get any payment from the MTP. The MTP loss ratio in Scenario 2 is the insurance loss ratio of 70%, since both conditions have been met. The payment to Littlesub is 5% or $50, since that is the excess over the retention that is covered by the MTP.

One other alternative that Littlesub could consider is MTP (III), a variation on MTP (II). Here, once both the triggering events occur, any payout depends not on the value of the insurance losses, but on the value of the investment portfolio.

The Benefits of MTPs

MTPs provide protection from disaster scenarios such as the occurrence of a devastating earthquake in the same financial year as price drops in equity or bond markets.

As we have demonstrated, MTPs also present substantial price advantages. But this aspect is only worth consideration if companies are sufficiently capitalized to be able to absorb any insurance and non-insurance losses that occur separately. These policyholders can use MTPs to reduce overinsurance and confine insurance cover to the simultaneous occurrence of an insurance and a non-insurance loss. On the other hand, companies with questionable financial strength, whose sole motive for introducing a second trigger is to save premiums, run a high risk if they use MTPs.

In practice, MTPs face the same hurdles as MMPs. High transaction costs and traditional organizational structures in corporate risk management, coupled with uncertainties concerning treatment under tax laws and accounting principles have all hindered their breakthrough to date.

THE NEXT STEP: ENTERPRISE EARNINGS PROTECTION?

Together with conventional insurance and derivative products, MMPs and MTPs represent the tools that enable a corporation to control how much risk it transfers and how much it retains. As we saw in Chapter 3, that is the first step in determining the optimal capital structure of the firm.

Corporations are concerned with managing financial performance. As we have seen in the examples above, MMPs and MTPs can be used to manage earnings volatility by hedging or insuring the underlying sources of that volatility. Is it possible to protect earnings volatility more directly and comprehensively?

The ultimate integrated product goes right to the bottom line: **enterprise earnings protection**. Such a product would promise to indemnify a company for deviations of earnings from projected levels, but would have exclusions that protect the insurer from the voluntary actions of corporate management, such as corporate restructurings. When designed properly, enterprise earnings protection may be able to provide an extremely efficient approach to the transfer of risks that would normally be hedged in the insurance and capital markets, and other risks for which hedging vehicles may not exist at all.

Earnings protection takes the integrated concept to the furthest extent possible—where all risks, both known and unknown, traditionally insurable and not, are hedged in a basket program. Unlike separate risk management programs, which may end up providing too much or too little protection for separately defined perils, a single block of insurance capacity is made available to meet these perils.

A number of designs are currently on the drawing board for earnings protection products. Some plan to protect against relatively minor deviations from projected earnings, whereas others may protect against catastrophic events, such as negative earnings in either quarterly or annual reports. All are based on strenuous underwriting of the insured company, including extensive risk management audits that are valuable in their own right, and all provide for coinsurance provisions in order to further align the interests of the insurer and the company.

Most of the earnings protection products under development do not contemplate that the insurer will bear the risk of an economic downturn and resulting declines in sales and earnings. One way to accomplish this is to adjust earnings upward when actual revenues fail to meet projected levels. These adjusted earnings are the basis for any indemnification on the part of the insurer. The remaining risks then more closely resemble the sorts of exposures that a company traditionally wishes to transfer, such as cost increases, plant explosions and lawsuits.

Once a company has such coverage in hand, it may need to reconsider the value provided by its conventional insurance and capital market hedges.

It is the great promise of these products that other hedges can be "wrapped into" the coverage at considerable cost savings. Perhaps it is possible that a company can end up paying less for insurance after putting such a program in place. The extent to which this is possible depends on how the product is designed, which in turn depends on the company's risk management objectives. If such programs can be developed successfully, they can become formidable tools in the risk management arsenal of a corporation.

Appendix 6A

An MMP Case Study

The process of developing an MMP for a multinational manufacturer ("the client") of durable and nondurable goods provides an excellent example of both the complexity and the potential benefits that may accrue from structuring an integrated risk management program. The manufacturer assembled a team of treasury, strategic planning, risk management and purchasing managers to identify and evaluate the firm's most significant operating and financial risks. The project team was headed by the treasurer and had received the approval of the board of directors. The company recognized that such an integrated program would require senior management support across key functional areas.

Typically, even sophisticated corporations hedge individual exposures (i.e. insurance, foreign exchange or interest rates) under separate programs. Hence, developing an optimal hedging program requires the input and collaboration of a variety of specialists within the firm. The cross-functional project team identified a broad array of risks, and sought to hedge those exposures that had the greatest impact on operating results. Initially, exposures from fourteen currencies, ten commodities, nine insurance risks and interest expense were identified as the most significant.

It was proposed that these insurance, financial and commodity risks would be combined under a three-year integrated risk management program. However, it was noted that limited or nonexistent forward markets, inadequate market liquidity, or exposure size were particularly problematic for several of the commodities and foreign currencies initially identified by the analysis. The client was particularly interested in obtaining coverage for unconventional and nontradable risks.

The reinsurer's team gathered loss experience data from the client for the insurance lines and evaluated market information for each of the financial and commodity risks. Loss curves were developed for each insurance risk to model the frequency and severity distribution of these risks. Ground-up loss distribution curves were generated for each of the exposures to quantify the expected losses. The insurance curves were aggregated into a single hazard risk curve.

Financial exposures including interest expense, foreign currencies and commodities were put into categories that reflected how effectively these risks could be managed over the life of the three-year cover. The risk categories were as follows:

- **Tradable for three years**—Financial risks placed in this category are characterized by liquid futures and forward markets. Exchange-traded and over-the-counter dealers as well as market participants are willing to make markets of substantial size. The following risks were placed in this category: interest rates, #2 heating oil, natural gas and 7 actively traded currencies.
- **Minimally tradable**—Financial risks placed in this category have limited futures and forward markets, typically six to twelve months in duration. Liquidity in these markets is occasionally limited and may be subject to volume constraints and supply and demand price volatility. In this category, the identified risks were electricity, soybeans and 7 less liquid currencies.
- **Spot market (no forwards)**—Financial risks placed in this category have historical price sources and a spot market. Futures and forward markets are non-existent. Given the lack of liquidity or forward yield curves, it would be extremely difficult to hedge these risks. In this category were placed ethylene, nickel and zinc.
- **Unconventional risks**—The financial risks placed in this category are characterized by unusual price dynamics (i.e. monopolistic or oligopolistic), unconventional supply and demand, or poorly-defined specifications. These risks were viewed as unacceptable and could not be included in the risk basket of covered perils under the program. Titanium dioxide was placed in this risk category.

Based on the evaluation of the financial risks associated with the ten commodities originally proposed for inclusion in the program, the client concluded that seven of the commodities could be managed in the program. However, additional economic research still would be required to include any of the minimally traded commodities in the program.

After considerable discussion, a three-year program was structured that included the client's most significant exposures. Eight currencies (AUD, NZD, MXP, DEM, FFR, JPY, GBP and CAD), four commodities (natural gas, #2 heating oil, electricity and soybeans) and interest expense were selected for inclusion. These financial and commodity risks were combined with nine insurance exposures (property including boiler and machinery, general liability, products liability, crime, directors and officers, workers' compensation, pension fund fiduciary liability, attorney errors and omissions and auto liability).

Because the structure was multi-year and the corporation was concerned about budgeted financial and commodity exposures in the second and third policy years, a "ratchet reset" feature was designed: the target values (budget) for the foreign exchange and commodity exposures were determined by multiplying the budget notional amounts by the average of monthly forward rates, observed prior to the end of the calendar year for the subsequent year. On this basis, the target values for the covered exposures were set based on at-the-money forward rates that aligned with the corporation's forecasts and budgeting cycle.

Based on the combined distribution curves, which quantified the probability of expected losses, and the corporation's risk appetite, an optimal retention level was determined. The MMP was structured as three-year coverage to provide net capacity of $100 million for losses on an annual basis, in excess of an aggregate retention of $25 million. In order to trigger a loss payment, the combined commodity, financial and insurance losses must exceed the combined $25 million retention level.

The MMP program incorporated the impact of the basket effect and the varying degrees of correlation between the individual exposures. Lower volatility, correlation, averaging effects and the aggregate retention from insuring combined exposures resulted in approximately 20% premium reduction when compared to coverage on an individual basis.

"Strong economic incentives stimulated
demand for blended covers..."

7

Finite Risk Reinsurance

Kai-Uwe Schanz and Prakash Shimpi

Finite risk reinsurance (or finite re) is based on the same instruments as traditional reinsurance. However, the essential characteristics of finite products, in particular the assumption of limited risk by the reinsurer,[1] the multi-year period of the contracts, the sharing of the result with the client, and the explicit inclusion of future investment income in the stipulation of the price, offer additional possibilities that are encountering growing interest among corporations. Among other things, finite products can:

- Stabilize reinsurance costs and the availability of capacity,
- Smooth fluctuations in results,
- Expand underwriting capacity,
- Provide (partial) protection against as yet unreported claims, and
- Optimize the balance sheet.

More and more, finite products are being combined with traditional reinsurance solutions in **blended covers,** which we describe in this chapter. This trend can be attributed to two things. First is the fact that in certain countries auditors, supervisory bodies and tax authorities refuse to recognize finite solutions as reinsurance unless they involve a substantial transfer of underwriting risk. Second, and presumably more important, are the advantages that the client can derive from combining traditional and finite risk reinsurance. In a single reinsurance program, reinsurers can arrange a price for each specific type of risk—not only for a period of several years, but increasingly for risks from a number of different lines of business. Firms

---

Several sections of this chapter also appear in: Swiss Re Economic Research & Consulting, "Alternative Risk Transfer via Finite Risk Reinsurance: An Effective Contribution to the Stability of the Insurance Industry," *sigma* 5 (1997).

utilizing such covers profit accordingly from reduced transaction costs for risk protection. Moreover, blended covers can be written to include risks that have traditionally been considered uninsurable.

Finite products also make sense from a macroeconomic standpoint in that they:

- Help to attenuate cyclical trends in the insurance market,
- Provide reinsurance capacity even for hard-to-insure risks,
- Promote the establishment of long-term relationships between corporations and reinsurers, and
- Facilitate corporations' access to risk capital.

WHAT IS FINITE RISK REINSURANCE?

Due to the diversity of the products available, it is difficult to find a widely accepted definition. In general, finite risk reinsurance represents a combination of risk transfer and risk financing, with emphasis on the time value of money. Instead of searching for a straightforward definition, it is more expedient to identify some features that are shared by most finite solutions:[2]

- **Assumption of limited risk by the reinsurer:** One essential characteristic is the assumption of limited (finite) risk by the reinsurer. In finite risk contracts, the corporation (referred to as the **cedent**) transfers two things. The first is the risk of unexpectedly rapid settlement of losses and commensurately reduced investment income from the relevant loss reserves. The second is a limited, yet significant underwriting risk, that the losses actually paid over the term of the finite contract may turn out to be greater than expected.
- **Multi-year contract term:** Another characteristic feature is a contractual period of several years, which contrasts with those of most traditional reinsurance contracts. Cedents can count on long-term cover under reliable conditions, and finite risk reinsurers with a continual flow of premiums. This not only provides both parties with considerably greater latitude for negotiating prices and conditions, but also gives them a basis for establishing a long-term partnership. As a rule, the risk spread is effected on a per-contract basis over time.[3]
- **Sharing the result with the cedent:** Profits accruing over a multi-year period are, to a substantial extent, paid back to the cedent so that there

is a close connection between the cedent's own loss experience and the actual cost of reinsurance. In this way, the cedent receives "compensation" for the limitation of the risk assumed by the finite risk reinsurer.

• **Future investment income as a pricing component:** Expected investment income is explicitly defined as a factor in the premium calculation. The consideration of the time value of money has an effect, especially in certain types of liability business where settlement may take decades.

Origins of Finite Risk Reinsurance

Finite risk reinsurance originated in the '60s, when a dearth of traditional covers for oil exploration and drilling operations prompted the London insurance market to develop alternative solutions. It was not until the early '80s, however, that finite risk reinsurance—at that time still referred to as financial reinsurance, due to its primarily financial orientation—achieved its real breakthrough in the United States, due to changing business conditions and the resultant changes in the needs of corporations. The following were the primary drivers of the development:

• **Increasing volatility of prices and capacities:** The intensifying cyclical nature of the reinsurance markets underscored the cedent need for more stable, and thus more reliably calculable, prices and capacities. In particular, the scarcity of traditional reinsurance protection and commensurate increase in prices in the mid-'80s promoted the rise of alternative covers—particularly for risks bordering on non-insurability.[4] The cedent need for stable cover is addressed through a number of forms, for example spread loss treaties (discussed later in this chapter). These treaties are concluded for periods of several years and are based on a fixed annual premium payment that, if necessary, is adapted to a cedent's individual claim development.

• **New trend in court decisions:** Until the late '70s, liability insurance played only a subordinate role in comparison with property insurance. As the tenor of court decisions changed, however, individuals and companies felt a growing need to protect themselves against the risk of incalculable liability claims. Liability insurance now accounts for about 55% of all non-life insurance premiums paid in the U.S.[5] This trend played a major role in accelerating the growth of finite risk reinsurance, because liability portfolios with significantly longer settlement periods than property insurance are especially suitable for finite covers, which offer contractual periods of several years and are based on the principle of the time value of money.

• **Downturn of underwriting results:** At the beginning of the '80s, most U.S. buyers of finite (more correctly: financial reinsurance) products were interested primarily in improving the key ratios of their balance sheets. This should be seen within the context of the underwriting results of the U.S. property and casualty insurers, which had deteriorated rapidly since the late '70s. The battle for market share at the cost of underwriting profit reached a preliminary peak in the early '80s. Many insurance companies had good cause to fear that they would lose their Best's[6] ratings, or would be unable to fulfill the solvency standards imposed by the National Association of Insurance Commissioners (NAIC). The stage had thus been set for the development of loss portfolio transfers and adverse development covers, which allowed cedents to remove "long-latent liabilities"[7] from their balance sheets and to avoid unpleasant surprises in the development of their loss reserves.

NEEDS OF FINITE RISK REINSURANCE BUYERS

The demand for finite products is based on a number of different client needs:

• **Smoothing of financial results:** One of the most important functions of finite risk reinsurance is to smooth fluctuations in the cedent's loss experience over the course of multi-year contracts. It addresses, therefore, the growing cedent need for stable capacity, available over the long term at calculable prices. Furthermore, it is not necessary to renegotiate contract terms every year. Changes reflect the cedent's individual loss experience and result from a mechanism that is contractually stipulated in advance for several years. The smoothing of the cedent's results and insulation from cyclical fluctuations in the traditional reinsurance markets are significant especially in countries where equalization reserves and/or hidden reserves either cannot be formed or are limited in size.

• **Optimization of balance sheet structure:** Finite solutions can allow cedents to improve their key balance-sheet figures. For insurers, the leverage ratios, i.e. the ratio of net premiums or loss reserves to equity capital, can be controlled by means of finite risk reinsurance. For non-insurance corporations, reserves for outstanding losses are generally not deductible as a business expense until the claims are actually paid. A firm that wants to retain a substantial portion of its risk may well be able to utilize finite risk reinsurance to get both balance sheet relief and a tax-deductible premium expense. At the same time, the cedent may be protected from timing risk on its liabilities, to the extent that the finite risk reinsurance policy specifies the loss payment schedule.

• **Increase in retentions:** In view of the high volatility of reinsurance prices and capacities on the one hand and reinsurers' limited readiness to accept risks on the other, the alternative of retaining risks for their own account has become attractive for some cedents. "Good" risks are less and less willing to pay for the losses of the market as a whole and instead seek individual finite solutions that efficiently protect their increased retentions.

• **Facilitation of acquisitions, mergers and corporate restructuring:** As a rule, such measures are successfully completed only in instances where there is a certain minimum degree of clarity regarding the financial consequences of long-latent liabilities. The partial assumption of these risks by one or more finite risk reinsurers provides investors and managers with the planning security they need. This aspect is discussed in greater detail in Chapter 8, Run-Off Solutions.

ELEMENTS OF FINITE RISK REINSURANCE

There are a number of finite risk reinsurance structures, several of which we will describe later in this chapter. Most of these structures share certain basic elements:

• **Limits:** The limits of liability can be stated in terms of limits per event, per risk, per annum or per duration of contract. The cedent usually retains a deductible, over which the limit applies. For example, a contract can state limits of $50 per event in excess of $20, with an annual limit of $100 and an aggregate limit of $150. Here the cedent retains the first $20 of each covered loss. The reinsurer then pays up to $50 on each loss, but no more than $100 in any year from all losses in that year. Over the lifetime of the policy, the reinsurer will pay no more than $150.

- **Risk transfer:** The finite risk reinsurer often assumes four types of risk:
  - —**underwriting risk** - losses incurred may be worse than expected,
  - —**timing risk** - claims payments may occur faster than expected,
  - —**interest rate** - risk is that the investment income may fall short of that assumed in pricing the policy, and
  - —**credit risk** - the cedent may default on repaying funds advanced under the policy.
- **Profit and loss sharing:** The cedent and the reinsurer share the profit or loss on the contract. One way to do this is through an **experience account** that tracks the cash flow of the contract. Premiums are paid in by the cedent and interest income is credited to the account. Losses and reinsurer's charges are deducted from it. Negative balances are paid down through additional premiums paid by the cedent. At the end of the contract term, the cedent and reinsurer share both negative and positive balances. (One of the examples below demonstrates how the experience account operates.)
- **Premium:** The premium paid by the cedent to the reinsurer is composed of three elements:
  - —**risk premium** - the charge for the underwriting risk assumed by the reinsurer, which is priced in the same way as traditional insurance risks,
  - —**reinsurer's margin** - includes charges for the other risks assumed (credit, timing, interest rate), the reinsurer's cost of capital and other administrative/expense charges, and
  - —**funding amount** - is to be placed in the experience account. This amount reflects a funding of losses that are expected to be paid over the term of the policy.

THE TYPES OF FINITE RISK REINSURANCE CONTRACTS

Considering the broad spectrum of client requirements, it is not surprising that there is also a wide variety of customized products available. Any attempt at classification is therefore inevitably a gross simplification. The most basic distinction can be made between **retrospective and prospective contracts** (Box 7.1).

Retrospective types of contracts cover losses that have already been incurred but are not yet settled. **Loss portfolio transfers** (LPTs) and **adverse**

Box 7.1   Types of finite risk reinsurance contracts.

Retrospective covers (past underwriting years)	Prospective covers (current & future underwriting years)
Loss portfolio transfer (LPT) Adverse development cover (ADC)	Finite quota share (FQS) Spread loss treaty (SLT)

development covers (ADCs) relate to past underwriting years. While through an LPT, a cedent transfers entire loss portfolios and the associated reserves to the reinsurer, the primary aim of an ADC is to provide protection against unexpected adverse development of the loss reserves (which remain with the cedent).

With prospective types of contracts, on the other hand, the coverage pertains to claims not yet incurred, but anticipated in the future. **Finite quota shares** (FQSs) and **spread loss treaties** (SLTs) cover risks of current and future underwriting years. FQSs are similar to traditional quota reinsurance,[8] but are able to handle the cedent's financial needs more flexibly and effectively. Through SLTs, the cedent reduces the fluctuations in its loss experience by paying scheduled annual or single premiums to the reinsurer, who then absorbs the fluctuations.

Each of these four major types of contracts is described in greater detail below. It is important to note that the examples below are simplified illustrations that highlight the main features of a contract. Since the application of any finite re technique depends heavily on local tax and accounting rules, some of the effects illustrated will not be possible in all jurisdictions.

Loss Portfolio Transfer (LPT)

Within the framework of an LPT, a company can cede future payment obligations resulting from past underwriting years. The finite risk reinsurer assumes the cedent's reserves for outstanding losses. The reinsurance premium is approximately equivalent to the net present value of the ceded loss reserves. The reinsurer also charges a profit and cost margin, as well as an underwriting-related risk premium, which reflects the timing and subsequent reserve risks assumed.

LPTs focus on the timing risk.[9] Along with the client's loss reserves, the reinsurer also assumes the risk relating to the settlement of these losses over time. This means that the reinsurer runs a substantial risk of loss in the event that settlement is unexpectedly rapid. It is of crucial importance, therefore, that the reinsurer prepares a projection of the payment pattern as precisely as possible.

LPTs provide buyers with a wide variety of benefits. In many jurisdictions, the most important balance sheet figures are markedly improved in the year in which the contract is concluded. First, for primary insurers, the **combined ratio**, i.e. the sum of the loss ratio and the expense ratio, is reduced because future income from investments is converted into current underwriting income. From the viewpoint of the cedent, this involves a trade-off between future income from investments and present income from underwriting. Second, LPTs can increase **solvency**, i.e. the ratio of equity to premium volume. Since the liabilities ceded are greater than the reinsurance premium, the implicit discounting of the loss reserves strengthens the client's equity base.

For non-insurance corporations, LPTs accelerate the settlement of self-insured outstanding claims, and possibly even the complete winding up of a captive company (e.g. after the sale of certain divisions or product lines). As we shall see in the next chapter, company mergers and acquisitions are made easier, since the rapid claims settlement risk associated with losses already incurred no longer presents a hurdle.

Example of LPT.   Growmore Corporation is expanding. Unfortunately, it had a civil liability judgement recently against one of its operations for an industrial accident that occurred 5 years ago. The judgement will require Growmore to make payments to claimants over the next 40 years. Growmore's accountants have estimated that the sum of the payments will be $200 million. Given the expected schedule of payments over time, they have estimated the present value of those liabilities to be $145 million, assuming a discount rate of 5%. Growmore recognizes that liability provision on its books.

In light of this new liability, Growmore's management is now reviewing the options it has to manage earnings. The key issues it faces are as follows:

- The schedule of payments used by the accountants is an actuarial estimate. The actual payments that will be made over time can vary considerably from year to year. Box 7.2 shows some sample claim payment scenarios and the impact on Growmore's after-tax income.

- Growmore is of the opinion that the accountants have placed a conservative value on the liability by using a discount rate of 5%. An increase in the discount rate would reduce the present value of the liabilities. Perhaps Growmore will be able to persuade its accountants to increase the rate. Of course, the accountants will review this rate every year, and as investment market conditions change, they are likely to change the discount rate from year to year, adding volatility to the financial statements.

Box 7.2   Growmore's income with loss portfolio transfer.

(In $ million) *Initial business plan*	Current year	1st year	2nd year	3rd year	4th year	5th year	6th year +
After-tax income	165	180	196	214	233	254	
Growth rate		9%	9%	9%	9%	9%	
Business plan adjusted for liability							
A. Pay claims from annual earnings							
Scenario 1: Expected claims NPV=130		10	50	10	50	10	70
After-tax income	165	174	165	204	199	241	
Growth rate		5%	–5%	24%	–2%	21%	
Scenario 2: Slower claims NPV=82		10	10	10	10	10	150
After-tax income	165	174	190	207	225	246	
Growth rate		5%	9%	9%	9%	9%	
Scenario 3: Faster claims NPV=171		10	90	50	20	20	10
After-tax income	165	174	141	178	212	231	
Growth rate		5	–19%	26%	19%	9%	
B. Loss portfolio transfer							
LPT premium NPV=130	130	0	0	0	0	0	
After-tax income	165	102	189	206	225	245	
Growth rate		–38%	85%	9%	9%	9%	

Assumptions:
7% discount rate
40% tax rate
After-tax income adjusts for investment income foregone on paid claims.

- The recent fall in Growmore's stock price represents a loss in value greater than management thinks appropriate for this liability. In discussions with key shareholders, Growmore learns that the uncertainty surrounding the annual earnings volatility and the possible drag on earnings are major concerns.

Although management had considered meeting the liability out of earnings in each year, it is now evaluating a solution that will place a better economic value on the liability and remove the earnings volatility from future years. An LPT proposed by Handy Re is a possible solution.

In exchange for a single premium of $130 million, Handy Re will take over the liabilities up to a sum (limit) of $200 million. Having analyzed the range of annual loss payments, Handy Re's actuaries and asset managers have determined that 7% is a reasonable discount rate that reflects achievable investment returns.

This LPT solution addresses Growmore's key issues: Handy Re absorbs the timing risk of the liability payments, the present value of the liability is fixed at a current market rate that is neither too conservative nor too liberal, and this source of earnings volatility is removed from Growmore's financial performance.

On the other hand, Growmore takes an immediate cash hit, since it is paying once for all the claims. Instead of a claim payment of $10 million, it pays out the full single premium of $130 million. However, since the premium is tax-deductible when paid, the tax relief of $52 million ($130 million × 40%) mitigates this hit. As Box 7.2 shows, the after-tax net income with an LPT is $102, which is $180 million from the initial business plan, reduced by the LPT premium of $130 million and increased by $52 million for the tax relief.

Depending on which scenario of claim payments ultimately emerges, the net present value (NPV) of claims will be either greater or less than $130 million. Since the LPT facility is designed to help finance losses over time, some element of that variation will have to return to Growmore through an experience account.

Another effect of the LPT is that Growmore shrinks both sides of its balance sheet. Its assets are reduced by the net cash payment (premium, adjusted for the tax effect) and its liabilities by the release of the liability provision. In this particular transaction, there is also an increase in Growmore's equity by $15 million, since the LPT premium of $130 million is less than the current liability provision of $145 million (Figure 7.1).

Adverse Development Cover (ADC)

ADCs (also known as retrospective excess of loss contracts) offer a broader spectrum of cover than LPTs. Unlike LPTs, no loss portfolios are ceded and there is no transfer of outstanding claims reserves. Instead, the focus is on the cedent's need for cover in excess of the loss reserves already formed. ADCs protect against the "nightmare" of inadequate loss reserves. In stop-loss or excess-of-loss contracts, the finite risk reinsurer absorbs part of these risks (Figure 7.2).

The premium to be paid by the cedent reflects the scope of the underwriting risks assumed, and takes into account the net present value of the loss payments expected during the term of the contract. Thus, the time value of money is also utilized in ADCs to put together more cost-effective covers.

Like loss portfolio transfers, ADCs also facilitate acquisitions or mergers of insurance companies, since they afford at least partial protection against (as yet unknown) long-latent claims.

Figure 7.1   Loss portfolio transfers: contraction of balance sheet and increase in equity.

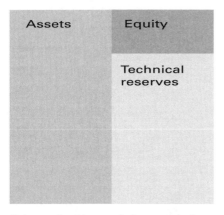

Balance sheet in year before conclusion   Balance sheet in year after conclusion

In addition, ADCs can have a positive effect on the client's stock market value. This is true particularly of clients that have liability obligations which are difficult to assess and which are lodged only after a number of years of delay. On the basis of ADCs, a kind of information arbitrage occurs: shareholders and rating agencies obtain a clearer picture of a company's exposure from losses incurred, but not reported. Furthermore, they can revise their expectations downward regarding the volatility of financial results, because the financial effects of long-latent claims are at least contained by the finite risk cover. All other things being equal, this lends impetus to the stock price. From the standpoint of the company management, this reduces the probability of (potentially hostile) takeover attempts.

In ADCs, the finite risk reinsurer can also assume the credit risk for the cedent by including protection if another reinsurer on a traditional reinsurance policy becomes insolvent. It is obvious that here the finite provider takes on hard-to-calculate risks and has to reckon with substantial costs for assessing the cedent's other reinsurance relationships.

Example of ADC.   Let us consider how Growmore can use an ADC. Having purchased an LPT cover, Growmore recognizes that it runs the risk that its estimate of the claim amount may be wrong. Although it has used its best estimates for developing the expected claim payments, there is a possibility

Figure 7.2   Illustration of adverse development cover.

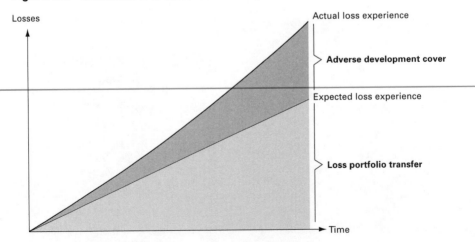

that the actual amount paid to claimants can exceed $200 million. Growmore does not want to retain that residual liability. It insures it by purchasing an ADC for $50 million in excess of $200 million. In other words, if losses exceed $200 million, then Handy Re will pay the excess up to a limit of $50 million. The single premium, reflecting the probability of a loss, is $5 million.

Finite Quota Share (FQS)

FQSs are one of the oldest forms of finite cover, and are utilized mainly by primary insurance companies. FQSs were developed to mitigate the distortions on the financial statements of insurers resulting from the requirement to recognize new policy acquisition costs immediately as expenses, even though the profits from these sales would emerge, and be recognized, over many years.

A practical example of FQSs is the solvency-oriented contract, which provides for the cession of part of the primary insurer's unearned premium to a finite risk reinsurer. In return, the cedent receives a commission which can be used to correct the temporary reduction in equity. In effect, the reinsurer provides an advance on the profit expected by the primary insurer in future business years. Unlike the traditional quota share contracts, FQSs are structured explicitly to limit the liability of the reinsurer.

The following example shows a form of FQS that helps a primary insurer to improve solvency, increase underwriting capacity and smooth underwriting results.

Example of FQS.   Smallish Insurance Company needs $20 million of support so that it will not have to show a negative result in the current year, 1999. It enters into an FQS with Handy Re. The FQS is structured as a three-year policy that addresses the cedent's need for a stable expense ratio, around 30%, and no negative results. An experience account will be used to share the result of the FQS. Box 7.3 shows Smallish's profit and loss (P&L) account before and after reinsurance. The expected loss ratio is 70%, so that on $400 million of premium, $280 million is expected in claims. In the first year, 1999, the expenses are high at $140 million, resulting in an expense ratio of 35%. In the subsequent years, the expenses are expected to be lower, at $100 million. Smallish shows a negative $20 million result in 1999. To eliminate this loss, Smallish reinsures 25% of the business under the FQS to Handy Re. This entails a transfer of $100 million in premium, with the corresponding claims of $70 million. Handy Re pays Smallish a ceding commission of $50 million in the first year and $20 million in the next two years. This structure eliminates the negative result in 1999 and, in exchange, lowers the result in the subsequent two years. In this example, the net effect is that the reinsurer will advance $20 million in 1999 and receive $10 million in both 2000 and 2001.[10] If the actual deviates from the expected loss experience, the experience account will track the differences and allocate the profit or loss shares to the cedent and reinsurer.

Spread Loss Treaty (SLT)

Many cedents face the problem that, even though they can estimate with relatively high reliability the total losses that will be incurred during a future period, the distribution of these losses in each individual year is uncertain. The main purpose of SLTs is to balance this timing risk.

Box 7.3   Smallish's profit and loss account with finite quota share.

(in $ million) Year	1999	2000	2001
Gross premium	400	400	400
−Gross claims	(280)	(280)	(280)
−Expenses	(140)	(100)	(100)
Result before reinsurance	(20)	20	20
−Premiums ceded to reinsurer	(100)	(100)	(100)
+Claims ceded to reinsurer	70	70	70
+Reinsurance commission	50	20	20
Result after reinsurance	0	10	10
Expense ratio before reinsurance	35%	25%	25%
Expense ratio after reinsurance	30%	27%	27%

$$\text{Expense ratio} = \frac{\text{Expenses} - \text{Reinsurance commission}}{\text{Gross Premium} - \text{Premiums ceded to reinsurer}}$$

In an SLT, the cedent pays either annual or single premiums to the reinsurer. These funds—less the reinsurer's margin—are transferred to what is known as an experience account, where they earn a contractually agreed rate of interest. Loss payments are paid from the experience account. The reinsurer is obliged to make claims payments even if they exceed the balance available in the account. To place a limit on its liability, the reinsurer sets a ceiling for the payments made within the course of a year or the entire term of the policy. Depending on the underwriting risk contained in the policy, the policyholder is obliged to settle in part or in full any negative balance in the experience account that is run up as a result of claims payments before the policy expires. The reinsurer carries the associated credit risk. If, on the other hand, the experience account shows a positive balance when the treaty expires, the cedent has a claim to a partial refund.

SLTs are characterized by two features. First, premiums are accumulated over the entire term of the treaty. Second, the incurred losses are distributed over a multi-year period. In this respect, the reinsurer acts as a short- to medium-term lender who provides advance financing for any negative balances in the experience account. Unlike a traditional bank credit line, though, the reinsurer also bears considerable underwriting risk.

From the cedent's standpoint, the most important aspect of SLTs is their ability to smooth the variation in annual incurred losses. Due to their design, SLTs enable the formation of an off-balance-sheet, flexible equalization reserve. They also serve as a tax-efficient tool for building up a fund to finance the deductible of traditional insurance covers or for the control of uninsurable risks over the medium term. In addition, the capital costs of captives can be decreased through SLTs, which reduce the captive's earnings volatility.

Example of SLT.   Stablefirm Corporation pays its captive insurer, Selfprotect Insurance Company, $30 million in premiums annually. The captive has annual operating expenses of $10 million. Stablefirm is concerned that its earnings would suffer from any volatility in Selfprotect's earnings. It authorizes Stablefirm to enter into an SLT with Handy Re to smooth its results.

The terms of the SLT are as follows. For each year of the 6-year contract, Selfprotect will pay Handy Re a premium of $10 million. Handy Re's liability is limited to a maximum of $30 million per year and to an aggregate total of $100 million over the 6-year term of the treaty. If the experience account has a negative balance, Selfprotect will make additional premium payments of $5 million per year for the remaining term until the deficit is paid off. The balance in the experience account accrues interest at a rate of 10% per annum. The premiums are paid at the beginning of the year, and the losses at the end of each year. If the experience account shows a positive balance when the treaty comes to an end, 50% of that balance is to be repaid to Self-protect. Likewise, 50% of a negative ending balance is to be borne by Self-protect. Box 7.4 and Figure 7.3 show how, in one possible scenario of losses, the underwriting result of the captive over the 6-year term is more stable with the SLT than without.

RISING DEMAND FOR BLENDED COVERS

Since the mid-'90s, there has been strong demand for solutions that combine finite and traditional reinsurance elements. Initially, these blended covers

Box 7.4   Selfprotect's underwriting account with spread loss treaty.

(in $ million) A. Without SLT	1st year	2nd year	3rd year	4th year	5th year	6th year
Premium income	30.0	30.0	30.0	30.0	30.0	30.0
Acquisition and operating expenses	10.0	10.0	10.0	10.0	10.0	10.0
Losses	20.0	30.0	0.0	0.0	20.0	0.0
Underwriting result	0.0	−10.0	20.0	20.0	0.0	20.0
B. With SLT						
Premium income	30.0	30.0	30.0	30.0	30.0	30.0
Acquisition and operating expenses	10.0	10.0	10.0	10.0	10.0	10.0
Reinsurance premium	10.0	15.0	15.0	15.0	10.0	15.0
Underwriting result	10.0	5.0	5.0	5.0	10.0	5.0
Experience account						
Opening balance	0.0	−9.0	−23.4	−9.2	6.3	−2.0
Reinsurance premium	10.0	15.0	15.0	15.0	10.0	15.0
Interest	1.0	0.6	−0.8	0.6	1.6	1.3
Losses	20.0	30.0	0.0	0.0	20.0	0.0
Ending balance	−9.0	−23.4	−9.2	6.3	−2.0	14.2
Final payment to Selfprotect						+7.1

Figure 7.3   Result-smoothing effect of Selfprotect's spread loss treaty.

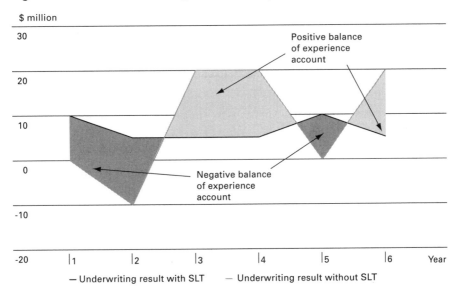

gained popularity because of changes in tax legislation and accounting principles that created an incentive for underwriting risks to be integrated more fully into finite risk solutions. Later, strong economic incentives stimulated demand for blended covers: An integrated solution can take a cedent's risk profile more efficiently, flexibly and precisely into account than many traditional covers.

Widely disparate risk types can be included within a single multi-year package, with the result that frequently recurring, easily predictable minor losses remain in the retention. Risks with financial consequences that can be estimated reliably for a multi-year period can be covered by means of finite solutions. Here, the reinsurer not only provides advance financing for relatively large losses suffered by the cedent, but also assumes significant underwriting risks. Traditional (catastrophe) excess of loss treaties are suitable for exposures that are life threatening and difficult to estimate.

The cedent's retention may be defined separately for each risk covered in the policy. In addition, its overall retention can be set for all the risks combined. This approach makes it possible to include even those risks that traditionally have been considered uninsurable under a single cover. Premium rates for the covered risks are set at such a level within a blended cover that the cedant only pays for what it actually needs: a smoothing of annual loss costs and the elimination of catastrophic perils.

Example of Blended Cover.   Mixit Corporation has completed a risk mapping exercise and has concluded that it can best manage its risks through a multi-year reinsurance policy that covers multiple risk exposures. It believes that it can manage its operations well and would like to self-insure a good portion of its risks. However, it is concerned that losses in any single year can exceed its estimates, and would like to purchase protection to smooth the effects of that risk. Mixit decides that it can retain $0.25 million for each loss event. It is also willing to retain an additional $10 million of aggregate losses in each year, and up to $30 million in losses over a 5-year term. It wants an insurance protection that will cover it for losses in excess of its retention.

Handy Re structures a 5-year blended cover for multiple risks.[11] The policy consists of an aggregate protection (Section 1) and an excess protection (Section 2) described in Box 7.5. Under this program, the cedent prefunds a portion of its self-insured retentions in the form of annual premium installments, which are paid during the term of the cover. The pre-funding portion is calculated as the annual premium less 35%, which represents Handy Re's expense and risk charge. In the first year, the net premium is $2.6 million ($4 million times 65%). This amount, less losses paid under Section 1 of the cover, is then accumulated with interest in an experience account.

To understand the mechanics of the program, consider a single loss event of $50 million. It is easiest to deal with Section 2 first, which pays $40 million (excess protection for claim over $10 million). The retention of $10 million is paid as dictated by Section 1. Mixit pays $0.25 million on the claim (the maintenance retention). Mixit then pays $5 million which represents its additional retention per claim. The remaining $4.75 million of the claim is paid under Section 1 of the blended cover (Box 7.6).

After the claim is paid, Mixit has exposure to additional losses under its self-insured retention. It has utilized $5 million of its $10 million program aggregate retention, leaving an exposure of $5 million. There is still insurance protection remaining under the policy. An aggregate limit of $25.25

Box 7.5   Multi-year blended cover for Mixit.

Insured risks
> Umbrella liability
> Directors & officers liability
> Employment practices liability
> Crime, errors & omissions
> Property

Term
> Five years

Section I: Aggregate protection
> $9.75 million for each occurrence/claim/annual aggregate
> Program limit: $30 million
> Coverage excess of $0.25 million maintenance retention each occurrence/claim
> Additional insured retention $5 million for each occurrence/claim/annual aggregate; $10 million program aggregate retention

Section 2: Excess protection
> $50 million excess $10 million for each occurrence/claim/annual aggregate
> Program limit: $100 million

Premium and profit share
> Premium: $4 million paid annually
> Profit feature: 65% of cumulative annual premium
>   less losses paid,
>   plus interest

million remains in Section 1 ($30 million − $4.75 million) and $60 million in Section 2 ($100 million − $40 million).

THE FUTURE OF FINITE RISK REINSURANCE

There is a place for finite risk reinsurance as a tool to manage some risks of a well-run corporation. Such a firm will retain those risks that have more predictable (high-frequency, low-severity) losses.

It will insure those risks that are less predictable and potentially more severe. Finite risk reinsurance will be used for exposures that can be anticipated and budgeted over a longer period of time, to smooth their effect on the firm's

Box 7.6   Impact of single large loss on Mixit's blended cover.

(in $ million)	
Loss amount:	50.00
Less: Insured maintenance retention	0.25
Less: Additional insured retention	5.00
Loss covered by insurance	44.75
Coverage Section 1:	4.75
Coverage Section 2:	40.00
Remaining insured retention and aggregate limits under the program:	
Insured retention:	5.00
Section 1 aggregate limit:	25.25
Section 2 aggregate limit:	60.00

financial statements. Uninsured risks will inevitably be borne by the firm, except to the extent that a blended cover, combining elements of traditional risk transfer and finite risk reinsurance, can be structured to cover them.

The popularity of finite risk reinsurance varies considerably from one region to the next and depends heavily on tax regimes and regulatory conditions. In most countries, the way these solutions are treated for both tax and financial statement purposes is not clearly formulated. As long as these uncertainties remain, finite risk reinsurance will not grow to the full extent possible, despite all the economic benefits it offers.

The United States is one of the few countries where the general accounting principles applicable to finite solutions have already been formulated. The foundation has been laid in Standards No. 60 and 113 of the U.S. Financial Accounting Standards Board (FASB). These directives, while reducing some of the accounting uncertainty about these transactions, have also diminished the tax and accounting motivations for initiating them.

Nevertheless, the finite re structures described here continue to provide real economic value to cedents—the benefits from increased accounting clarity outweigh any reduction in tax or accounting incentives. The focus for these transactions has shifted correspondingly. It is therefore hardly surprising that finite risk reinsurance solutions are most advanced in the U.S.

Appendix 7A

Overview of Forms of Reinsurance

There are basically two types of traditional non-life reinsurance contracts: proportional and non-proportional.

Proportional Reinsurance

There are two types of proportional reinsurance:

- **Quota share treaties:** The primary insurer cedes a defined percentage of all premium income from the relevant portfolio to the reinsurer, who pays the same percentage of each loss that occurs. There is thus a proportional relationship between the premiums ceded by the primary insurer and the losses paid by the reinsurer.
- **Surplus treaties:** The primary insurer cedes each risk in the reinsurance treaty individually. The distribution of premiums and losses between the primary insurer and the reinsurer is determined by the ratio of the retention to the sum insured and therefore varies from one risk to another.

Non-Proportional Reinsurance

In non-proportional reinsurance, there is no proportionality between premiums and share of loss. The determining factor is not the premium but the level of loss. If a loss exceeds the retention—referred to as the "priority" in non-proportional business—the reinsurer pays, up to a certain limit. The priority may be defined as:

- An individual loss per risk, known as "working excess of loss (XL) cover,"
- The sum of all individual losses resulting from a (catastrophic) event, known as a "catastrophic XL cover," or
- The annual loss ratio of a portfolio, known as a "stop-loss cover."

"They were perceived to be short-term
phenomena that would have little impact..."

8

Run-Off Solutions

Diane Houghton and Prakash Shimpi

Risks that arise in the normal course of a business activity do not necessarily disappear when that activity ceases. Liabilities from past activities can surface as corporate obligations if the losses were incurred when the company was responsible for those activities. The other chapters in this book tend to focus on risks arising from ongoing activities of the firm. In this chapter, we consider how a firm can act to address earnings volatility arising from past activities.

The term **run-off** is used to refer to the management of **retrospective liabilities**, i.e. losses arising from past activities. For example, a corporation might use a run-off solution to move payments for a product liability claim cleanly off its books rather than having to make payments of varying amounts over the next 40 years. Similarly, an insurance company might use a run-off solution to bring finality to a line of business that it is no longer underwriting, but in which claims may have been incurred.

DEVELOPMENT OF THE RUN-OFF MARKET

There are a number of factors that can lead a company to use a run-off solution. Some of these are:

- **Company-specific:** liabilities arising from corporate activities, mergers or acquisitions, mispricing or underestimating risks, closing lines of business, or cleaning up a balance sheet as part of a corporate restructuring;

- **Market-related:** changes in the value of a liability due to financial market volatility (interest rates, exchange rates) and inflation;
- **Structural:** management of liabilities driven by changes in regulation and accounting or tax considerations; and
- **Legal:** court judgements for claims on specific types of liabilities such as asbestos and environmental (A&E), tobacco or breast implants.

It is important to recognize that a run-off liability is not necessarily "bad business," although it can be. The biggest run-off transactions to date have involved either A&E or workers' compensation (WC) liabilities. Yet, new WC and environmental impairment liability policies continue to be written.[1]

RUN-OFF STRATEGIES

Up until the mid-'80s, most companies faced with retrospective liabilities chose to handle them internally by either ignoring them or by managing the claims within the stream of normal business. It was common practice for most companies to ignore these liabilities; they were perceived to be short-term phenomena that would have little impact on a firm's financial health.

Box 8.1   Retrospective liability management strategies.

Ignore:	- Hope that liability is temporary and under control - Depend on current income to pay claims
Segregate:	- Control the liability separately, within the corporation - Hope for no negative impact on new business activity
Ring-fence:	- Control liability in separate legal entity - Hope to capture value in new business activity
Run-off:	- Transfer liability to reinsurer - Remove uncertainty arising from past liability

The second alternative that companies chose, after they realized that ignoring these liabilities only made them worse, was to segregate them into a separate operation or into a separate division. This offered an operational solution, but not a financial solution or the finalization of the liabilities.

Some companies have employed the **ring-fence** technique, which not only separates the liabilities, but also puts them into a separate company in an attempt to limit the associated liabilities. Another popular term for this technique is the "good bank—bad bank" approach, reflecting the strategy that some banks used when they put all their bad risks in one company (the bad bank) so that another company (the good bank) could operate with a clean bill of health. This technique can offer a solution, but may be subject to problematic regulatory issues and approval.

The run-off approach that has emerged recently captures additional value by managing the liabilities systematically. These run-off solutions are customized to the needs of a corporation and can bring finality to their exposure, and possibly extract value from the run-off liabilities. A total solution can include substantial risk capacity through conventional and finite risk reinsurance, or a structured solution through the capital markets—in effect utilizing the full array of conventional insurance products and the new tools described in this book.

A run-off solution can be utilized by insurance companies, public entities and other corporations. Typically, solutions need to recognize the different accounting, regulatory and other needs of these institutions. By drawing on the experience and resources of a professional run-off reinsurer, the institution will be able to manage its past liabilities more effectively, allowing management, shareholders and others to shift their attention from past problems to focus on current business.

Among the variety of techniques that can be employed, two common solutions are finite risk reinsurance (discussed in Chapter 7) and the total transfer of a company. The **total transfer** of a company is a final solution that offers a complete transfer of all liabilities, with no future repercussions. It includes the transfer of both the liabilities and the operations of the run-off.

Claims Management

Since a run-off solution entails the transfer of liabilities from a corporation to a reinsurer, a proper assessment of the liabilities at inception and professional claims management thereafter are critical elements in the transaction. To do so requires a thorough analysis of the liabilities and recognition of all the inherent risk exposures.

An in-depth analysis of the liability portfolio's operational and claims management issues can lead to the identification of previously overlooked efficiencies. Depending on the nature of the liabilities, the reinsurer or a third party can take over the entire operation and make decisions on responses to claimants. Alternatively, claims management can be done in partnership with the corporation. In that case, it is important to make sure the interests of the corporation and reinsurer are aligned, so that claims settlement takes place as contemplated at the inception of the run-off transaction.

Since there is uncertainty in the timing of claims and the ultimate losses that can emerge, proper procedures need to be established to deal quickly with any worsening claims. Run-off operations should also ensure that sufficient cash flow and liquidity are generated from the assets backing the liabilities, so that claims will be paid when due.

Case Studies

The following case studies illustrate some of the run-off solutions actually executed. Because of the inherent complexity of such transactions, we have opted to provide only thumbnail sketches that highlight the key objective of the corporation.

Key Objective: Remove Uncertainty of Environmental Liabilities

A leading building materials group took on major environmental liabilities after acquiring a company with long-tail exposures in the United States.

Despite its balance sheet provisions and efficient management of the contaminated sites, the company continued to face skepticism from the investment community on its management of those liabilities. To safeguard its financial strength and balance sheet, the company obtained reinsurance protection that included $400 million in conventional and finite risk reinsurance. The program applied portfolio underwriting techniques that rewarded the company for its effective management of the exposures. On the day the coverage was announced, the company's stock rose 13%, despite a deep decline in the overall market. A leading equity analyst, in explaining an "accumulate" recommendation, noted, "We expect this solution to finally put to bed any concerns investors still harbor on the environmental liabilities front."[2] By entering into this solution, the company's management was able to focus on new business growth without the drag of the past liabilities.

Key Objective: Finality on Asbestos Liabilities to Enhance Stock Valuation

A U.K.-based manufacturer of automotive components suffered from depressed share valuation that it attributed to stock market perceptions of its high potential exposure to asbestos liabilities. The manufacturer had mined and manufactured asbestos earlier in the century, selling its last asbestos operation three decades earlier. However, it was still subject to asbestos-related claims. A run-off solution provided £500 million of excess of loss reinsurance coverage. On the days following the transaction's announcement, the company's stock rose nearly one-third on the London Stock Exchange, increasing the company's capitalization by more than £250 million.

Key Objective: Change in Ownership through Demutualization

To prepare for demutualization, a large Australian mutual insurance and fund management company needed to restructure parts of its operations to ensure that it would be fairly valued. An integral part of the restructuring was the effort to reduce the uncertainty of its overseas long-tail portfolio, which consisted of asbestos and environmental liabilities. A run-off solution provided reinsurance coverage of $500 million. The coverage sharply reduced the uncertainty for policyholders and future stockholders. On their first trading day, the shares finished significantly higher than originally priced.

Key Objective: Exit Strategy for New Ownership

A U.K. insurance company was placed in run-off because of long-tail U.S. casualty losses. To help its current owners exit the business, a run-off solution was provided through a finite risk reinsurance agreement with timed retrocession and additional cover for uncollectible reinsurance. An integral part of the solution was the transfer of the company to a third party.

Key Objective: Privatization of Workers' Compensation Residual Market

A U.S. state had established a residual market entity for workers' compensation. This entity stopped writing policies after the state reformed its program in 1993. The state sought to exit the business while, among other things, ensuring that claims from approximately 10,000 injured workers were handled effectively. A reinsurer worked with the state to privatize the program and provided aggregate stop loss reinsurance, creating a total of $1.2 billion of coverage for claimants. The transaction also freed numerous insurance companies from the threat of future assessments. The transaction was the first successful privatization of this kind and reflected a growing global trend by governments to extract themselves from businesses that can be managed more efficiently by the private sector.

THE VIRTUES OF ACTIVE MANAGEMENT

Managing the bottom-line impact of retrospective liabilities has become a major financial challenge for insurers and corporations around the world.

Taking a pro-active approach to managing these liabilities can now be done in a more comprehensive manner. CFOs, in particular, are recognizing the value in run-off solutions to optimize the capital structure of the firm, re-move uncertainties in the valuation of liabilities, and re-focus management on the generation of new business.

"… a cross between virtual capital and just-in-time capital."

9

Contingent Capital

DAVID COLAROSSI AND PRAKASH SHIMPI

Contingent capital (CC) instruments are relatively new phenomena based on a tried-and-true technique. In essence, a contingent capital instrument is an option to raise capital, subject to certain conditions. In its simplest form, it is a bank line of credit that a firm can draw on for most of its business needs, as specified by agreement with the bank. Once drawn, the funds are treated as corporate debt and increase the capital leverage of the firm. Commercial and investment banks routinely offer such products as letters of credit and revolving credit facilities.

In the current risk management environment, contingent capital refers to instruments that are somewhat more complex than the conventional products offered by banks. The terms that dictate when and how much additional funds can be drawn go beyond the conventional covenants and pledges usually associated with raising capital. These "conditions precedent" or triggers may be related to natural hazard and financial market risks, among others. If the risk can be quantified, it can be a trigger. These risk triggers, integrated into conventional credit-based capital instruments, create an opportunity for a corporation to raise capital more efficiently.

It is important to recognize that contingent capital is not an insurance product, but a product that is structured and priced using a combination of insurance and capital markets techniques. It is an instrument that allows a corporation to raise equity or debt (or other on-balance-sheet, paid-up capital) upon the occurrence of a pre-agreed event. The providers of this capital do not carry the risk of the event, they simply finance any losses once the event has occurred. The capital providers expect to be repaid, with interest.

Referring to the capital structure and risk management resources discussed in Chapter 3, a contingent capital instrument:

- Helps a corporation manage its retained risks,
- Provides off-balance-sheet capital to cover those risks, and
- Is usually structured as an option to issue a security.

THE NATURE OF THE CC OPTION

A contingent capital instrument is an option. An option is the right to buy or sell something at a fixed price (the strike price) for a fixed period of time. It is a right, not an obligation, and because of that an option has value. The right to sell something is called a put option. Contingent capital is a put option—the "something" is securities.

The corporation that owns the contingent capital option has the right to sell its own securities at a fixed price for a fixed period of time. This is the manner in which the company raises capital. These securities may take the form of equity, debt or some hybrid of the two. The provider (**writer**) of the contingent capital option is obligated to buy the securities at the discretion of the option owner, if all conditions precedent are met.

The features of a contingent capital option would make it similar to a derivative product known as a knock-in option. We touched on knock-in options briefly in Chapter 6. We discuss them again here to highlight the parallel with contingent capital instruments.

Standard options give the owner the right to buy or sell an asset. With a knock-in option, the right doesn't exist until a trigger has been hit, knocking the option into value. For example, assume you own 100 shares of TKO Company stock and the stock is currently selling at $50 per share. If you want to protect yourself against drops in the price of that stock, you can buy a put option on the TKO stock that would give you the right to sell the stock at $50. However, a less expensive alternative might be to purchase a knock-in option to sell the TKO stock at $50 per share, but only if the stock first drops to $45 per share. If the stock price drops to $47 you cannot exercise the option, because it hasn't yet knocked in. As soon as the stock price drops to $45, you would have the right to sell it at $50. The knock-in option costs less than a standard option because the trigger ensures that it can be exercised in fewer circumstances. The decision to purchase a knock-in or standard option depends on the value placed on the ability to exercise the option between $45 and $50.

The difference between a normal knock-in option and a contingent capital option is that the contingency or trigger for a contingent capital option is a different risk than that of the asset underlying the option. In this respect, a contingent capital option is similar to the multi-trigger products (MTPs) that we discussed in Chapter 6 (in both, the trigger risk differs from the underlying option's risk). The key difference between an MTP and CC is that the MTP transfers the risk of the corporation, whereas the CC does not. Although both provide cash to the firm when the triggering events occur, only the CC results in new paid-up capital.

In the example above, $45 was the trigger and $50 was the strike price. Both relate to the price of the underlying stock, and as such are highly correlated. With a contingent capital option the underlying will be a security (e.g. stock of the firm), but the trigger will be related to a different risk, such as an economic variable or catastrophic event. There might be some correlation between these trigger events and the price of the security underlying the option, but the correlation will not be as pronounced. Thus, the cost savings of purchasing a contingent option should be greater than when purchasing a conventional knock-in option.

How a CC Instrument Works

A CC instrument is a multi-year option that gives a corporation the right, but not the obligation, to raise paid-up, on-balance-sheet capital after the occurrence of a defined triggering event. It is structured as a put option and is written, or sold, by a put option writer. The corporation purchases the put option and pays an option premium, either once up front or periodically over the **option period**, T (Figure 9.1).

Figure 9.1   Timeline for contingent capital option.

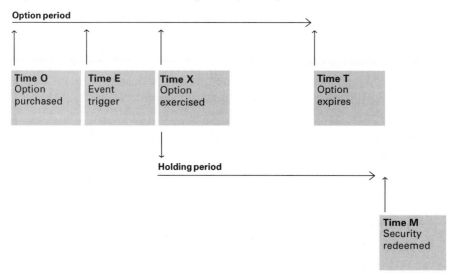

The option is not available to be exercised until an event defined in the CC instrument occurs at time E, during the option period. If no event occurs, the option is not available for exercise and the corporation has no access to the capital. If an event occurs, the option is available for the remainder of the option period.

If the firm exercises the option at time X, within the option period, it then places the security underlying the CC instrument with the option writer and receives the previously determined amount. This amount becomes new capital to the firm. There is a **holding period**, M, during which the option writer (who is now the capital provider) receives dividends or interest on the security, as previously agreed. At the end of the holding period, the firm redeems the security and repays the capital. If the firm is unable or unwilling to do so, then the option writer has other alternatives that enable it to recover its capital.

To summarize, the option period runs from 0 to T. During that period, both the event trigger must occur (at E) and the option must be exercised (at

X). At X, capital moves from the option writer to the firm. Later, at the end of the holding period, M, the security is redeemed and the capital repaid.

FEATURES OF CC INSTRUMENTS

There are no standard CC instruments. Each one is customized, and there is a great deal of flexibility. Nevertheless, the description above highlights a few key features common to most CC instruments that are worth discussing further:

• **Option period:** The option period should be long enough to allow for the triggering event to occur and for management to make a decision on exercising the CC option. Although deals of less than a year have been discussed, all the public deals that have been done to date have multi-year option periods. In effect, the corporations that have utilized contingent capital as a substitute for paid-up capital have done so over several accounting periods.

• **Holding period:** The holding period extends to the date when the security is due to be redeemed. It is common to measure the holding period from the exercise date. One alternative might be to measure it from the end of the option period.

• **Trigger events:** The first CC transactions were executed by (re)insurance companies that wanted to protect themselves from catastrophic events. Triggers for insurers are usually based on insurance losses, either for a single event or for a collection of events. However, the events can be broadly defined and run the range from earthquakes of a specific magnitude and investment performance to policy surrender rates. Now, non-insurance corporations have been evaluating how to implement such CC facilities. For these corporations, the choice of triggers is wider. It can include economic indicators such as inflation, gross domestic product and house prices, financial market indicators such as S&P 500 and foreign exchange rates, potential liabilities such as extraordinary taxes and civil liabilities, or revenue indicators such as ticket sales and product sales.

• **Type of security:** The security underlying the CC option can be any of the securities that a firm uses to raise paid-up capital, for example common equity, preferred equity or senior debt. The choice often depends on the regulatory environment of the corporation. For example, firms that need to demonstrate financial strength to regulators would use securities that qualify as regulatory capital. An insurance company is more inclined to use common or preferred equity, since these will be counted as capital for solvency purposes. A manufacturer, on the other hand, does not face the same regulatory scrutiny and would prefer to issue debt if the triggering event were to occur. If the corporation has securities that are publicly traded and have adequate liquidity, then those securities are candidates to be used in a CC instrument. If there are no such securities, then the choice of security is that much more challenging. Without a liquid market in the underlying security or another security of the firm, the termination at the end of the holding period is riskier for the option writer. If the firm does not redeem the security as agreed, the option writer will have to dispose of an illiquid security of uncertain value.

- **Conditions of availability:** Although the triggering event defines the moment when the option becomes available for exercise, the firm will still need to meet several other conditions to actually receive any funds at the exercise date. These conditions, commonly called **covenants**, are standard in the market for bank loans. They relate to various conditions that the firm has to meet at the exercise date and on certain other dates during the holding period.

At the exercise date, the firm will have to demonstrate that it is at least financially viable. If a triggering event also bankrupts the firm immediately, then the option writer is not likely to advance funds—it has no hope of being repaid. A covenant could, for example, require that the firm on the exercise date demonstrate a certain minimum net worth before any funds are advanced. Other covenants restrict the activities of the firm during the holding period to protect the interests of the option writer. Any breach of these covenants could trigger a reduction of the holding period, and the firm would have to redeem its security ahead of schedule. One common condition refers to a change of control. If the control of the firm passes to new management, then the option writer may have the right to be repaid sooner.

- **Redemption alternatives:** The objective of the option writer is to provide a CC facility; it is not to acquire a permanent shareholding of the corporation. CC instruments are structured to include an exit strategy for the option writer. The alternatives can be to have a security that:

  - forces payback of the capital (e.g. maturity of debt),
  - converts into a liquid tradable asset (e.g. conversion to common stock), or
  - provides a share of future profits of a specified line of business (e.g. reinsurance of certain insurance risks).

- **Cost components:** The cost of the CC instrument is made up of two components: the **option premium** and the **financing rate** on the security if the option is exercised. The firm can pay a higher option premium and reasonably expect a lower financing rate, or vice versa. The choice depends on the firm's perception of the likelihood of both the occurrence of the triggering event and the need to exercise the option once the trigger occurs. The option premium can be paid once up-front, or it can be spread over the term of the option. The financing rate can be fixed or floating (probably with a cap), and can be tied to the credit rating of the firm.

An application of CC:
The Case of Manufact Corporation

Having described the mechanics and the features in general terms, let us consider an example to put all the pieces together.

Manufact Corporation is a manufacturer serving a small number of industries. It has plants in five locations in the U.S. that supply its customers. It has been serving these customers for a number of years and has shared in their growth. It is a well-respected, publicly traded company. It has done an analysis of its revenues and is concerned about a low-probability event that could affect its earnings significantly. If one of its ten best customers (one that generates $50 million in revenues annually) goes out of business, Manufact has sufficient capital and liquidity to weather the storm. However, if two or more of these customers go out of business, Manufact will be impacted severely. It will have continuing expenses without the matching revenues for the failed customers' orders. At the same time, it will need to bid for new assignments more aggressively, and probably have to invest in retooling its plant and upgrading its facilities. Furthermore, if this happens, management will not be able to devote the time required to raise new capital.

Conticap Re is a reinsurance company specializing in contingent capital facilities. It structures a three-year CC instrument in the form of a contingent equity put option for Manufact. In the event that any two of the ten named customers go out of business, the option is triggered. Once triggered, Manufact has the right to sell up to $100 million of step-up convertible preferred shares to Conticap Re.

If Manufact exercises its option, Conticap pays $100 million in exchange for the step-up convertible preferred shares. Before Conticap will advance any funds, Manufact has to demonstrate GAAP net worth of $500 million. During the holding period, i.e. while Conticap owns the shares, Manufact pays it scheduled dividends.

Manufact has the right to redeem these shares after the first 12 months. Redemption before the end of 36 months will require Manufact to pay a call premium to Conticap. If Manufact fails to redeem the shares by the end of 36 months, the dividend rate of the shares steps up to a higher rate. The higher rate is an incentive for Manufact to redeem the shares prior to 36 months. If Manufact does not do so, then the step-up dividend mitigates the liquidity risk of having to sell the securities on the open market.

For this CC arrangement, Manufact will pay Conticap an annual option premium, reflecting the probability of the occurrence of the triggering event. Figure 9.2 illustrates this example.

SOURCE OF CAPITAL

The source of capital is an important consideration when developing a CC. The contingent nature of the instrument means that the capital can only be raised at some time in the future. Therefore, the corporation has credit risk exposure to the capital provider. Clearly, the corporation needs to be assured that the capital provider will be able to pay when the cash has to be raised. Who provides this capital?

Figure 9.2   Contingent capital for Manufact.

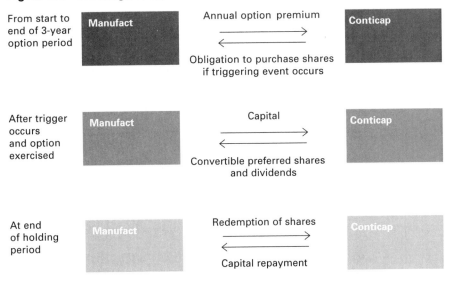

The obvious choices are banks and (re)insurers, who are both financial intermediaries, and the capital markets at large. Let us consider each of these in turn.

- **Banks:** CC options embody a number of risks, not all of which are hedgeable in the liquid capital markets. Since this is not a hedgeable product, it must be provided by an entity willing to accept and keep risk for several years. With the exception (until recently) of credit risk, banks are not in the business of keeping risk. As we discussed in Chapter 5, banks will take some risk, but most risk will be passed on to others.

- **(Re)insurers:** In the example above, we used Conticap Re, a strong reinsurance company, as the capital provider. In the transactions that have been executed so far, both insurers and reinsurers have been active as providers of capital. The combination of different risks in a CC option is attractive to the insurance markets. (Re)insurance companies are in the business of taking risk. Traditionally, they do not hedge their insurance risks; they diversify. In the past, those risks have been somewhat limited to the traditional "insurable" risks, but times are changing. Certainly, the insurance markets are no strangers to credit risk. Besides the risks taken by the large credit insurance market, (re)insurers have large capital and asset bases that must be invested. The vast majority of these investments are stocks and bonds, backed only by the full faith and credit of the issuers. In a contingent capital product, credit risk is integrated with other risks. Some of these other risks may be attractive as diversifiers of the (re)insurer's book of risks. The technology already developed for MMPs and MTPs that we discussed in Chapter 6 can be employed to evaluate the interaction of these diverse risks and price a CC option. It seems natural, therefore, for insurers and reinsurers to write CC options.

• **Capital markets:** Other investors could do the same as the insurers, but, in most cases, they are not going to have the same broad band of expertise to look at the variety of risks faced by a corporation. It is important to note, however, that since this is an option product and not an insurance product, other non-insurance investors are free to participate as capital providers. One way for them to do so is to follow the lead of the insurance markets in these investments. Just as securitization of insurance risks (discussed in Chapter 10) allowed capital markets investors to put their capital at risk against traditionally insured risks, contingent capital products allow the capital markets to participate in this form of risk financing. If investors are able to participate in a significant way, then this opens up a huge source of capital. The size of the market for debt securities alone is over $31 trillion worldwide.[1]

THE VALUE OF CC TO A CORPORATION

If a corporation determines that it may need some capital in the future, it has two choices. It can either raise the capital immediately or later. If it raises it immediately and cannot fully deploy it in its operations, that capital will not earn the requisite return and, as we discussed in Chapter 3, will be a drag on the company's ROE. It would prefer to defer raising the capital to later, when it is able to use it. The risk then is that the firm may not be in the best condition to raise capital at that point in time. For example, after a major loss, the firm may not be able to demonstrate the same level of financial strength as before, and new capital will be more expensive.

If the firm wants to retain the risk of low-probability, high-severity events, the conventional choices have been to raise new equity or debt—either immediately or later. Equity is expensive, and likely to be even more so after a high-severity event. A lower ROE will not meet shareholder expectations. Debt capital costs less but faces the same issues as new equity. In addition, new debt increases leverage ratios, which could have a detrimental effect on the firm's credit rating. A CC instrument can be structured to provide an alternative choice, one that commits a capital resource but does not raise the capital until needed. The immediate cost is lower than debt or equity, and it is not likely to have a detrimental effect on the firm's financial ratios.

A corporation's current paid-up capital structure is likely to influence its ongoing business strategy. If a company is undercapitalized, but sees real opportunity to do more business, contingent capital can support the added volatility of the expansion. This would allow the company to improve its bottom line without dragging down return on equity or increasing its debt ratio. If a company is overcapitalized, its results will be poor relative to investors' required return on equity. Such a company would be better off returning some of the capital to its shareholders in the form of dividends or share buybacks. If it does have a remote need for the excess capital, then the purchase of a contingent capital option would be a viable alternative. Doing so would reduce the company's equity and increase its return on equity, without increasing its risk profile—it has access to capital if it needs.

Contingent capital can also act as a credit enhancement for a corporation, since it increases the firm's potential capital base. It demonstrates that the firm can withstand greater losses than it previously could have and, as stated earlier, it does so at a minimal cost. Companies that wish to improve their credit conditions, for example to satisfy rating agencies, might find contingent capital an efficient solution. The only added risk is the credit risk of the contingent capital option writer, which can be mitigated by selecting only highly rated, creditworthy entities.

CC COMPARED TO OTHER FORMS OF CAPITAL

Contingent capital is a risk financing product, not a risk transfer product. It has features of an option, yet the underlying security is conventional corporate paid-up capital. The major capital providers to date have been from the insurance industry. To understand better where contingent capital lies between insurance and bank debt, we take a closer look at the differences between these instruments. First we compare CC to insurance and debt. We then compare CC to some alternatives such as bank letters of credit and pre- and post-event bonds.

CC vs. Insurance

Traditional insurance products are usually one-year contracts that indemnify a corporation against losses. For this, the insurer receives an insurance premium. Payments made by the insurer to the corporation cannot exceed losses incurred by the firm. The corporation has no obligation to pay back any money received in settlement of a claim. Contingent capital has very different expected cash flows from insurance, and a very different risk profile. A firm purchasing a contingent capital product pays an annual option premium. The term of the option is usually several years, but need not be. If the option is triggered, for example by a large, traditionally insurable loss, the firm has the right to demand capital from the option writer. However, in this case the option writer receives an asset (a security) in return. The option writer receives dividends or interest on the capital it has provided until the security is redeemed, repaying the capital.

Both traditional insurance and CC products require the payment of a premium. For the same layer of loss, however, the insurance premium should be more expensive than the option premium. Intuitively this makes sense, since on a loss, the corporation keeps insurance recoveries, whereas it would have to pay back the CC. Whenever a firm pays to transfer risk, it is paying for the expected loss plus a risk premium. Risk takers want to make a profit over the long term. The risk premium they charge may be greater than that which the firm itself would assess. The firm may have a better understanding of the risks involved and how those risks affect its bottom line. It knows what risk mitigants have been put in place to prevent losses and how effective they are. In such a case, the firm would be inclined to bear the risks itself, if it had enough capital resources. This is where CC facilities work better than conventional insurance. It enables a firm that feels it understands its own risks to finance losses over time without paying a risk premium for transferring them.

CC does not smooth accounting earnings like its insurance counterpart, finite reinsurance. It smoothes cash flows.

CC vs. Bank Debt

A firm's cost of debt is equal to the rate that is charged by investors and/or banks for loaning the company money. Debt has after-tax benefits, since the rate is paid out in the form of tax-deductible interest. The cost of debt can be broken down into two components: a risk-free rate for the actual use of cash and a risk premium that reflects the credit risk of the firm. With CC, apart from the initial option premium, no cash changes hands immediately, so there is no rate charged for cash until the CC option is exercised.

CC option writers face two forms of risk. The first is the contingency trigger and the second is the credit risk (default) of the firm. The CC option would likely be structured around a trigger event that would hurt the firm, but would be far from bankrupting it. As the likelihood of two non-correlated events occurring is less than the likelihood of either one of the events occurring, the risk premium paid for contingent capital should be less than the risk premium paid on standard debt securities. This makes intuitive sense, since the capital will not be available in all situations.

If the corporation can isolate the one or two major risks it believes could have the greatest effect on its financial well-being, and define those as the triggering events, then CC facilities can be cheaper than debt capital, without giving up any real benefits. And, like interest paid on debt, the option premium paid by the company is also tax-deductible.

Another advantage over debt is that contingent capital does not add debt immediately to a company's balance sheet, and allows debt ratios to remain lower. This can be a very important factor in the eyes of investors, analysts, rating agencies and regulators.

CC vs. Bank Letters of Credit (LOC)

With a bank letter of credit (LOC), a company will pay a small commitment premium until it draws cash, at which time it pays a larger amount as interest. This is very similar to CC, and quite often the commitment fee may be competitive with or even less than the option premium for CC. The reason for this is that LOCs tend to have much more restrictive covenants. Banks often look solely at their credit exposure to the company and judge that risk. If they charge less, it is because they do not expect to have that credit exposure if things start to go badly for the firm. The covenants associated with the LOC may specifically protect them from that possibility by making the LOC unavailable if significant events occur. Also, the cost of LOCs will rarely, if ever, recognize the reduced risk of drawing funds by adding a non-credit-related risk trigger. Conversely, one of the main benefits of a CC option is that it is triggered when things have not gone well and the company needs capital. Of course, even CC option writers will need some protection. Since the primary objective of a CC option is to provide capital when needed, the restrictive covenants must be somewhat flexible.

CC vs. Pre- and Post-Event Bonds

Pre- and post-event bonds developed concurrently with CC instruments. They came as a response to the need to finance losses associated with high-severity events. Pre- and post-event bonds are straight debt securities. Their names indicate only when they are issued. Pre-event bonds are one way to capitalize a company, but they are paid-up corporate debt. The capital must be used in an effective way to produce a profit, but it will increase the company's debt ratio. One advantage for a company new to the debt markets is that it will make the company's name familiar to investors, so that a post-event bond will be a that much easier to place in the capital markets. However, no matter how familiar investors are with a company, the evaluation of a post-event bond will be based on the financial condition of the company after some major event has occurred to weaken it. This is the worst time to raise funds, but nonetheless it is the time additional funds are needed. By contrast, CC facilities also raise funds when needed, but that arrangement is made well in advance.

DEVELOPMENT OF THE CC MARKET

Thus far, the majority of CC transactions have been done for insurance or reinsurance companies, which were the first to recognize the benefit of these products. Although the details of each transaction differed, they were all CC products as described in this chapter.

CC seems almost tailor-made for insurance and reinsurance companies, because of the cyclical nature of their business. An insurer needs a strong capital base to absorb losses, and also to underwrite new risks. After a major catastrophe, an insurer will have to pay large claims, thereby reducing its capital—and its ability to write new business. By setting up a CC facility in advance, the insurer can have the additional capital available immediately after a catastrophe so that it can continue to write new, profitable business. It is therefore no surprise that insurers and reinsurers were the first to purchase these options. As it turns out, another set of insurers and reinsurers were the major writers of these options. Although the risks covered under these options have broadened, the development has remained strongly within the insurance industry.

Contingent capital is a cross between virtual capital and just-in-time capital. It is virtual because it is visible as a resource to the firm, yet the capital is not paid-up. It is just-in-time because it arrives in the firm only when it is needed, as determined by the firm's management. Because of these attributes, CC is gaining momentum outside the insurance industry. Another development, also starting with the insurance industry and spreading to corporations at large, is contingent insurance or reinsurance. Recognizing that insurance is a form of capital, contingent insurance allows a firm to buy insurance coverage at pre-determined terms, on the occurrence of a triggering event. This product is still in its infancy, but appears to have gathered some interest from a variety of companies.

Contingent capital brings with it many benefits: low cost of capital, effective risk financing and credit enhancement, increased ROE, and structural flexibility. More companies are beginning to enjoy these benefits, as they recognize contingent capital's potential as a tool in risk management and corporate finance.

"Standardization and transparency
also affect pricing."

10

Insurance-Linked Securities

GAIL BELONSKY, DAVID DURBIN, AND DAVID LASTER

Since 1997, approximately $3 billion in worldwide insurance and reinsurance capacity has been created through the issuance of capital market instruments including:

- Over-the-counter swaps,
- Exchange-traded and over-the-counter options, and
- Private placement bonds.

Although still small in comparison to 1998 worldwide reinsurance industry premiums of $121 billion, this new class of "insurance-linked" securities (ILSs) has broken new ground in the insurance and financial markets. By bridging the insurance and capital markets, ILSs are creating a range of attractive investment opportunities previously unavailable to those outside of the insurance industry. The securities also constitute a potential new source of competitively priced insurance coverage, especially at times when such coverage is in short supply. Participants who recognize the potential of these securities and position themselves accordingly will help shape the market's development and will stand to profit the most from it.

Although insurance and reinsurance companies have led the initial wave of activity, other corporations can also securitize their insurance risk. If a corporation merely insures a conventional risk and relies on its insurer to execute the securitization, the transaction will have minimal impact on its capital structure. If, however, the corporation uses securitization to make its

Excerpted from Swiss Re New Markets, *Insurance-Linked Securities* (Zurich: Swiss Re New Markets, 1999).

risk management program more comprehensive, or if it takes a direct role in the issuance of ILSs, the impact can be wide-ranging.

The plan of the chapter is as follows: First, we consider how insurance-linked securities work and describe some deals that have already come to market. Next, we explain how these securities facilitate a mutually beneficial transfer of risk, allowing issuers to tap into new sources of funds and investors to diversify their portfolios and boost risk-adjusted returns. We then examine the modeling and quantification of catastrophe risk, both processes vital to the pricing of insurance-linked securities. Finally, we offer some insights into how the market for these securities might develop in coming years.

How Insurance-Linked Securities Work

The majority of ILS transactions to date have involved **catastrophe bonds**, commonly called "cat bonds," whose coupon and principal payments depend on the performance of a pool or index of natural catastrophe risk. Insurance-linked securities such as cat bonds can be structured to hedge the risks of many types of institutions, ranging from global corporations to local insurers, from whose perspective the securities behave like a reinsurance contract.

Consider, by way of example, a simple one-year structure collateralized by a bond issue that provides capital to cover losses in the event of a hurricane (Figure 10.1). The illustrated transaction involves three parties: investors, the cedent and the issuer. Investors purchase bonds from the issuer, a special purpose reinsurance vehicle (SPV) that simultaneously enters into a reinsurance contract with the cedent. The SPV is typically structured as an independent, charitably owned trust that is licensed as a reinsurer in an offshore location such as the Cayman Islands or Bermuda. Its sole purpose is

Figure 10.1 Catastrophe bond payment structure.

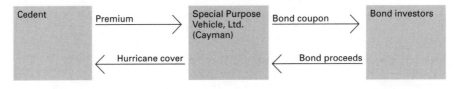

Cedent		Special Purpose Vehicle, Ltd. (Cayman)		Bond investors
	Premium →		Bond coupon →	
	← Hurricane cover		← Bond proceeds	

to engage in the business relating to the securitization. This exclusive focus on a single transaction minimizes the risk to which the SPV exposes its counterparties.[1] Thus, the SPV resembles a single-parent captive that is created to serve the reinsurance needs of its parent.

Figure 10.2 depicts the timing of cash flows in a typical transaction. The funds provided by the bond investors are initially deposited in a trust account with restrictions on how its assets are invested and when they can be withdrawn. The investment earnings on this initial deposit as well as the premium the cedent pays for insurance coverage are periodically (often, semiannually) paid to investors as a bond coupon. In the typical structure, there is a possible extension period following the maturity date, called the **loss development period,** during which the amount of losses payable under the cover is determined. If there have been no qualifying events during the year, the principal amount is returned to the bond investors with their final coupon payment. If there has been an event, the amount due the cedent under the coverage definition is paid at the end of the loss development period and any balance of the funds goes back to investors as a return of principal.

The simple structure depicted in Figure 10.1 can be modified. Often, there is a reinsurance company acting as an intermediary between the cedent and the SPV. This reinsurer can retain some risk before retroceding to the SPV. An insurance company may, for example, recover based on its own losses, while the reinsurer enters into a contract with the SPV based on an index of losses. In another variation, a bond issue can have one or

Figure 10.2   Catastrophe bond cash flows timing.

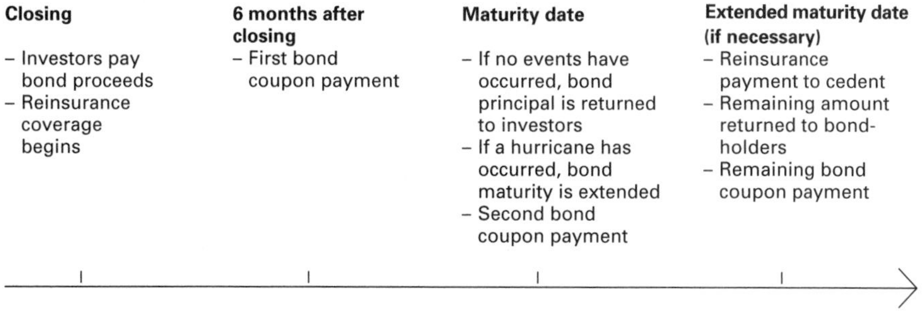

Closing	**6 months after closing**	**Maturity date**	**Extended maturity date (if necessary)**
– Investors pay bond proceeds – Reinsurance coverage begins	– First bond coupon payment	– If no events have occurred, bond principal is returned to investors – If a hurricane has occurred, bond maturity is extended – Second bond coupon payment	– Reinsurance payment to cedent – Remaining amount returned to bondholders – Remaining bond coupon payment

more classes that are guaranteed to return to investors some percentage of principal, a feature known as defeasance. These bonds can be structured so that investors receive the guaranteed portion of the principal at the regular maturity date if no catastrophic loss occurs. If a loss does occur, the full principal is repaid but at a later date. This delayed repayment is funded by zero coupon securities that the issuer purchases at the maturity date using the guaranteed portion of the bond proceeds.

Cat bond structures involve an offshore issuer, management agents and trustees, as well as other parties. An alternative way to transfer catastrophe risk is through a swap transaction, in which a series of fixed, predefined payments is exchanged for a series of floating payments whose values depend on the occurrence of an insured event. The swap, by design, offers benefits to both sides, permitting a cedent to lay off insurance risk to a counterparty better equipped to manage it. The cedent can enter into the swap directly with counterparties or through a financial intermediary (Figure 10.3). In some jurisdictions, the counterparties need not be insurers. New York state insurance regulators ruled in the summer of 1998 that insurance-linked swaps whose payments are not based on the cedent's actual losses are financial contracts and can therefore be entered into by non-insurers.

EXAMPLES OF SPECIFIC DEALS

Three transactions—an **index bond**, a **physical trigger bond** and a **physical trigger swap**—illustrate how deals can be structured so that their payouts are based on indices rather than actual losses. Basing a deal on an index rather than a book of business allows the cedent to protect proprietary information from disclosure to competitors and makes the deal more transparent to investors. Index-based deals also raise fewer investor concerns about

Figure 10.3   Cat swap payment structure.

adverse selection (the fear that an insurer is trying to cede precisely those risks that it privately deems the most problematic), moral hazard (the problem that ceding risk might alter the behavioral incentives of the primary insurer), and unsound underwriting practices. These advantages must be weighed against the advantages of indemnity-based deals, which are based on a book of business. Indemnity-based deals resemble other risk management techniques already in place and are not subject to basis risk, the risk of a mismatch between a firm's book of business and the index to which a particular transaction is linked. If the mismatch in an index deal is substantial, the cedent might remain exposed to the risks against which it sought to hedge. To date, index-based transactions have comprised 20% of the market, as measured by risk capital raised.

Industry Index Bond

In a transaction completed July 16, 1997, a SPV named SR Earthquake Fund, Ltd. simultaneously issued $137 million notes and entered into a $112.2 million contract with Swiss Re based on an industry-wide index of California earthquake losses. The index was based on the largest insured loss from a single earthquake over the two-year risk period, as determined by PCS (Property Claim Services), a leading provider of loss estimates for the insurance industry.

In response to the varying risk appetites among investors, the bond issue was divided into four classes, or "tranches." The first two classes (A-1 and A-2) are the first insurance-linked notes ever to be rated investment grade (Baa3 by Moody's and BBB– by Fitch) based on their expected loss as measured by a catastrophe loss probability model. Only 60% of the bond principal is at risk; the remainder is invested in Treasury notes maturing before the end of the two-year risk period. A-1 pays a fixed interest rate of 8.645%; A-2 has a floating rate equal to 3 month LIBOR plus 255 basis points (hundredths of a %). Class B notes (rated Ba1 by Moody's and BB by Fitch), which have 100% of principal at risk, pay a fixed interest rate of 10.493%. If a qualifying earthquake occurs in California during the risk period, these three classes suffer loss of principal because the issuer would have to pay funds to Swiss Re for their coverage. The resulting loss to bondholders would depend on the level of insured losses, as estimated by PCS (Table 10.1). Class C notes (not rated), whose coupon is 11.952%, entail greater risk. They lose all principal if the largest California earthquake exceeds $12 billion of insured losses.

The annual expected principal loss is 0.46% to Class A-1 and Class A-2 note holders, 0.76% to Class B note holders, and 2.40% to Class C note holders.[2] The maximum losses to the $62 million of Class A-1 and A-2 notes provide $37.2 million of coverage to Swiss Re. In addition, the $60 million of Class B notes and $14.7 million of Class C notes provide further coverage to Swiss Re in those amounts.

The use of the PCS loss index benefited both the reinsured and the note holders. Because Swiss Re writes residential and commercial earthquake coverage that closely mirrors the California market, using the PCS loss index exposed Swiss Re's capital to minimal basis risk. In exchange for that risk, the company was able to limit the amount of information it disclosed about its book while minimizing any potential adverse selection and moral hazard issues for investors. The parties to the transaction were comfortable using this index over the two-year period. If the risk period were significantly longer, however, the issuer would have sought a mechanism that would allow the effective coverage to vary in response to changes in general conditions and its own exposure to the California insurance market.

Table 10.1   Payout schedule for SR Earthquake Fund issue.

PCS estimated insured losses from largest earthquake	Classes A-1, A-2 Principal loss*	Class B Principal loss*	Class C Principal loss*	Annual probability of loss this magnitude
$12.0 billion or greater	0%	0%	100%	2.40%
$18.5 billion or greater	20%	33%	100%	1.00%
$21.0 billion or greater	40%	66%	100%	0.76%
$24.0 billion or greater	60%	100%	100%	0.52%

*as % of original principal

Another issue especially relevant to earthquake bonds is the development period. Before the Northridge earthquake in 1994, many industry participants would have estimated the period between the occurrence of a natural disaster and the bulk of the loss claims at six months for earthquakes and slightly less for hurricanes. Northridge, however, was very different. The original PCS estimate for claims was $7.2 billion after six months and did not develop to the full insurance loss estimate of $12.5 billion until twenty months after the event.

Reinsurers accept the trickling in of claims over time; investors, however, have collateralized the potential loss payout and would like the flexibility to reallocate their principal to other assets once the risk period is over. (Investors receive the full premium only during the risk period; during the development period, they receive interest rates pegged at either the LIBOR rate or at LIBOR plus a nominal spread.) Once the principal is returned to investors, however, it cannot be retrieved. To strike a balance between returning principal too soon (before all losses have been accounted for) and holding it too long (which would reduce the return to investors), a stratified extension period was developed that has been used as a standard for payouts on several subsequent index transactions. Over the development period, which is one year at maximum, the latest estimate of insured losses is periodically compared to an increasing benchmark level. If losses build steadily, the trust account keeps the money on deposit. If the losses stabilize below predetermined trigger levels, additional principal is returned to investors.

Physical Trigger Bond

Tokio Marine, a major writer of Japanese earthquake policies, faced different challenges when purchasing coverage for its earthquake exposure. The company wanted to lock in reinsurance capacity at a fixed price over ten years, which would facilitate an increase in its underwriting activity. Because the company planned to amortize its issuance costs over the life of the deal, the long risk period also reduced the prospective annual cost of the transaction. (**Issuance costs** are a one-time expense as compared to the annual costs of reinsurance, such as brokerage fees.) Determining which policies to model for an indemnity transaction would have been difficult because Tokio Marine's book of business was expected to change over time. Another difficulty was the absence of a generally accepted reporter of loss estimates in Japan. (More generally, the lack of industry loss reporting outside the U.S. makes it difficult to arrange index transactions based on non-United States risk.) Finally, even if a reporter of loss estimates did exist, the prospect of the insurance environment changing over the course of a decade created additional uncertainty.

To overcome these obstacles, a first-of-its-kind transaction finalized on November 19, 1997, was structured on the basis of a true physical index. The potential losses in the transaction, which involves a bond issuance by Parametric Re, Ltd. (a Cayman Island SPV), are based on the magnitude of earthquakes in and around Tokyo. The reinsurance cover, written by Parametric Re, was contingent on the magnitude of earthquake activity in the region as measured by the Japan Meteorological Agency (JMA). An earthquake registering a JMA Magnitude of 7.1, for example, would have a recovery of 25% if the earthquake were to occur in the inner grid but zero were it to occur in the outer grid (Figures 10.4 & 10.5). The bonds issued by Parametric Re were divided into two classes, units and notes. Notes with

Figure 10.4   Parametric Re inner and outer grids.

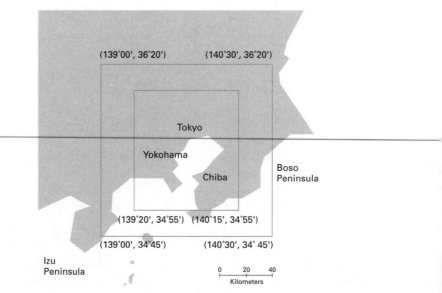

Figure 10.5   Parametric Re loss trigger.

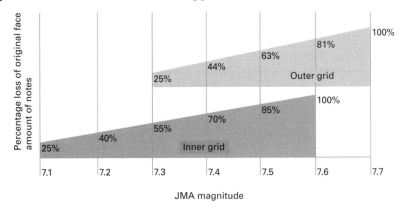

a face value of $80 million were fully exposed to earthquake risk (rated Ba2 by Moody's and BB by Duff and Phelp's). Units worth $20 million risk (rated Baa3 by Moody's and BBB– by Duff and Phelp's) were comprised of $10 million of defeasance certificates unexposed to earthquake risk and $10 million of notes exposed to earthquake risk.

A major advantage of the magnitude trigger is that it permits standardization: A single trigger can be used in multiple transactions. If other companies issue magnitude trigger bonds based on the same index, investors will be able to reuse their analyses of the original transaction. Traditional indemnity-based transactions, by contrast, require investors to analyze each company's book of business. Transactions based on a magnitude trigger also offer investors greater certainty and objectivity. Moreover, because payouts depend on a quickly determined, well-defined standard rather than the settlement of actual claims, investors can receive their funds more quickly.

Physical Trigger Swap

On April 1, 1998, Mitsui Marine arranged coverage through a swap transaction based on the same earthquake parameters as the Parametric Re bond offering. The insurer wanted to develop an alternative source of reinsurance capacity for a portion of its Japanese earthquake exposure. Because the amount of coverage it sought was $30 million, and because of timing constraints, a swap was determined to be the best alternative. As a general rule swap executions involve fewer intermediaries and less documentation, usually resulting in quicker, more cost-effective transactions.

Periodically, Mitsui Marine pays a premium, which is in turn paid to counterparties. Because the notional amount of a swap is not always on deposit with a bank, the deal can expose the cedent to credit risk, just as would be the case for a reinsurance contract. To reduce this risk, the counterparties can be required to pledge collateral.

NATURAL CATASTROPHE RISK ANALYSIS[3]

A basic prerequisite for the securitization of insurance risk is a reliable estimate of expected losses and the likelihood of different loss outcomes. For a peril such as fire, estimates of the expected losses to a portfolio of insured objects are usually based on claims statistics from past years. Historical losses are indexed to current price levels and adjusted to reflect changes in the amount of exposed values. This method is often inapplicable, however, to natural catastrophes. Because the return periods for significant events can be decades or even centuries, there is usually no representative claims experience for a given portfolio of catastrophe risks. It is difficult, moreover, to index past loss events because the geographical distribution and the quality of the insured objects may change considerably over time. Complicating matters further, many catastrophe-prone areas in the United States have experienced rapid increases in population. Because most of the ILS activity to date has been related to natural catastrophes, we take the opportunity here to describe how the assessment of risk for rare events may be done.

One way to develop estimates of the risk from earthquakes or windstorms despite these difficulties is to simulate a representative set of events that might affect a portfolio of risks. For each of the simulated events, insured losses and the frequency of occurrence are estimated. The simulation results are then used to construct an "artificial loss experience," which substitutes for an actual history of losses. The simulations take into account four elements:

- Hazard,
- Vulnerability of the insured properties,

- Distribution of the insured values with respect to location and risk class, and
- Insurance conditions applying to the original cover.

Hazard refers to how often earthquakes or windstorms of a given intensity can be expected to occur in a particular region, irrespective of the coverage in place. A hazard model is based on historical records of past events and scientific information specifying the perils. Regarding earthquakes, tectonic and palaeoseismic information can be used to improve estimates of recurrence rates. Moreover, the attenuation of earthquake waves from a fault rupture has to be modeled and geological data are needed to consider local site effects amplifying or damping the amount of ground shaking. Regarding storms, wind models characterizing the propagation of hurricanes and the spatial distribution of wind speed have to be compiled. After a tropical cyclone has made landfall, natural surface roughness from mountains or man-made roughness created by large cities have to be considered to avoid overestimating wind intensities.

Long-term average recurrence estimates might be inadequate for assessing the risk of a certain event occurring over a short period of time such as a few months. One reason is that the probability of a specific earthquake fault rupturing in the near future depends on the time elapsed since the last event. In the case of atmospheric perils such as hurricanes, analysts must consider short-term changes in occurrence probabilities due to changes in climate.

Vulnerability relates to the degree of destruction that an insured property or a portfolio of insured objects is expected to sustain from an earthquake or windstorm of a given intensity. Analysis of past catastrophe losses permits the quantification of relationships between natural hazard parameters (e.g. earthquake magnitude or hurricane wind speed), specific risk characteristics (e.g. line of business, type of buildings) and the expected damage. These relationships can then be applied to portfolios lacking specific loss experience.

The **distribution of insured values** with respect to risk characteristics and geographical zones (e.g. counties, towns or even individual sites) is central to the analysis of natural catastrophe risks. This information allows one to assess what values are affected by a given event and to consider aspects of site-specific hazard and vulnerability.

The total amount of insured loss arising from an event is also heavily influenced by the **insurance conditions**—like deductibles or limits—that apply to the original cover. If many of the losses that a natural disaster causes are less than the deductible, the total insured loss is significantly reduced.

Finally, additional factors such as underinsurance (a level of coverage less than actual replacement costs), claims handling practices, moral hazard, and the sharp increases in building costs that occur in the wake of a disaster should carefully be considered.

Setting up such a natural catastrophe model involves estimating a wide variety of parameters based on incomplete data and knowledge. Given the level of uncertainty inherent in such an exercise, a thorough analysis requires simulations based on many alternative parameter estimates to test for robustness. These simulations, because of their complexity, can only be carried out with the help of computer programs. Based on the representative set of simulated events and their estimated occurrence frequencies, the probability of each loss level is computed. This is summarized in a "loss frequency" or "exceedence probability" curve. These curves provide estimates of expected annual losses as well as the probabilities of attachment for different reinsurance layers.

The loss frequency curve in Figure 10.6, for example, provides the following information:

- A loss amounting to 0.8% or more of the total portfolio values should be expected about once every ten years (annual frequency 0.1),
- A loss ratio of 20% or more will occur on average once every 140 years (annual frequency 0.007), and
- Some degree of damage can be expected to occur every five years.

Several leading reinsurance companies first developed natural catastrophe risk assessment programs in the '80s. Reinsurers bear a significant share of insured catastrophe losses and therefore have a vital interest in understanding the risks. More recently, a few specialized catastrophe consulting firms have begun providing similar tools to the insurance industry. Several large corporations with heavy risk concentrations have also developed their own models.

Figure 10.6   Loss frequency curve.

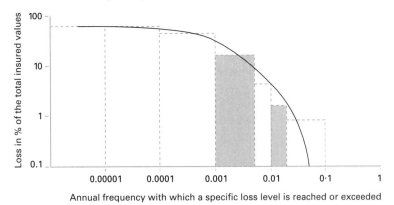

Annual frequency with which a specific loss level is reached or exceeded

ISSUER'S PERSPECTIVE

Insurance-linked securities offer several potential benefits to issuers, including attractive pricing (whether now or in the future), additional reinsurance capacity, credit enhancement and greater leverage. We discuss each of these in turn.

Pricing

Insurance-linked securities can provide a viable alternative to traditional insurance and reinsurance, although the cost advantage will vary throughout the insurance underwriting cycle. In some periods, such as after a major disaster, industry capital may be in short supply, pressuring insurers and reinsurers to boost premiums to rebuild surplus. At other times, when there is excess capacity in the industry, insurers might aggressively compete for business by lowering their rates. The status of the cycle is thus a major determinant of the attractiveness of ILSs. If, moreover, the timing of the insurance cycle varies by line of business, so too will the potential cost savings associated with securitization. The tighter the market for a particular line of reinsurance business becomes, the more compelling will be the case for securitization in that line of business.

Standardization and transparency also affect pricing. As the market matures, some types of contracts will become easier to standardize, bundle and explain to investors. Standardization simplifies issuance and reduces transaction costs. As investors grow comfortable with particular ILS structures, moreover, they will require less explanation for each particular deal. The more transparent the securities are, the lower the premium issuers will need to pay. The yield spread between ILSs and Treasury securities should therefore narrow over time, just as they have for other financial instruments such as mortgage-backed securities.

The maturation of the ILS market should also improve its liquidity. If there is no secondary market for a particular instrument, it will attract only a limited clientele; namely, investors prepared to buy and hold until maturity. Issuers will therefore have to pay a liquidity premium above and beyond the risk premium. Once a more active secondary market for the securities develops, ILSs will become more attractive to a broad range of investors, who will therefore require a lower rate of return to hold them.

A final point for potential issuers to note is that in weighing the costs of securitization, what matters is not just today's cost of reinsurance, but also tomorrow's cost. Assembling the data and documentation needed to issue ILSs typically requires several months. If the reinsurance market firms up, such as after a major catastrophe, issuers will face a considerable delay in making their initial entrance into the ILS market because many others will be trying to do the same. Firms with prior experience at issuing ILSs will have a much easier time accessing the market. Thus, even if issuing ILSs is somewhat more expensive than conventional reinsurance, the transaction might ultimately prove cost effective because it affords the issuer the opportunity to enter the ILS market more readily in the future.

Other Considerations

Capacity.   Another advantage ILSs offer issuers is that they provide additional reinsurance capacity. Some participants feel that the catastrophe reinsurance market lacks the capacity to provide them adequate protection against major events. Their response is to hold a substantial buffer of extra capital in lieu of reinsurance. Other firms face a separate concern: When the market tightens, reinsurance contract attachment levels rise in response, effectively providing less coverage. In this context, the ILS market has begun to offer additional reinsurance capacity in the late '90s, just as the Bermuda market began to do in the late '80s and early '90s.

Credit Quality.   Purchasers of reinsurance seriously consider counterparty risk because the situations in which the coverage is most needed are often times of industry distress. This is why insurers generally purchase reinsurance from several companies simultaneously. Reinsurance capacity varies in credit quality. According to a tabulation by Standard & Poor's, less than half of the global reinsurance contracts written in 1996 were by AAA-rated reinsurers; more than a quarter of contracts were issued by firms rated A or below (Figure 10.7). ILSs can be structured to minimize counterparty risk. When issuing catastrophe bonds, for example, a firm can specify that the principal be invested in highly rated investment-grade securities to be held as collateral in an SPV. Arrangements such as this may provide greater credit quality than conventional reinsurance.

Leverage.   One of the traditional uses of reinsurance is to permit a direct insurer to leverage its balance sheet and its underwriting expertise so that it

Figure 10.7   1996 market share of global reinsurance industry by rating category.

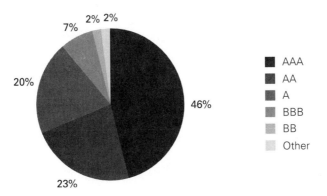

Source: Standard and Poor's Global Reinsurance Highlights 1997

can underwrite more risk with a given level of capital. A mature ILS market might offer some direct insurers even greater latitude to employ leverage. An insurer could, for example, pursue a strategy of underwriting a certain type of policy—be it homeowners, auto or term life—in large volumes, packaging these policies, and selling them to an intermediary. This strategy might appeal to firms whose competitive advantage in marketing and processing applications enables them to earn a satisfactory return on underwriting. Indeed, a mature ILS market might stimulate the formation of such firms.

Finally, there are **strategic reasons** for some firms to issue ILSs. A company's risk manager, or credit rating agency, may be uncomfortable with its level of exposure to a particular peril. In response to such concerns, an additional layer above traditional reinsurance can provide an extra margin of safety. Early participation in the market will signal to investors and policyholders that a company is proactive, innovative, and willing to assume a leadership role. If, moreover, the ILS market evolves so that there are profitable niches for various participants, the first firms to issue the securities will be in the best position to learn how the process works and to determine what role they might play in the market.

INVESTOR'S PERSPECTIVE

Insurance-linked securities can offer investors attractive returns while providing a way of reducing the overall risk of their portfolios.

Market Yields

Insurance-linked securities offer investors the opportunity to earn high expected returns for several reasons. In their early stages of development, ILSs will be priced to yield a "newness premium." Catastrophe bonds with a given credit rating, for example, have yielded a spread over LIBOR that is higher than that of other comparably rated fixed-income securities (Figure 10.8). If the securities become more accepted by investors, the newness premium would disappear or at least shrink, causing the securities to appreciate in value.

Even after the market has matured, investors will still have opportunities to earn high returns. Experts who can discern which ILS issues are

Figure 10.8   Comparative pricing at issue.

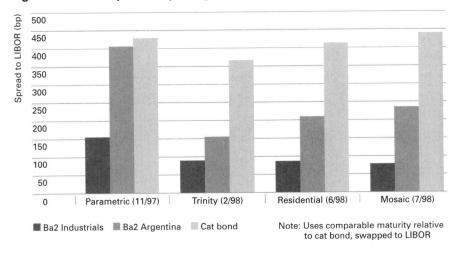

undervalued will be able to profit from their specialized knowledge. Profitable opportunities will also arise when a tight reinsurance market causes the industry to conserve its scarce capital by pricing coverage at abnormally high levels. In such high-rate environments, issuers will be willing to compensate investors more generously than under normal market conditions, raising the expected return to investing in ILSs.

Diversification Opportunities

Because, as empirical analyses have shown, the occurrence of insurance-related events is uncorrelated with the returns to stocks and bonds, investing in ILSs reduces the overall risk of a diversified portfolio. Indeed, if ILSs represent a limited share of an investor's overall holdings, their inclusion reduces portfolio risk by almost as much as the purchase of a risk-free security. Thus, an ILS need only earn an expected return slightly above the risk-free rate to improve the risk-return profile of a portfolio.

To demonstrate this point, consider a hypothetical ILS structure that pays an agreed-upon yield if no catastrophe occurs but suffers a total loss of principal in the event of a catastrophe, whose probability can be estimated. The greater the probability of catastrophe, the higher the variance of returns to the security.[4] This probability therefore determines the extent to which holding the security reduces overall portfolio risk.

To illustrate, let us compare four securities: a risk-free security (such as a Treasury bill) and three ILSs whose percentage probabilities of total loss of principal are, respectively, 0.5, 1.0 and 2.0. How effectively does each security reduce risk when added to a portfolio of risky assets?

As is well established in the finance literature, adding a risk-free security to a risky portfolio causes a linear reduction in the risk of that portfolio, as measured by the standard deviation of returns (Figure 10.9, solid line). Thus, a 10% allocation to a risk-free security reduces portfolio risk by 10% (point A), a 20% allocation reduces portfolio risk by 20% (point B), and so forth. As Figure 10.9 shows, each of the three ILSs provides nearly as much portfolio risk reduction as does the risk-free asset for allocations of 10% or less. For larger allocations, however, the risk reduction facilitated by these securities is substantially weaker. Because ILSs are still a new and unfamiliar asset class, we will concentrate on cases in which investors allocate less than 10% of their portfolios to them.

Figure 10.9   Risk reduction properties of ILSs.

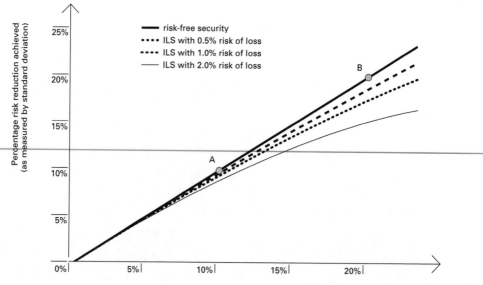

One way to express the amount of portfolio risk reduction achieved by investing in an ILS is as a proportion of the portfolio risk reduction realizable through investing the same funds in a risk-free security. Thus, allocating 5% of a portfolio to an ILS securitizing a catastrophe risk whose probability of occurrence is 1% reduces portfolio risk by 97.4% as much as would allocating the same funds to a risk-free security (Table 10.2, Panel A, shaded cell). More generally, for asset allocations of 1 to 10%, the three ILSs realize anywhere from 89.0% to 99.7% of the risk reduction achievable by investing in a risk-free security.

This, in turn, has implications for the spread above the risk-free rate that an investor will require in order to be indifferent between holding an ILS and a risk-free security. Taking the same example, a 113 basis point (bp) spread would provide a sufficient incentive for investors to allocate 5% of their portfolios to the ILS (Table 10.2, Panel B, shaded cell).[5] Of this amount, 100 bp would compensate for the expected loss while 13 bp would compensate for the marginally smaller amount of risk reduction achieved.

These calculations suggest that ILSs pay investors a premium that more than compensates them for the risk of loss. For example, Class A securities of the SR Earthquake Fund issue had a risk of loss of less than 1% yet paid an annual yield of 255 bp over LIBOR.

Table 10.2   Risk reduction facilitated by investing in an ILS.

Portfolio allocation to ILS (in %)	Panel A: Reduction achieved relative to a risk-free security			Panel B: Yield spread above risk-free rate needed to compensate investor for added risk (in basis points)		
	Percentage probability of catastrophe			Percentage probability of catastrophe		
	.5	1.0	2.0	.5	1.0	2.0
1	.997	.995	.990	51	103	205
5	.987	.974	.947	57	113	226
10	.972	.945	.890	64	128	255

Note: Figures in Panel B assume that risky portfolio earns expected return of 5% above risk-free rate.

Thus, investors received a spread above the risk-free rate that was far higher than our calculations indicate. The discrepancy was even greater than this comparison suggests, moreover, because our calculation assumed a total loss of principal in the event of a major earthquake, whereas the security's potential loss was capped at 60%.

The difference between the actual and the theoretical spread likely reflects several considerations, including newness and liquidity premiums (previously discussed), as well as compensation for model and parameter uncertainty. **Model uncertainty** reflects our inability to know how faithfully the catastrophe model being used to rate a transaction captures all of its relevant risks. **Parameter uncertainty** is a concern because even if a model is conceptually perfect, it might still be misestimated due to insufficient data.

To summarize, investors who substitute ILSs for a portion of their holdings in Treasury securities can achieve a higher expected return on their portfolios for a given level of risk. The high coupons that ILSs pay reflect several distinct factors, which should become less relevant as the market for these securities matures.

One final point to note is that the analysis assumes that an investor buys just a single ILS issue. In actuality, many investors will assemble diversified portfolios of these securities, thereby reducing their risk exposure to any particular event. If buying a single ILS represents an attractive opportunity, owning a diversified portfolio of several such securities would be better still.

Potential Non-Cat Lines of Business

The discussion so far has focused on the securitization of catastrophe risks. What other types of insurance risk might be amenable to securitization?

To gain some perspective, let us first note some of the qualities that typically characterize asset-backed securitization transactions:

- Historical basis for pricing or quantitative analysis of future income,
- Segmentation of business lines,
- Regulatory or tax advantage,
- General industry motivation to transfer a portion of risk, and
- Need for capital combined with high cost of capital for general corporate risk.

Catastrophe-linked securities satisfy all but the regulatory or tax advantage (same advantage is accomplished by an existing vehicle, reinsurance) although the other characteristics may only be satisfied weakly. One of the stronger motivations is the industry need to handle large, infrequent catastrophes. While other lines of insurance, such as marine and aviation, have been covered through securitizations, the coverage has been small relative to catastrophe coverage obtained in the market.

Another insurance risk that has been securitized in significant size is life insurance. The transactions to date have been motivated by a need for capital to finance acquisitions of existing books of business. Securitization may work well for life insurance because many of the risks that would cause a mismatch between assets and liabilities (policies) are risks that are well understood. The securitization raises money based on the present value of the emerging surplus of the business. Other risks embedded in the surplus include mortality and lapse risk, both of which have a historical basis for analysis. Each transaction differs based on the types of policies included. More of these types of transactions should occur in the future.

Several other lines of business seem well suited for securitization. Workers' compensation and auto insurance are often mentioned because of their historical pricing basis. Mortgage insurance and residual value insurance have both been securitized in the last year. Asbestos and pollution are additional, albeit more challenging, potential lines of business. Although there have been many historical surprises in the loss development of these risks, some of the uncertainty in development patterns has been reduced. Further, the size of future claims in the industry remains quite large, making it an attractive candidate for securitization. Credit insurance, a large European line, is very well suited for securitization because of the existence of capital markets pricing comparables. Finally, securitization may also be attractive for some of the high-severity, low-frequency types of political risks that are now being integrated into coverage.

MARKET EVOLUTION

Although the issuance of insurance-linked securities has begun in earnest, the extent to which the market will grow over the next decade and beyond remains uncertain. We can, however, gain insight into this new market by considering the development of other financial innovations. Especially instructive is the emergence of a market for mortgage-backed securities as well as other asset-backed securities that combine and repackage individual cash flows. Drawing in part on this history, we offer a few observations.

"Early Adapters"

Just as the success of a new consumer good often depends on the acceptance of "early adapters" (trendsetters inclined to try a new product) so too have ILSs had some natural constituencies in the early going: mutual funds, investors with industry knowledge, and hedge funds. The number of participants in these categories seems poised to increase. One such set of investors is yield-conscious bond fund managers. Bond funds, of which there are now thousands, have become a commodity product. Because funds within a given subcategory hold very similar securities, managers seeking to differentiate themselves from their peers actively seek new instruments that provide some pick-up in yield. Insurance-linked securities, in limited quantities, might fit the bill.

Another class of early investors includes firms and individuals with institutional knowledge of insurance markets. The securities offer insurers and reinsurers a simple way of entering a particular market (line of business or region) without building costly infrastructure. Similarly, individuals who have worked in the insurance field, whether as underwriters, actuaries or security analysts, might open asset management boutiques investing exclusively in these instruments. Finally, hedge funds, which have the flexibility to invest in a wide range of assets, could also take more of an interest in these securities.

Lucrative Niches Should Emerge in the ILS Market

A major accomplishment of the mortgage-backed securities (MBS) market is that it reduces the costs of underwriting a mortgage by permitting a more efficient allocation of capital and division of labor through specialization. Before the market developed, banks would typically make mortgage loans, carry them on their books, and service them for the life of the loan. Although they might occasionally swap or sell off a block of loans to another bank, this was a cumbersome activity. Today with the advent of the MBS market, a bank typically makes a loan and then sells it to an agency, such as Fannie Mae or Freddie Mac, which in turn bundles the mortgages, offers credit enhancement, and services the loans.

A similar development may be in store for insurance-linked securities. Today, primary insurers generally sell policies, invest the premiums, service the policies and manage the liability. In coming years, an established market for insurance-linked securities would allow different industry players to assume more focused roles. Some firms can become "virtual insurers," marketing policies by direct mail or phone and then immediately selling off the policies once the sale is made (banks, for example, might find this role attractive).

Other firms might be the securitizers, purchasing policies from a variety of direct insurers, packaging them in ways that appeal to investors (perhaps offering credit enhancements), and then reselling them. Major reinsurers or firms with experience in securitizing assets might be naturals for the role. A third market niche would involve servicing the individual policies—collecting premiums and processing claims, for which a service fee can be collected. Firms with efficient, low-cost back-office capabilities might be especially suited to the role.

Finally, firms that can effectively sell ILSs to clients will stand to earn commissions or placement fees. Investment banks, retail brokers and reinsurers are candidates for this role. In short, a lesson to be learned from other financial innovations is that there is money to be made by those who successfully specialize in particular securitization-related activities rather than doing everything themselves.

Catalysts for Market Development

Potential catalysts for market development include a major stock market downturn, the increased participation of the rating agencies, and favorable regulatory treatment.

A plunge in securities prices would accelerate the development of the ILS market. Investors, whose expectations have been colored by an extraordinary

15-year bull market in U.S. equities, would grow disillusioned, reduce their equity holdings, and look to other asset classes for new investment opportunities.

The involvement of credit rating agencies and regulators can also stimulate the development of the ILS market. As they have begun evaluating deals, the rating agencies have increased the credibility of the securities in the eyes of investors who lack the experience or resources to investigate the details of the security. By assigning ratings to the deals and explaining their evaluation methodologies to the investment community, the rating agencies provide a simple way to compare the risk of different ILSs while inviting comparisons between ILSs and other fixed income securities.

Regulatory reaction to the new securities is important for two reasons. First, if regulators indicate that the risks underlying the securities are adequately disclosed, more investors would feel comfortable owning them. Second, depending on how insurance and banking regulators classify the securities, their owners will receive more or less favorable treatment with respect to taxes and capital requirements. A favorable tax ruling on a particular mortgage-backed structure known as "REMICs" made it a preferred alternative for many issuers and investors in that market.

PROSPECTS

The potential scale of the ILS market is substantial. Under conservative assumptions, domestic U.S. ILS issuance could reach $10 billion per year within the next decade. The current scale of the U.S. property/casualty market offers a rough sense of the potential markets for ILSs. For example, in 1998 net written premiums were $48 billion for multiple peril insurance, $135 billion for commercial and personal automobile insurance, $23 billion for workers' compensation, and $64 billion for all other lines.

If over the next decade securitizations grew to 5% of multiple peril, 2% of automotive, 1% of workers' compensation, and 2% for all other lines (including the longer tailed liability lines), they would total $6.6 billion assuming no growth in direct premium volumes. Annual premium growth of 3–4% over the next ten years would bring this to between $9–10 billion in the United States alone, or nearly five times the recent $2 billion annual pace of issuance. Thus, while still a relatively small piece of the overall insurance market, it seems quite plausible that ILSs will grow to become an important risk-financing tool.

An interesting question is the extent to which these securities will create new financing possibilities, as opposed to substituting for more traditional insurance and reinsurance financing. If securitization starts to replace traditional insurance financing, insurers and reinsurers will need to either develop expertise in a particular area—be it ILS structuring, risk assessment, or sales and distribution—or face the prospect of declining market share and obsolescence.

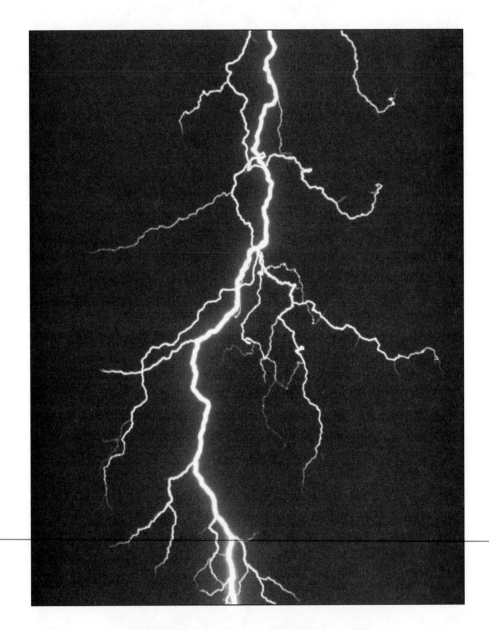

"Weathermen were put on this earth
to make economists look good."

11

Weather Risk Management

PRAKASH SHIMPI AND SCOTT TURNER

It seems rather trivial to say so, but the weather affects us all. There are those of us who stay in the warm indoors on a cold winter's night instead of heading out to the movies. And then there are major corporations whose earnings rise or fall depending on weather conditions. So far, all we have been able to do is shrug our shoulders and complain about the weather when it bothers us, and enjoy it when it does not. Those days are over.

Until recently, companies either retained their weather risks or tried to hedge them with financial or commodity products. Now a growing part of the economy can face weather risk head-on. For many companies, weather is a major influence on earnings volatility. Today, tools and techniques are available to address the variety of ways in which weather can affect earnings, allowing a company to transfer weather-related earnings volatility off its books. As we saw in Chapter 1, the best companies are able to manage their earnings volatility.

Although practitioners are already looking at other types of weather risks such as rainfall, snowfall, water flow and humidity, the weather derivative market covers predominately temperature risk. As we stated in Chapter 5, weather risk management is an example of the use of capital markets techniques to expand the limits of insurability. In this chapter we will examine in detail tools to manage exposure to temperature variations.

It is difficult to get an estimate of the size of the over-the-counter (OTC) market that has developed since weather derivatives were first traded in 1996. One recent estimate suggests that as much as $3 billion in transactions has already been executed.[1] How large is the market likely to get? One figure reported is $70 to $100 billion.[2] However, the best estimates simply say "very large." The U.S. Department of Energy estimates that roughly $1 trillion of the $7 trillion U.S. economy is subject to weather risk. Even if a small fraction of that risk is actively manageable, it indicates that the potential market is very large indeed.

To date, the U.S. is the dominant market for weather derivatives. However, a handful of transactions have been done in Europe and there is growing interest in Asia and Latin America as well.

A growing number of players, notably major energy companies and (re)insurance companies, have made a strong commitment to this market. Intuition tells us that energy companies are affected significantly by the weather, and are therefore natural participants in the market. The interest of the insurance industry is not as obvious, so we shall spend some time in this chapter discussing it.

Shareholders, financial analysts and rating agencies are aware that weather has an impact on corporate earnings. In response, CFOs, treasurers and risk managers may find it necessary to measure this impact and address it. This requires the quantitative and qualitative analysis described in Chapter 4 on risk mapping. The logical first step is to analyze historical revenues against historical meteorological data and establish a connection. Once the risk is understood, steps can be taken to manage weather-related earnings volatility.

Currently, the OTC market consists primarily of customized products that meet the specific needs of each buyer. Standardized products, however, are appearing on the exchanges. This risk is usually managed through a weather derivative. However, coverage can also be structured as insurance and reinsurance policies.

The Development of a New Market

Weather derivatives are an example of the fourth degree of integration (Chapter 5): Beyond the desire of a corporation to manage its risks, the markets need to be ready to accept these risks.

Deregulation of the energy industry was a major driver behind the first trades. Electric utilities, for example, now have both regulated and unregulated businesses. Without going through the technical distinctions between each business, it is sufficient to recognize that each carries its own set of risks.

Ultimately, these companies deal in electricity, from its generation to its delivery. There are a variety of ways to generate electricity. The cost of generation is a factor in the price of electricity all through the delivery chain. Conventionally, the energy industry has hedged the price risk related to the physical commodities used in generation such as coal, heating oil and natural gas. However, hydroelectricity, wind power, solar energy and nuclear plants generate electricity without using these physical commodities, and therefore these producers cannot hedge price risk the same way. It also means that the price of electricity is not as strongly correlated to the price of physical commodities as one might need for an effective hedge. More recently, contracts based directly on electricity price have emerged in the market. But price hedges are only part of the story.

For a utility or an energy company, profitability is also strongly dependent on the moment-to-moment supply and demand dynamics of electricity. A hot summer increases the demand for electricity, possibly beyond the supply available. Unlike physical commodities such as natural gas, electricity cannot be stored for a sunny day. It is consumed as it is generated. The volume of energy demand (and consequently the supply) is therefore a major risk exposure. Weather derivatives evolved as a response to the exposure of energy companies to fluctuations in demand volume.

Initially, transactions were done bilaterally between utility companies. Subsequently insurers and reinsurers broadened the market. The growing number of participants in this market now includes other players that have recognized that they, too, have exposure to weather risk, for example the agriculture sector, tourism industry, beverage producers and municipalities.

IMPACT OF WEATHER ON CORPORATE EARNINGS

The energy industry, utilities in particular, has the clearest exposure to unexpected weather conditions. Through sheer necessity, they have been pioneers in the development of the weather derivatives market. As we indicated above, demand volume is affected by weather; a cooler-than-expected summer or a warmer-than-expected winter will reduce demand and lead to a reduction in revenues for a local utility company.

The impact of weather outside the energy industry is usually just as clear, but sometimes not. Consider, for example, a large manufacturer in the Midwest. It has a contract that allows its power supplier to interrupt its electricity supply in peak periods. A few isolated plant closedowns might be manageable. But a prolonged heat wave could cut into profitability. Although the hedger in this case is the manufacturer, the underlying risk is the same as that of the power supplier (although with the opposite position), i.e. the temperature. The manufacturer will buy a hedge, say an option, that pays when the number of very hot days is greater than some threshold number.

Another example is a theme park in New Jersey. It relies on good summer weather to bring in the crowds. Rainy days are costly, and can cut revenues by $100,000 per day. Excessive humidity during summer can also cut attendance, but perhaps affecting revenues only by $50,000 per day. Here, part of the risk can be managed by purchasing an option that pays up to $100,000 per rainy day during the period. The other part of the risk can be managed by purchasing an option that pays $50,000 per humid day. As we learned in Chapter 6, there may be an opportunity to combine these two options into a basket option, thereby fine-tuning both structure and cost of the option.

It is not difficult to come up with more examples. But of the two examples above, only one so far has developed into an active market—the temperature-related hedge. For the rest of this chapter, we focus on the impact of temperature risk on an energy producer to discuss alternative hedging structures. The first step, then, is to develop an understanding of the technical features of this weather risk.

CHARACTERISTICS OF WEATHER RISK

Weather risk is the uncertainty in corporate earnings and cashflows caused by uncertainty in the weather.

The revenue generated by a company from the sale of a good is the product of the price of the good and the volume sold. Earnings volatility can therefore arise from volatility in both the good's price and in the volume of sales. Weather derivatives focus on managing the exposure to volume risk. As mentioned above, the profitability of an energy company is strongly dependent on the moment-to-moment supply and demand dynamics of electricity. Other companies are also recognizing that they have weather-related exposures that are more strongly correlated to the volume of electricity consumed than to its price. Of course at some point, a significant change in volume will also affect the price—thereby making risk management all the more challenging.

Even in these early days of the weather risk management market, some characteristics of weather risk have emerged that can help us understand its nature:

- **Variety of measures:** The first thing to recognize is that there are many aspects of weather, such as temperature, humidity, rainfall, snowfall or wind speed. In any one of these categories, there are different ways to measure the weather. For example with temperature, one could select the average temperature over a certain number of days, or the minimum and maximum temperatures during a defined period. The market has embraced the concept of a "degree-day," which we will describe in greater detail below.

- **No physical markets:** Although some methods of generating electricity utilize physical commodities, electricity itself is not a physical commodity. It cannot be stored for a sunny day, rainy day, cold day or any other type of day. And much as we wish, we cannot take delivery of two weeks of Cancun weather in Chicago in February.

- **Local geographic exposure:** The impact of weather on electricity demand depends on specific local conditions. There is no benchmark location that will serve as a proxy for all exposures. The basis risk in using such a benchmark would be so large as to make any hedge ineffective.

- **Time-specific exposure:** Moment-by-moment changes in weather affect electricity demand. Risk exposure is therefore a combination of high-frequency, low-severity weather fluctuations over an expected norm, and low-frequency, high-severity peak (or freak) weather conditions.

- **User-specific exposure:** Weather risk does not affect everyone the same way. This feature helps create an active market of natural buyers and sellers.

- **No moral hazard:** Contrary to science fiction movies, the weather truly is beyond the control of any individual. It cannot be influenced or manipulated, and therefore cannot be controlled by any group of countries or manufacturers.

- **Data availability:** A variety of weather information is available for hundreds of local sites in most of the developed world. The data is usually collected by a local government agency and is generally available to anyone who wants it, although recently some countries have started to charge commercial rates for access to and use of the data. The challenge is to discover which components of weather drive earnings volatility. Chances are there is ample data to do so, and to support a liquid derivatives market.
- **Difficult to forecast:** Weathermen were put on this earth to make economists look good.

UNDERSTANDING DEGREE-DAYS

The earnings of most energy companies correlate well with how far the temperature is from a comfortable level on a day-to-day basis. Depending on how far the temperature is from that level, the electricity demand can be higher or lower, affecting profitability. To capture this risk exposure to daily average temperature, the concept of a degree-day emerged and is now the standard measure for the bulk of the transactions. It is a fairly straightforward measure and is defined below.

A **degree-day (DD)** is a unit of measure in a weather derivative contract. Premiums, strikes and limits are expressed in DD. Each DD's value is negotiated between buyer and seller, as are the premium and limit. For example, a buyer may seek to purchase a contract with 300 DD in limit, with each DD worth $50,000 (the value of each DD is the "**tick**"). This creates a potential recovery of $15 million, i.e. 300 DD × $50,000 per DD = $15 million maximum cover.

An **energy degree-day (EDD)** is one degree of difference in average daily temperature above or below 65°F. Historically in the U.S., 65°F has been the temperature at which furnaces would be switched on, and is taken by the utility industry to be the temperature that represents optimum human comfort. The assumption today is that most households will turn on their air conditioners if the temperature goes above 65°F and turn on their heaters if it falls below 65°F. Temperatures other than 65°F have been used in the U.S., but these are exceptions. The benchmark need not be 65°F in other countries. For example, 18°C has been used in Europe.

This leads naturally to the definition of two other terms that are part of the standard vocabulary of the weather derivatives market. When a day's average temperature is less than 65°F, the degree-day difference is referred to in terms of **heating degree-day (HDD)**. When a day's average temperature is greater than 65°F, the degree-day difference is referred to in terms of **cooling degree-day (CDD)**. The terminology is natural because in low temperatures, the heating comes on, hence HDD, and in high temperatures, the cooling comes on, hence CDD.

In a contract, one would define for any single day:

Daily HDD = Maximum of (0, 65°F − daily average temperature)
Daily CDD = Maximum of (0, daily average temperature − 65°F)

A day with average temperature of 41°F has 24 HDD and 0 CDD. Likewise, a day with an average temperature of 72°F has 7 CDD and 0 HDD.

Over any period, the EDD is the absolute number of degrees that the average temperature has been above and below 65°F (i.e. the absolute sum of HDD and CDD), reflecting the total opportunity for comfort-related energy sales. For the two days in the illustration above, the EDD is 31, which is the sum of 7 CDD and 24 HDD.

The **strike** for an option is an agreed-upon number of DD (either HDD, CDD or EDD) that triggers the option. The buyer is paid on the difference between the strike and the actual number of DD in the period.

The **limit** in a transaction is the maximum number of DD covered. As we saw in the example above, this effectively limits the maximum dollar payout possible in the transaction.

TRANSACTION STRUCTURES

We now have sufficient knowledge to look at some transaction structures. Although we will use examples of DD-based contracts, the basic structures are common in other derivative markets and are therefore likely to be just as valid for other weather-related risks such as rainfall and humidity.

Swaps and options are the building blocks of these structures. Combinations of these building blocks create more exotic structures such as collars, strangles, baskets and knock-ins. We look at a small selection of these structures below.

Degree-Day Floor or Cap

The most common covers are floors and caps. In a DD cap contract, the buyer is paid when the number of DD in a period is above the strike. In a DD floor option, the buyer is paid when the number of DD is below the strike.

An energy producer has lower sales, and hence lower profits, in a mild winter. It wants to buy an option to protect itself against this risk. Here, the producer runs the risk that the heating may be on for fewer days than expected. It needs to make up for lost operating revenue when the number of HDD is low. Therefore, the appropriate contract is an HDD floor option. Figure 11.1 shows the familiar option payoff diagram. The company establishes a minimum revenue stream while maintaining all of the upside potential. Of course, a premium has to be paid to purchase this option.

Box 11.1 sets out the terms of the floor. The energy producer supplying to the New York/La Guardia area calculates that the typical number of HDD during the option period from November to March is 6350, with a historical standard deviation of 1300. Its models show that the marginal revenue lost for each drop in HDD is $7500, which is the value used for the tick. Protection is sought for half a standard deviation variation from the mean HDD. This establishes the strike level of 5700 HDD. The maximum

Box 11.1   Degree-day floor option.

Location	New York/La Guardia	
Period	November 1 to March 31	
Tick	$7500 per HDD	
HDD mean	6350	
HDD standard deviation	1300	
HDD strike	5700	(= Mean − 0.5 x standard deviation)
Coverage limit	$6 million	
HDD limit	800	(= Coverage limit ÷ tick)
Premium	$1.5 million	(= 25% Rate on limit)

Figure 11.1 Heating degree-day floor option.

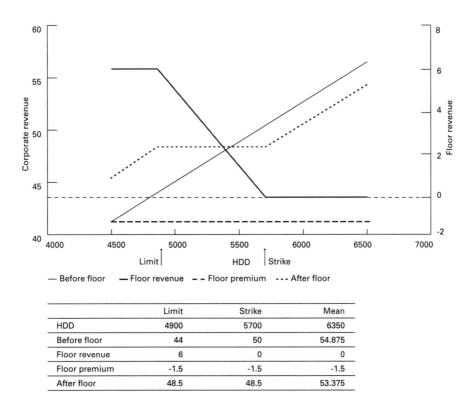

	Limit	Strike	Mean
HDD	4900	5700	6350
Before floor	44	50	54.875
Floor revenue	6	0	0
Floor premium	-1.5	-1.5	-1.5
After floor	48.5	48.5	53.375

payable under the cover is the limit of $6 million, which translates to 800 HDD. If the total HDD during the option period is 5300, the option pays off 400 HDD, or $3 million.

The floor option premium for this level of protection ranges between about 5% to 30% of the limit. In this example, if the premium is 25% of the limit, then the cost is $1.5 million.

A cap is a mirror image of the floor, with the cap paying off in colder weather.

Degree-Day Collar

A collar combines the purchase of a floor and the sale of a cap (or the sale of a floor and purchase of a cap), accomplishing two things. First, it reduces the cash outlay, since some of the premium received from the sale of the cap reduces the premium that has to be paid to buy the floor. Second, it limits both the downside and the upside revenue potential.

Continuing the example above, the energy producer makes a profit if the weather is unusually cold. It is willing to sell some of that profit in order to pay for the downside protection. It decides to sell a cap that pays if greater than half a standard deviation of HDD occur. It uses the cap premium to purchase the same floor as before. The structure it selects is symmetrical, with the same limits applying to both the floor and cap parts of the collar. Box 11.2 sets out the terms, and Figure 11.2 shows the payoff diagram for the collar. If the structure is designed so that the prices of both pieces of the collar are the same, then the net cost to the hedger is $0. Such a structure is known as a "costless collar."

If the total HDD during the option period is 4900, then the collar pays the purchaser the limit of 800 HDD, or $6 million. On the other hand, if the total HDD is 7800, then the purchaser has to pay out the limit of 800 HDD, or $6 million. If the total HDD is anywhere between 5700 and 7000, the purchaser receives nothing.

Degree-Day Basket Option

Weather affects each local area differently. Hedges should therefore reflect these differences as well. A significant number of transactions that have been executed specify a number of locations in the same basket option. The hedge pays off when the sum of the HDD from all the locations crosses the strike.

Box 11.2   Degree-day collar.

Location	New York/La Guardia	
Period	November 1 to March 31	
Tick	$7500 per HDD	
HDD mean	6350	
HDD standard deviation	1300	
HDD low strike	5700	(= Mean – 0.5 x standard deviation)
HDD high strike	7000	(= Mean + 0.5 x standard deviation)
Coverage limit	$6 million	
HDD limit	800	(= Coverage limit ÷ tick)
Premium	$0	

Figure 11.2   Heating degree-day collar.

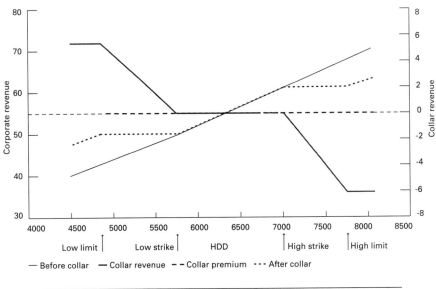

	Low limit	Low strike	Mean	High strike	High limit
HDD	4900	5700	6350	7000	7800
Before collar	44	50	54.875	59.75	65.75
Collar revenue	6	0	0	0	-6
Collar premium	0	0	0	0	0
After collar	50	50	54.875	59.75	59.75

If our energy producer also supplied Newark, New York/Central Park and Boston, then a basket option such as the one illustrated in Box 11.3 may be appropriate. The sums of the HDD means and standard deviations for each location are used to specify the basket option terms. The basket is essentially a sum of four floor contracts, except that the limit is payable even if the variation comes entirely from one location.[3] For simplicity, we have just made this contract four times larger than the degree-day floor shown earlier. Hence, the payoff diagram has the same shape as Figure 11.1.

Another cost-efficient contract is a strangle, in which a floor and a cap are purchased simultaneously. This structure may be particularly appropriate for multi-year transactions for which forecasts are completely unreliable. Also, strangles protect buyers who suffer economic loss when weather results deviate in either direction from the norm. Since a loss can occur only on

Box 11.3   Degree-day basket floor option.

Location	HDD mean	HDD standard deviation
New York/La Guardia	6350	1300
New York/Central Park	6400	1300
Newark, NJ	6200	1250
Boston, MA	6450	1350
Total	25400	5200

Period	November 1 to March 31	
Tick	$7500 per HDD	
HDD mean	25400	
HDD standard deviation	5200	
HDD strike	22800	(= Mean – 0.5 x standard deviation)
Coverage limit	$24 million	
HDD limit	800	(= Coverage limit ÷ tick)
Premium	$6 million	(= 25% Rate on limit)

either the floor or cap side for any given period, the premium for the strangle can be significantly less than the sum of the individual floor and cap premiums.

Degree-Day Compound Option

The final example that we will show is a compound option, or an option to enter into an option. In such a structure, the purchaser has the right to enter into a degree-day cap or floor at some later date within the contract period. The purchaser pays the compound option premium immediately. If it exercises the option and enters into the cap or floor, it then pays that option premium. If it does not exercise the option, then no further payments are due.

Such a contract provides tremendous flexibility to the energy company. For instance, the energy producer may wish to see how the first few months of the heating season go before committing to a floor option.

Box 11.4 sets out the terms of such an option. The compound option premium is $0.11 million. If the purchaser decides to exercise that option, it pays a further $0.8 million to enter into the floor option. Notice that in

Box 11.4 Degree-day compound option.

Location	Philadelphia, PA
First option expiration	December 31
First option premium	$0.11 million
Second option type	Floor option
Period	November 1 to March 31
Tick	$10000 per HDD
HDD mean	4000
HDD standard deviation	330
HDD strike	3800 (= Mean – 0.6 x standard deviation)
Coverage limit	$4 million
HDD limit	400 (= Coverage limit ÷ tick)
Premium	$0.8 million (= 20% Rate on limit)

this example, the HDD in the underlying floor option are calculated for the entire HDD period from November to March.

DATA AND PRICING[4]

The ready availability of data in the U.S. has aided the market's expansion tremendously by providing common data for the assessment of risk magnitude and frequency. More than 1000 data collection sites nationwide are monitored by the National Climatic Data Center, an independent government source. Weather data collected includes: maximum and minimum temperature, dew point, precipitation, snow and ice depth, barometric pressure, and wind speed. Such reliable primary sources of weather data provide up-to-the-hour, computerized measurements. Their historical banks of data sometimes extend as far back as the 19th century, and typically at least 25 years. Data in other developed countries is also extensive and of high quality, which makes the development of those markets inevitable.

Given the abundance of data, one might expect that pricing would be straightforward. Indeed, weather derivative products are priced using both an analysis of historic weather trends and a probabilistic analysis of future events.

As yet, however, there is no uniform approach to pricing temperature transactions. There seem to be two camps, the traders and the (re)insurers. Each is active in a different sector of the market, and therefore analyzes the data differently. Typically, the traders focus on a shorter historical period, usually ten years. Reinsurers and insurers tend to look at longer periods. For both, the actual period used to determine the final price depends on the specifics of a transaction. Below are examples of HDD results for two different locations for the November through March period, each using a different pricing approach.

There is no discernable trend in the Charleston, WV, data (Figure 11.3). While there is volatility from year to year, there is no movement towards a higher or lower HDD level. In this case, the tendency would be to use as much data as available in the pricing (for example 50 years) to capture all relevant information.

In contrast, the Las Vegas, NV, data illustrates a situation where there appears to be a trend (Figure 11.4). Dependent upon the degree of trend

Figure 11.3   HDD for Charleston, WV.

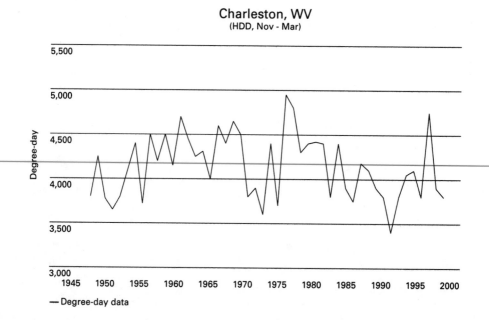

observed and the confidence with which the trend is expected to continue, a shorter period of time would be used (i.e. 5 to 25 years).

The final price is determined by more than the apparent existence, or absence, of a trend. These factors include movement of the measurement station, seasonal climatic events (e.g. El Niño, La Niña and the Clipper Effect), the period to be covered (e.g. the number of months, single or multi-year contract), and available forecasts.

As the market grows, both data analysis and pricing technology are likely to see rapid development akin to that in the financial derivatives market. One step in that direction was the recent announcement to develop such technology jointly by two companies serving very different industries. One provides satellite weather data and forecast information to the energy and agriculture industries, and the other has expertise in risk assessment and catastrophe modeling for the insurance and reinsurance industries.

Figure 11.4   HDD for Las Vegas, NV.

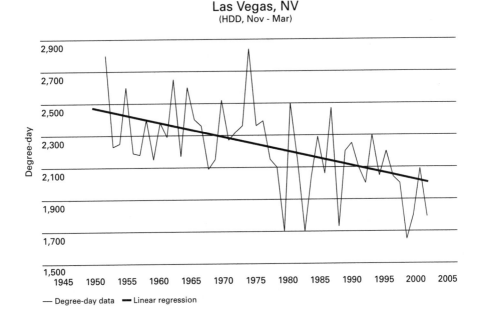

MARKET PARTICIPANTS

The major players in this market are large power companies with significant power marketing operations and a number of regional utilities. As discussed earlier, they have a natural role in this marketplace. These companies have existing positions in weather risk. They are net sellers of the risk, and the market has developed so that other participants with opposite positions are natural buyers. Non-energy corporations are recognizing their weather exposure, and are similarly motivated to come to the market to hedge. By and large, their position is opposite to the energy companies, which makes for a good trading market. At this point, however, the risk management needs of the energy companies exceed that provided by the hedging activity of non-energy companies.

A very small number of investment banks have entered the market to facilitate trading between counterparties. However, banks do not have natural exposure to weather and they do not have an appetite to keep a significant amount of such risk on their books. They do not have as much to offer this market as they do, for example, in hedging financial risks.

A growing number of (re)insurance companies are now strong participants. Unlike the banks, the insurance industry does have risk exposure to weather, and is accustomed to keeping risks on its books.

To fulfill their roles as risk capital providers, some (re)insurers have identified demand outside the traditional insurance market, and are applying their knowledge of hazard risk analysis to structure flexible and appropriately priced weather products. Some (re)insurers are committing large blocks of capacity to absorb weather risk. The insurance industry's participation serves to broaden the market and make it more liquid.

Reinsurers are well positioned to provide risk-bearing capital to offset weather risks. The industry was the first to use historical data to try to predict the future through probability and statistical analyses. Its core competency is the risk management of hazardous events through the provision of capital on a contingent basis to clients, thus enabling them to bear risk. *Weather risk is a natural extension of what the insurance industry is already doing.*

Many insurers and reinsurers have already invested in derivatives operations to develop the new integrated products we discussed in Chapter 5. This technology is now being applied to weather risks.

Expanding the Weather Market

In the actively traded market, many deals have closed for limits from half a million dollars up to $6 million. Deals are frequently written on a short-term basis, with some covering "precipitation in May" or the "snowfall in the second week of November." They make weather risk management more accessible to corporations. The energy brokers and traders are able to execute such transactions efficiently.

However, for companies looking for long-term management of weather risk and high limits of coverage on an annual or multi-year basis, such coverage is generally available only from large net capacity providers such as (re)insurers. Indeed, trading houses have found the participation of (re)insurers helps complete very large transactions, adding liquidity and capacity to the market.

Markets outside the U.S., primarily in Europe and Japan, are starting activity and are poised for significant growth as well.

The exchanges, absent in the first phase of the market development, are about to launch their products. The Chicago Mercantile Exchange (CME) has announced that it will be launching HDD and CDD futures and options on futures contracts based on its HDD/CDD Index.[5] If they are successful, other exchange-traded products are sure to follow.

Part III
The Future

"Efficiency and strategic reasons are
the main incentives."

12

Global Outlook

ESTHER BAUER AND KAI-UWE SCHANZ

Apart from the popularity of the captive concept in industrialized countries, the ART market is still in its formative stages. Against an international backdrop of greater emphasis on maximizing shareholder value, as well as the convergence of banks, insurance companies and capital markets, risk management will increasingly take a holistic approach. In the medium term we can therefore expect to see a sharp rise in demand for the various ART solutions and their eventual breakthrough into the market. They will not replace traditional commercial insurance covers; rather, they will supplement them in areas where traditional covers do not offer efficient solutions.

Important factors influencing the expansion of ART solutions include risk management culture, the importance of the capital market for corporate financing, and industrial structure. These vary significantly across the globe. The more important a country's capital market is for corporate financing in its national economy, the more influence institutional investors have, and the more important the shareholder value principle is for companies (Figures 12.1 and 12.2). In what follows we shall discuss the most important driving forces and hurdles to ART solutions in different regions, and provide estimates for their growth potential.

Excerpted from *sigma 2* (1999).

**Figure 12.1   The importance of the capital market for corporate financing:
Market capitalization in % of GDP.**

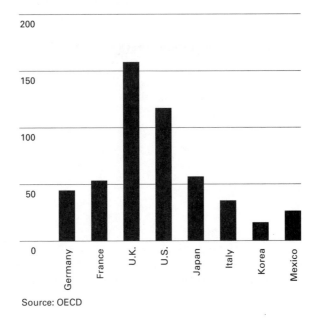

Source: OECD

UNITED STATES

The United States has taken a leading role in the area of alternative risk financing solutions. Different forms of self-insurance have steadily gained importance in the last 20 years, while over the same period the premium volume of traditional commercial insurance as a share of gross domestic product (GDP) has stagnated (Figure 12.3). Self-insurance, with an estimated volume of $128 billion, is already almost as important as traditional commercial insurance at $158 billion.[1] Problems in the area of liability insurance (such as product liability, workers' compensation and environmental liability) have repeatedly triggered a search for alternative solutions. Although traditional covers are available at very favorable

Figure 12.2   The importance of the capital market for corporate financing: Equity ownership.

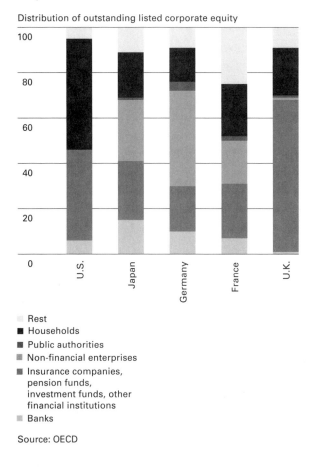

Distribution of outstanding listed corporate equity

Rest
Households
Public authorities
Non-financial enterprises
Insurance companies,
pension funds,
investment funds, other
financial institutions
Banks

Source: OECD

rates in the current insurance cycle, the alternative market is enjoying dynamic growth.

Although the formation of new captives has slowed, their use continues to grow. Mid- and small-sized companies are increasingly exploiting the possibilities of rent-a-captives, while other existing captives are being used for a broader range of purposes. Efficiency and strategic reasons are the main incentives. As offshore locations lose some of their attraction as tax havens, more captives are being formed in the U.S. A number of U.S. states have

Figure 12.3   Commercial insurance in the United States.

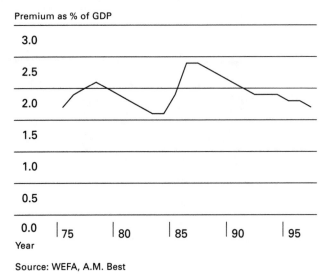

Premium as % of GDP

Source: WEFA, A.M. Best

established themselves as captive domiciles by providing attractive regulatory environments.

Both the increasing importance of the capital markets in corporate financing, and the integration of risk management tasks within companies, promise enormous potential for alternative risk transfer solutions. This is especially so for finite risk solutions, which combine traditional risk transfer with alternative risk financing mechanisms. It is becoming increasingly important to minimize the earnings uncertainty that arises from risks unrelated to a company's core business, and for which traditional covers are not available. Simply disclosing these risks is not enough to satisfy investors.[2]

Although the risk management culture in the U.S. is comparatively advanced, holistic risk management is still in its infancy. A survey conducted by the Risk and Insurance Management Society (RIMS) confirms that although there is much interest in integrated risk management, it still does not play a significant role in the formulation of risk financing programs.[3] Activities to date in this area have been conducted by only a handful of large organizations.

Most insurance securitization transactions concluded so far deal with U.S. earthquake or storm risk. Insurance derivatives have been traded only in Chicago and Bermuda, and the electronic exchange CATEX is licensed for business in New York and Bermuda. At present, the main purpose of these initiatives is to expand reinsurance capacity. In the medium term we can expect companies increasingly to transfer their risks directly to the capital markets. The challenge is to identify a portfolio of risks for an individual company that investors can understand and assess, increasing their willingness to invest.

EUROPE

The importance of alternative risk financing solutions varies considerably across Europe. In the U.K. their development is relatively advanced, while in continental Europe they are still in their infancy. This distinction applies less to the world's biggest industrial and service companies.[4] Because they face intense global competitive pressure, these companies have similar risk management practices wherever they are domiciled.

The main differences from the U.S. market include a lesser importance of the capital markets for corporate financing, less shareholder pressure and conservative balance sheet practices that permit the use of hidden reserves. In the medium term, Europe is likely to experience significant growth for ART solutions. The European regulatory and tax environment and accounting principles are more favorable to innovation in alternative risk transfer than in the U.S.

The growth potential for captives is less clear: Low penetration by captives in many European countries implies that there is still room for growth. Indeed, the number of captive domiciles continues to increase. Nonetheless, deregulation of insurance markets has not yet triggered the expected boom in captives. With more flexible structuring of insurance tariffs, in some cases there is no longer even any need for a captive. In the U.K., the market is showing signs of saturation. The continuous reduction of tax incentives will dampen captive growth in future. As the profits of captives are increasingly being taxed by their home countries, the tax-free creation of reserves in the captive domiciles is becoming increasingly difficult.

Demand for finite solutions and integrated covers for different types of risks should be boosted above all by a greater focus on the concept of shareholder value and the change this brings to the risk management culture. The introduction of the euro has created a single capital market in Europe that is second in size only to that of the U.S. The European capital market is therefore likely to become more transparent and more liquid, with greater product diversity and a more prominent role for corporate financing. We can already observe a trend toward a reduction in cross-shareholdings between industrial, insurance and banking groups. The introduction of the euro will intensify the competitive pressure that has already been unleashed by the deregulation of many markets. Further deregulation is expected in sectors that have traditionally been heavily regulated (telecommunications, energy, health care).

European countries should increasingly fall in line with international accounting standards that make it more difficult to form hidden reserves and require a more transparent disclosure of a company's financial status.

ASIA

Alternative forms of risk transfer for corporate clients are still in the early stages in Asia. This slow development compared with other regions can be attributed to the close interdependencies between industrial companies and property and casualty insurers, as well as the relatively underdeveloped risk management culture.

Captive insurers owned by a company do not play a significant role in Asia, except in Australia, for the reasons given. Even in Japan, where the technical and physical standards are very high, the function of risk management within organizations remains very underdeveloped and tends to be considered an administrative task. Another reason is the relationships between industrial companies and property and casualty insurers mentioned above. In Japan, for example, the four biggest non-life insurers, whose market share totals almost 50%, belong to associations known as "Keiretsu." Since a large proportion of commercial insurance is arranged within these groups of companies, the competitive pressure and prospects for (external) ART providers have not been very good to date.

This picture is starting to change. The enduring stagnation in Japan and the economic and financial crisis that has gripped much of Asia have loosened many of the formal and informal networks. Competitive pressure is also increasing as the market opens up more quickly to foreign competitors. Both factors increase the need for corporate risk management to become more professional and cost efficient. In Japan, for example, finance departments are becoming interested in how risk management affects company earnings. This environment will likely provide a boost to captives in the region, especially since Hong Kong is in the process of building itself into a second regional captive centre alongside Singapore.

The foregoing observations largely apply to finite and integrated solutions as well. We are not likely to see an actual breakthrough (especially in the area of prospective finite solutions), since the current risk management practices still encourage traditional risk transfer in many countries. There is likely to be more (short-term) potential in the area of loss portfolio transfers and retrospective excess of loss covers. They may accompany and even accelerate the trend toward restructuring and consolidation now occurring in many parts of Asia.

Transactions that transfer insurance risks to capital market investors have been limited to Japan so far. Against a backdrop of deregulation of cover restrictions in the commercial business, the three biggest Japanese non-life insurers have placed part of their earthquake and storm risks in the capital market. This is intended to create additional capacity for covering a company's natural catastrophe risks. A large Japanese car company has concluded one of the first capital market transactions hedging auto residual value risk. Other companies will likely follow suit.

Latin America

In Latin America, too, alternative risk transfer is still in its infancy. The role of the risk manager—if there is one at all—has so far been limited to monitoring safety standards and purchasing insurance cover. Apart from the underdeveloped risk management culture, the close interdependencies of holdings between industrial companies and insurers probably play a role, as in Asia. Because the capital markets are immature, the shareholder pressure to maximize earnings is not as pronounced as in the U.S. With extensive economic reform, gradual changes are occurring. Since the start of the '90s many markets have been deregulated and opened to foreign providers, entire branches of the economy have been privatized and monopolies abolished. These developments are forcing companies to address new risks. As a result of the shock of new competition, extensive restructuring is now going on in most industries. The insurance industry itself has been largely deregulated. Prices and insurance conditions have been more or less fully deregulated since the start of the '90s, making greater product diversity possible. Foreign (re)insurers, brokers and risk management consultants are also promoting the transfer of know-how. Changes in the risk landscape due to the region's ongoing integration into the global economy (e.g. liability risks) and the privatization of social security benefits (e.g. workers' compensation insurance) have prompted a new understanding of risk management's role.

Large industrial companies are very interested in captives. Forty-two companies already have a captive abroad. In view of the obvious potential, Panama is attempting to establish itself as a regional location for captives. Regulatory and tax authorities tend to be rather hostile to captives and finite solutions, which they suspect serve mainly as a means of tax avoidance and capital flight. In this spirit, Mexico recently passed a directive imposing a 40% tax on premiums paid to foreign captives.

In the medium term the trend should shift mainly toward higher deductibles and simple multi-line, multi-year covers that combine various traditionally insurable risks.

Capacity in the international (re)insurance markets for earthquake and storm covers is currently adequate. The problem lies rather in the fact that only a small proportion of exposed assets are insured at all. The damage to the national economy, which ultimately has to be covered by the state, can assume enormous proportions, as hurricanes Georges and Mitch recently demonstrated. International and regional development banks, together with governments, are therefore becoming increasingly interested in alternative mechanisms for catastrophe financing. There is also growing interest in seeking protection against weather risks in the agricultural sector. Because farming is a significant source of income in many countries, the El Niño phenomenon and its devastating effect have raised awareness in this area.

"The 'old school' may be uncomfortable
 with this."

13

Prospects and Challenges

DAVID DURBIN

The markets for integrated risk management (IRM) processes and products are in their infancy. As the earlier chapters have discussed, many innovative approaches are being developed. Technical advances in risk assessment and pricing, as well as the desire to improve risk management processes are both important forces underlying the development of new products and markets for IRM. Yet the market development is dependent on much more than the ability to create some new derivative or security; it depends on the needs of customers and their ability to understand and make efficient use of the products. This chapter discusses the prospects and challenges facing IRM market development. It pays particular attention to larger economic and social trends affecting the IRM environment.

There are three parts to the discussion of IRM market development. The first discusses potential catalysts—general trends affecting the risk markets that make IRM processes and products more attractive to users. The second discusses potential barriers. It is fair to say that IRM market growth and development have been modest. There are several reasons for this, including the current soft insurance market and the complexity of many of the IRM products. These challenges will need to be overcome if IRM is to catch on and become a vibrant, sustainable market. The final part discusses prospects and challenges. It also suggests possible market growth paths.

POTENTIAL CATALYSTS FOR IRM GROWTH

The business landscape is changing rapidly for insurers, reinsurers, other financial institutions and their corporate customers. Many of these changes will require corporate managers to change the way they analyze and manage the risks facing their enterprises. This is not only a competitive issue; other stakeholders also have a strong interest in a firm's risk management practices. Shareholders are concerned about the efficient use of their funds and the creation of wealth. Public officials are concerned about protecting consumer, shareholder and (for insurers) policyholder interests. Rating agencies and other financial intermediaries are concerned about the broader risk management abilities of managers. Simply stated, managing volatility—no matter what its source—is an important job for managers. Customers, owners and public officials, among others, are concerned about the processes managers employ.

Broad trends in several areas are important contributors to IRM growth: risk management and professional standards, technological progress, legal and regulatory standards, rating agency scrutiny, education and training, financial market developments, insurance market development and major watershed events. Each of these will be addressed in turn.

Risk Management and Professional Standards

Standardization of risk management practices has the potential to accelerate interest in and adoption of IRM techniques and programs. This standardization has occurred on several fronts. Two specific areas are analytical models and professional standards.

Over the past few years a number of advances have been made in the analytical models that measure various types of risk. These tools have become quite common, especially for financial institutions. Examples include:

- JP Morgan's RiskMetrics, which provides a consistent framework for measuring and managing market risk,
- CreditMetrics, also by JP Morgan, which measures and helps manage credit risk,
- Value-at-risk (VAR) models, commonly used by asset and trading risk managers (also regulators) to measure the probability distribution of potential losses from trades or positions over a set time period (e.g. a day or week),

- Aasset-liability matching (ALM) models, commonly used by insurers to limit interest rate risk by checking whether a firm might be adversely affected by changes in the yield curve or other economic factors, and
- Dynamic financial analysis (DFA) models, used mostly in the insurance industry, which seek, in probabilistic terms, to simulate the effect of alternative underwriting, financing and asset management decisions on a firm's balance sheet.

These approaches generally rely on historical relationships, and attempt to identify the probability distribution of potential outcomes. The models usually include some worst case or maximal possible loss scenarios. Some of the newer DFA models also incorporate macroeconomic projections of the possible business environment. Their strengths lie in identifying situations or trading positions that may lead to unintended adverse results. The firm can then set aside sufficient risk capital to provide a cushion against possible worst cases. The use and sophistication of the models has dramatically increased recently. There are now a number of software and analytical firms offering to install such analytical risk measurement tools. This will increase the penetration of these models, which will encourage firms to think of risk holistically.

It is fair to say that there is still much more work needed in developing rigorous quantitative models, especially those that evaluate multiple risk categories. Problems remain, such as the lack of credible information on historical correlations and on the important high-severity, low-frequency events (i.e. the "tail" of the probability distribution). Advances in modeling or simulating structural changes are also required. However, it is also important to realize that there will always be a role for professional judgment and qualitative assessments. Blind reliance on quantitative approaches neglects the human dimension, organizational structures and corporate culture that are also fundamental to an enterprise's appetite for risk and risk management. These issues are vital to the growth of IRM, and there is a growing awareness of their importance. Indeed, more firms understand that "everyone is a risk manager." This trend is expected to continue.

At the same time as the growth in analytical models, there have been advances in professional standards. Firms have realized that they face many types of risks that may be more efficiently managed together. In some large firms, the job of risk manager has evolved from buying insurance to managing a wide array of insurable and uninsurable risks. Other firms (mostly financial) have in the last several years appointed chief risk officers (CROs) with dedicated responsibility for measuring and managing enterprise-wide risk. In addition, professional associations like the Risk Insurance Managers Society, the Global Association of Risk Professionals, and the U.K.-based Institute of Risk Management have emerged or evolved to promote holistic risk thinking. They provide important sources for promoting standards, sponsoring education and innovation, and communicating ideas. The growth in membership for these organizations is a good sign for the evolution of IRM.

In this effort we believe that the Insurative Model, described in Chapter 3, helps tie these various disciplines and points of view together.

Technological Progress

Several technological developments make it easier to adopt IRM processes and products. Ongoing advances and the declining cost of computing power have made possible sophisticated risk management systems that were unimaginable just 10 to 15 years ago. Computer networks now allow firms to collect, store and distribute information about risk exposures and coverage more quickly and to wider groups. Improved technology has also facilitated the development of increasingly complex derivative securities, which are a useful risk management tool (although these introduce risk that itself must be managed).

Legal and Regulatory Standards

There has been growing awareness and interest by various public authorities in the risk management processes of financial institutions. This is driven in part by their role in protecting the interests of consumers and shareholders. It is also driven by the realization that business systems are much more complex than they have ever been, and that there is a need to implement risk management systems and processes in order to identify and understand better the risks businesses face. Several notable market disruptions and firm failures have also caught the eye of the public officials. The increased attention of officials has and should continue to stimulate interest in IRM.

For example, bank supervisors in the United States (including the Federal Reserve) have begun to look more closely at ways in which banks manage risk. Banks actively involved in trading have balance sheets that fluctuate so widely that evaluating their assets and liabilities at any one point in time is insufficient. To supplement this traditional approach, bank examiners have begun reviewing risk management processes as well as the risk portfolio.

In recent years, auditors, managers, accountants and legislators have devoted increased attention to internal control. The Financial Accounting Standards Board (FASB) has issued guidelines encouraging fuller disclosure by companies of what they perceive to be their most serious risks, how they manage those risks, and who in particular is responsible for risk management.

Groups of regulators and practitioners have issued important guidelines regarding internal controls and the management of risk. Some notable efforts include:

- **The COSO report (1992)**, drafted by U.S. accounting professionals, sets out standards for internal controls that ensure efficient operations, reliable financial reporting, and legal compliance. Among the aspects of internal control it describes in detail are risk assessment and monitoring.

- **The Cadbury report (1992)**, a U.K. document, recommends that directors should confirm in their company's annual report that they have reviewed the effectiveness of corporate internal controls. It has been the foundation for more specific professional standards for boards of directors.

- **The Basle Committee on Banking Supervision**, an international organization, has conducted extensive research and issued guidelines intended to improve risk management standards in banks. Its three most recent reports, issued in October 1998, are *Enhancing Bank Transparency, Operational Risk Management,* and *Framework for Internal Control Systems of Banking Organisations.*

For insurers, there are precedents requiring disclosure of risk exposures to various regulatory authorities. The National Association of Insurance

Commissioners, the oversight organization for the individual state insurance regulators, requires insurers to calculate and disclose their risk-based capital (RBC) measures. These measures, which differ for life and non-life insurers, take into consideration the performance, volatility, composition and growth of both assets and liabilities. Firms with more long-tail insurance liabilities, more volatile growth, and that hold a higher level of equities as a proportion of their invested assets are assessed higher risk-based capital charges. The RBC is compared to a firm's capital position to measure its relative financial health. If capital relative to RBC drops too low, the regulators may take actions such as putting the company under watch, into receivership, or in severe cases into bankruptcy.

Additionally, in the U.S., the state of New York requires life insurers to provide the results of several stress tests on their asset and liability portfolios. In Canada, effective January 1, 1999, property and casualty insurers must conduct "dynamic capital adequacy testing," which forecasts an insurer's financial condition through plausible adverse scenarios. This variant of DFA requires an insurer to analyze the impact of various events jointly on all its assets and liabilities. Once again, this should encourage holistic thinking and processes.

Rating Agency Scrutiny

Rating agencies play an increasingly important role in today's business environment. Investors, counterparties and business partners look to the agencies to provide important intelligence about the financial strength of organizations. A company can demonstrate that it understands its risk exposures and their correlations by providing the rating agencies with the results of its risk measurement and management models.

There are some important trends to watch for over the next few years. Credit rating agencies may play an important role, especially if they start explicitly taking into consideration whether a firm is using IRM tools and processes. This is not an unlikely event. Consider that, in 1995, Standard and Poor's Insurance Rating Group added to its capital adequacy model a risk charge for mortgage-backed securities. This factor helped crush new issuance as many insurers effectively stopped purchasing these securities because of the potential for downgrades. If a rating agency established similar penalties for not employing integrated risk management, the market would likely take off. In addition, some rating agencies appear to be exploring the use of DFA for rating insurers.

Education and Training

As previously mentioned, there are a growing number of professional risk management organizations, whose mission is to broaden the definition of risk management and to promote education and the exchange of ideas. There has been a significant growth in academic research and writing on risk management. As this newer material makes its way into the academic mainstream over the next several years, the next generation of managers will increasingly be exposed to IRM and financial engineering through their courses of study. There is also a burgeoning conference circuit, where various experts and practitioners extol the virtues of IRM and provide how-to primers. Again, as more of today's and tomorrow's top managers are exposed to IRM concepts and case studies, and as the risk measurement and management tools become more sophisticated yet easier to use and communicate, we expect to see greater interest in exploring and implementing IRM solutions.

The Casualty Actuarial Society in the U.S. has also taken an active role. Part of the curriculum now includes DFA models, which broaden the scope of the actuary's analysis to include not only liability estimation but also the entire balance sheet and the firm's business plans. The actuarial profession must begin to deepen its knowledge of assets, off-balance-sheet risk, capital structures and other factors such as economic cycles, changes in capital markets, and the development of new types of risk transfer products.

Financial Market Developments

Developments in financial markets will play a powerful role in the development of IRM products and solutions. There are a number of important trends:

- The derivatives markets have been a hotbed of innovation. The explosion in the types and use of derivatives is one of the major capital markets events of the late 20th century. Increasingly, firms are able to use these tools to hedge various market, credit and interest-rate risks. The growth in these markets means that they are quite liquid, allowing firms more comfort in taking different positions. At the same time, there has been notable growth in over-the-counter and off-balance-sheet markets, where specialized risks and circumstances might be handled. Growth in these instruments will clearly play a role in IRM market development as it becomes easier to design appropriate market hedges.

- There has been significant development of basket options, which bundle different risks or cash flows. This is fundamental to IRM.

- Insurance-linked securities, described in Chapter 10, provide a new channel through which the capital markets and investors can provide additional capacity to support various liabilities. Catastrophe bonds have become an attractive new asset class, offering risk and returns that are not correlated with many other assets. They also provide access to a much larger capital base than traditionally has been available to support the insurance industry. For example, in the United States as of the end of 1998, there was approximately $333 billion of capital and surplus for the property/casualty insurance industry. There is more than $31 *trillion* available in the capital markets.

- The financial sector is undergoing significant consolidation. A number of large players in financial services are banding together with multiple capabilities and skill sets. Distinctions between distribution, structuring and capital provisions, while still important, are beginning to blur. Similar distinctions between banking and insurance are also slowly eroding. Financial giants such as Citigroup and State Farm now offer a whole portfolio of products and services, and hope to capitalize on cross-selling of insurance, banking and credit products. This will make the provision of IRM products and services easier and more efficient.

Insurance Market Developments

A number of important developments in the insurance markets point to increased interest in IRM. Most of the developments involve product or joint venture announcements; there have only been a few major IRM deals announced. In addition, with top-line growth expected to be quite modest in traditional lines of business (a function of slower economic growth and significant price competition), insurers, reinsurers and brokers are beginning to feel significant expense and cost pressures. These players are all seeking ways to expand revenues and earnings, and the attraction of designing risk transfer and financing programs for previously uninsurable risk classes is powerful. Current market conditions are such that revenue growth is quite difficult without the acquisition of other firms, unless the IRM markets can be developed. Indeed, one of the interesting market developments is that the insurance industry through various IRM-type products may actually be taking risks out of or away from the capital markets.

Combining traditional lines of insurance into multi-line policies is not a new concept. This practice has been in use, especially for commercial lines, for more than 20 years. The development of multi-line and multi-year insurance policies has also been around for awhile. Indeed, most of what is called IRM in the market really refers only to these types of covers. Introducing other risks (mostly financial) into the cover is really quite new and is gradually becoming the standard definition of IRM in the marketplace. At the most extreme is the concept of enterprise-wide risk management, which purports, as the term suggests, to incorporate all risks into a consistent risk management framework. The argument is that by incorporating potentially uncorrelated or negatively correlated risks, the "portfolio effect" will permit companies to manage more efficiently their entire risk profile. Perhaps the ultimate IRM product has recently been introduced into the market. This product, called earnings protection insurance, is being touted as a way to guarantee, almost virtually, smooth earnings. It will be quite interesting to observe the market's acceptance of this product; it certainly is an important development for IRM.

As indicated above, the major insurance brokers, consultants, reinsurers and insurers are all dipping their toes into the IRM market. Since about 1997, there has been a proliferation of IRM product, consulting and software announcements.

Major Watershed Events

Major events or notable failures that focus attention on failed systems or processes often drive market developments. Over the past several years there have been a handful of major corporate failures due to collapses in risk management. These have generally involved trading operations where the extent of positions was unknown, there was misuse of certain derivative securities, or management failed to supervise properly the actions of staff. Examples include Barings Bank, Orange County, Procter and Gamble, Sumitomo Bank and Long Term Capital Management.

Looking to the near future, there are two current events that have the potential to cause major disruptions—the year 2000 computer problem and the conversion to the single currency (euro) in the European Union. Both involve significant changes to computer systems that, if not handled properly, could seriously impair the ability of some firms to function. If such meltdowns occur, it is quite conceivable that there will be greater demand for IRM thinking and solutions as corporations seek to avoid catastrophic events that shut down operations.

Similarly, major events such as a prolonged and serious stock or bond market crash, which remove risk-bearing capital from the markets, will cause firms to look for alternative solutions for their risk management needs. As of the middle of 1999, there certainly appeared to be too much capital in the traditional insurance markets, resulting in significant price competition to retain and attract business. Any major event, such as a market crash or natural catastrophe (as with Hurricane Andrew and the Northridge Earthquake), that removes capital from the insurance markets with a resulting hardening of insurance prices will cause corporations to seek alternative risk transfer and risk management solutions. It was just these sorts of shocks that facilitated the growth of the Bermuda insurance market in the late '80s and early '90s.

Potential Barriers to IRM Development

While there has certainly been a fair amount of press and conference buzz, there have been quite few "true" (i.e. those combining traditional insurance with financial risks) IRM deals. There have been two major reasons for this: corporate governance and culture issues, and pricing (including transactions costs) issues.

Corporate Governance and Culture Issues

As with any new way of thinking or new process, there is very often a resistance to change. Bureaucratic inertia and strong vested interests in the status quo present large barriers. This is certainly the case with IRM, especially as the risks a corporation faces cross functional lines within an organization. In addition, as a new model for risk management that requires corporate finance and traditional insurance acumen, there is a significant educational barrier. Specific issues include:

- **Corporate silo effect:** The age of specialization has spawned insurance and traditional risk managers, treasurers, accountants, financial traders and human resource managers. Each operates within its own sub-unit and historically has had few reasons to communicate with the other units. In many organizations, breaking down these silos is a very difficult task. In extreme cases, introducing IRM may make transparent the inefficiencies of the silos and may even result in job losses. It is natural that resistance to this sort of change will occur.
- **Absence of a coordinated and powerful IRM champion:** It follows from the silo problem that, in order for IRM to be embraced, there needs to be a senior level officer of the company willing to push this concept. The CEO or CFO needs to be actively engaged in this process in order for it to succeed. This requires an innovative individual comfortable with both corporate finance and insurance issues.
- **Technology and education issues:** IRM may require newer and more sophisticated IT systems. It will also require at least some people to have some exposure to and expertise with corporate finance. The

"old school" may be uncomfortable with this. IRM may require centralized information and management systems that may conflict with the notion of decentralized profit centers. This is especially important for larger and more diverse companies. IRM may also be viewed as a cost center.

Barriers to Sale of IRM Products

There are several features of the current insurance and financial market environment that have dampened the demand for IRM products. These stem primarily from the current soft market in insurance and the complexity of understanding and implementing IRM products.

- **Pricing:** Currently, the soft markets for traditional insurance products, driven by excess capital and significant price competition, make IRM products unattractive. Unlike the liability crises in the late '80s, or the high periods of medical inflation of the late '80s and early '90s, corporations can secure insurance for modest prices. There have actually been price decreases in some lines of business over the past few years. Consequently, there is no compelling price need to seek alternative solutions.
- **High transactions costs:** The due diligence required to understand, negotiate and then sell the concept to senior management is significant. With only modest savings (at best) given the current pricing environment, no manager wants to be in the position to have to explain to the board how it had made sense to increase risk retention when now, post-event, they have to pay out $1 million for a fire that could have been covered for $20,000.
- **Product complexity:** IRM products and their pricing can be complicated. Understanding how various triggers work, the correlations between them, and how they affect the distribution of expected losses may not be easy. The amount of coordination and information needed are potential barriers to product implementation.
- **Regulatory and accounting uncertainty:** The regulatory and accounting treatment for IRM products is evolving. It is also a new

framework for public officials. The booking of liabilities and expenses can be subject to differing interpretations. This can affect the attractiveness of IRM.

PROSPECTS AND CHALLENGES

IRM and enterprise-wide risk management are concepts offering great promise. The potential to rethink risk management and reap the benefits of modern portfolio theory, applied across broader categories of liabilities and assets, is appealing. Yet, a variety of cultural and market forces are present that have slowed IRM market penetration. Looking to the future the relevant questions are: Will these barriers diminish, and will IRM become the dominant risk management philosophy and the basis for risk transfer and risk financing products?

The critical challenges for IRM providers lie in making the value of these products more apparent. Currently, the economics of deals are not always favorable, especially given the soft traditional insurance market and high transaction costs. Historically, however, similar conditions have existed with the introduction of new investment and financial risk management tools. The derivatives markets started modestly and then experienced explosive growth. Mortgage-backed securities, developed in the early '80s, needed several years, including the S&L crises, to develop. Now they are an important component of the mortgage markets. The market for insurance-linked securities might develop in a similar fashion, as discussed in Chapter 10. Often people think in terms of an "S" curve for the use and acceptance of new product innovations: a period of slow growth followed by explosive growth and then product maturity. There are a number of reasons to think that this type of growth might be possible for IRM. The most important question is: What would trigger the explosive growth?

History also suggests that hard insurance markets will return, and that the speed of technological progress will increase. A critical issue for IRM market development is timing. If hard markets do not return to insurance within the next 3–5 years, IRM market development will likely be incremental over the next decade. If the hard market returns, and analytical tools advance that permit a simple articulation of the IRM value proposition, then

IRM growth will likely be significant. That is, pricing has to become more attractive and transaction costs have to be reduced. One way to reduce transaction costs will be the commoditization of risk products. Similar to mortgage-backed securities or other asset classes, the development of tools to combine, package and trade bundles of risk will be critical. Liquidity in these markets will also be required.

To win widespread acceptance, the new instruments must find a proper structure or paradigm. Insurance risk can be packaged in a variety of forms. Although each alternative form is merely a different way of dividing the same pool of risk, how the risk is parceled out determines what types of capital providers will find the instruments attractive. Insurance risk packaged as a bond will appeal to a different class of investors than it would if packaged as an option or swap. The choice of structure also has legal, regulatory and tax consequences. Because there is no scientific way to determine which financial product design will prove most popular, underwriters will need to experiment with a variety of structures in order to discover which ones appeal most to capital providers and risk owners.

Economic developments could make specific industries major purchasers of IRM products and services. Financial institutions are themselves more likely to embrace IRM because of shareholder and regulatory pressures. Deregulation in the energy sector may well bolster demand for IRM.

Macroeconomic shocks could be important. Significant declines in equity markets, perhaps accompanied by a rise in interest rates, would affect the amount and cost of capital available to the insurance industry. In the past, such conditions have provided the impetus for product innovations and the restructuring of the market. The liability crises of the '80s helped foster a burgeoning ART and captive market. The major natural catastrophes of the early '90s provided the opportunity for growth in the Bermuda markets. The workers' compensation problems of the late '80s and early '90s gave rise to growth in self-insurance vehicles; it also provided an inroad and lucrative market for managed care companies, which were looking to grow their market shares.

THE SHAPE OF THINGS TO COME

A great deal of IRM research and development activity is underway. This is an exciting time, with the launch of many new products and markets that treat the risks facing firms in more comprehensive and integrated ways. Efficient and better use of capital is the prime motivation. However, these developments are new and are still evolving.

Over the next few years, market and product developments should remain brisk, and while the widespread acceptance and market penetration of IRM remains years into the future, there are some signposts available to provide insights into how the markets might develop. As discussed above, the language of IRM remains elusive and fuzzy. It means different things to different people, although there are (as with this book) a number of ongoing attempts to codify consistent terminology and definitions. As these efforts begin to bear fruit, both suppliers and consumers of IRM products and services will be better able to communicate their needs and product offerings.

At present, the supply side of the IRM markets is quite fragmented. It is useful to segregate IRM suppliers into two segments: (1) IRM processes and (2) IRM risk financing. In the first segment, there are a number of firms offering various risk landscaping services, enterprise-wide software, consulting services, value-at-risk models, and risk-adjusted capital measurement tools. They all focus on thinking about and measuring risk—in all its manifestations—in an integrated fashion.

The second segment takes this one step further and provides risk structuring and risk transfer products that capitalize on the diversification and portfolio effects of risk management. Right now, the IRM process and consulting market is more developed and active than the risk transfer market. In part this is due to the relative newness of IRM risk transfer products. In part it is also due to the current health and state of the world-wide insurance and reinsurance markets, where prices are relatively low and insurance coverage widely available. There is little market demand for innovative products that, in many cases, require up-front investments of time and resources to understand their features and applications. The supply side is much further along than the demand or customer side in terms of product and market development. The demand side remains either quite wary or uninterested in exploring IRM risk transfer. As the economics of IRM products become clearer, and as the products demonstrate their utility under adverse market conditions, the demand for IRM risk transfer products is expected to grow substantially.

There are some additional factors to consider when analyzing the market potential for IRM risk transfer products, especially those that might be labeled second, third and fourth degree integration products. Although the following relate specifically to the U.S. market, they are likely relevant to most industrialized countries:

- There is no reliable information on the total cost of all forms of business risk. Anecdotal information suggests only 10–20% of total risk is insured or actively managed. Thus, there is a great deal of potential for IRM products that include traditionally uninsured risks.
- There are economies of scale in risk management: larger firms have lower costs of risk per dollar of revenue than mid- and small-sized firms.
- The macroeconomic shift from manufacturing to service industries is likely to increase the level of liability risk and its associated costs.
- Finally, economic growth in the U.S. is coming from service- and technology-related firms that also tend to be mid- and small-sized. This should increase the aggregate level of risk in the economy.

As mentioned above, the actual markets for IRM risk transfer have been quite modest. According to a recent joint survey, only about one in ten U.S. firms, generally large, have considered an integrated approach. In total, only about 1% of the firms have actually bound a program. The most frequently considered exposures for integration include property, general liability, foreign exchange and credit risk. Under some conservative assumptions regarding the total proportion of risk included in the bound programs, the size of the IRM risk transfer market in the U.S. for 1998 was probably on the order of $0.5–1 billion in premiums.

If over the next 10–12 years up to 10% of firms embrace an integrated approach for at least some portion of their total risks, and given modest continued growth in the overall economy, the IRM risk transfer market could be as large as $10–12 billion in premiums per year. Note this would imply close to a 25% compound annual growth rate, which is quite robust. Yet, even with this significant growth, the overall IRM market will, absent a major event or series of events, remain a small piece of the overall property/

casualty market (presently in the U.S. at approximately $280 billion in premiums in 1998, growing perhaps to $410 billion by 2010).

The IRM risk transfer markets are likely to be comprised of large and well-capitalized insurers, reinsurers and perhaps investment banks serving large and sophisticated corporate clients with considerable financial expertise or exposures (banks, pharmaceutical companies and insurance companies themselves). It remains to be seen whether mid- and small-sized firms will embrace IRM. Important for the development of those markets will be commodity products, perhaps delivered via the Internet or other e-commerce distribution system. If successful, this market segment has the potential to be many times larger than the IRM markets for large corporations. However, at present, the realization of this market is quite uncertain and, if it happens, will likely be many years into the future.

"At some level these discussions take
on an almost evangelical air..."

14

Migrating to the New Environment

DAVID DURBIN

One of the major goals of this book has been to catalog the emerging risk management paradigm shift. Arguments have been presented about the benefits of integrating risk management, whether it's of the first, second, third or fourth degree. Exciting advances in risk modeling and applications of modern portfolio theory have been presented, and discussions provided about individual products and forces likely to impact overall market development. At some level these discussions take on an almost evangelical air: Adopt integrated risk management and your company or job (if not necessarily your soul) will be "saved" (or at least vastly improved). Yet there remain some very important practical implications to consider. Importantly, we have not yet discussed the steps individuals can take to promote and implement an integrated approach to overall corporate risk management. This chapter outlines some practical guides to these issues.

Chapter 13 provides some insight into several critical barriers to successful integration of corporate risk management. The section on page 241 titled "Corporate Governance and Culture Issues," provides a roadmap for individuals interested in integrating risk management within their firm. To reiterate, the corporate silo effect, absence of a coordinated effort or a powerful IRM champion, technology and education issues, and possible need for centralized information and management systems all present possible impediments to successful IRM implementation. As such, these are the areas that individuals can address in order to promote IRM within their own organizations. Broader forces such as the health and performance of the equity or insurance markets or other important economic developments are almost by definition not amenable to change by individual actions.

GOING FULL BANDWIDTH

In an interesting series of articles and interviews,[1] Scott Lange, former director of risk management for Microsoft, in a phrase appropriate for Microsoft's industry and culture, labeled the process of changing a corporate culture as "Going Full Bandwidth." Lange provides a number of suggestions for inculcating IRM through all levels of an organization. The goal is to remove the corporate silos and enhance knowledge, information and tools important for IRM. Lange specifically recommends that individual managers:

- Recognize the relationship between finance and risk management, and learn the jargon of corporate finance. Issues such as the optimal and efficient use of capital are vitally important for senior management, shareholders and regulators. Speaking the same language as the financial experts will elevate the status of risk management and demonstrate its importance.
- Develop a better sense for the full array of risk financing methods available, including the accounting treatments that may be applicable. As above, this places risk management in the context of financial management.
- Develop better quantitative risk models. As discussed in previous sections of the book, there is a growing demand for risk measurement by various constituents. Experience from the banking and trading industries (VAR models) and insurance industry (risk-based capital and dynamic financial analysis) suggests that information demands will only grow, especially as the financial worlds continue to converge. Better models and information should translate into competitive advantages.
- Broaden their scope. Given the modest but notable trend toward total organizational risk and use of capital market tools for risk financing, there are opportunities for individuals who can solve problems beyond their traditional areas of expertise.
- Be attentive to needs of all customers, be they external or internal. External clients may need risk transfer and financing, but internal members of senior management also look to use the firm's capital in the most efficient manner to enhance shareholder value.

These steps may be fairly obvious, though perhaps difficult to implement. Breaking down corporate silos and bureaucratic processes is never easy. Communication, in a language the listener can understand and identify with, is a powerful tool. Very often specialists, be they traditional corporate risk managers or financial traders, communicate in a code that only their brethren can appreciate. The power of providing a broader perspective to senior managers and other important stakeholders in a language they understand should not be underestimated. This is especially important for discussions about risk assessment, risk measurement and risk financing.

PREPARING FOR THE NEW ENVIRONMENT

There is another, perhaps more practical, dimension to investing in knowledge about IRM sooner rather than later, and developing a common language and corporate philosophy about risk management. While current insurance market conditions make traditional products relatively attractive, these markets are notoriously volatile and cyclical. Familiarity and understanding of IRM will be potentially quite valuable when insurance prices rise and certain types of insurance become less available. Individuals and firms who make investments in corporate infrastructure and human capital will be in a better position to change their risk management programs quickly.

There is a case to be made that, similar to the markets for many asset-backed securities, the entire insurance business system (at least as applied to most large and medium corporate clients) will change from a product orientation to a functional orientation. A recent report[2] stated that, instead of investment banks handling market risk, commercial banks credit risk, and (re)insurers hazard risk, "The financial services industry of the future will have firms that are specialized by function and integrated across risk types: risk brokers for origination and customer service, conduits for underwriting and balance sheet management, integrated investment banks for capital markets risk transfer, and portfolio managers of financial and insurance securities."

The report defines four prerequisites for this transformation to functional specialization:

1. Insurers realize that underwriting techniques can be expanded across risk types. This has already begun.
2. Risk packaging and transfer to the capital markets becomes more common and is applied to different risk types. This has also begun to happen today.
3. Investors appreciate that insurance risk can be an attractive asset class which can help diversify a portfolio and provide attractive risk-adjusted returns that are uncorrelated with other asset classes. Although the volume of transactions has been modest, this appears to be the case with cat bonds and other insurance-linked securities.
4. Corporate finance theory recognizes that certain entities have comparative advantages in retaining risk, enabling firms to move risks off their balance sheets to others who may handle them more efficiently.

Clearly, then, forward-thinking managers need to watch these signposts as leading indicators for the future. They also need think about their own human capital and the structure of their own organizations. In the future, "risk transformers" will likely become more important than product managers, especially for the financial services industry. Successful transformers will have a broader knowledge of the environmental and economic forces affecting an organization's businesses. Technical expertise will still matter; it will just be broader in scope.

Broadening Your Toolbox

Information needs will also continue to evolve and change. Currently, most management information is product-based and not specific enough. There is a need for more sophisticated ways of viewing risk-return relationships across all levels of an organization and across broader risk classes. Individuals who can provide these tools will not only enhance their organization but will also enhance their own value and reputation as well.

There are some other issues that may be in the self-interest of today's specialists. Broadening one's toolbox and developing the ability to speak the financial language of the CEO and large shareholders will likely provide more long-term career and professional growth. With margin pressures, cost efficiency, and short-term earnings expectations driving a lot of business decision-making, managers who can significantly affect a firm's cost structure will have a comparative advantage. By dealing with more than just traditional insurance issues, risk managers can add spice to a profession that is traditionally viewed as boring. The creation of new programs that use shareholder capital more efficiently can overcome the perception that risk management is a cost center and not a profit center.

As mentioned above, quantitative measures of risk are still being developed. Firms also often have an asymmetric view of risk: Corporations will often take $50–$100 million retention on property exposures, but will use financial hedges for exposures as low as $1 million. Risk mapping and measurement will identify this asymmetry, which is also indicative of inefficient use of capital. The development of benchmarks within an organization and the identification of the best practices within an industry will provide useful tools for senior management.

There are a growing number of software vendors and consultants offering risk identification, measurement, and management tools and services. In today's dynamic business environment, analysts and managers need to continuously update and upgrade their skills. With the growth in IRM research, seminars, training programs and trade associations such as GARP and RIMS, IRM is a concept that can only grow in importance. In this environment, skills that are not routinely updated will quickly become obsolete.

It is apparent from the current business and financial markets that innovations do not take long to pass into common use. Markets quickly adopt new tools, processes and products. Recent examples include the Black-Scholes option pricing model, the development of asset-backed securities, and trading in derivatives and futures. Sitting on the sidelines as new markets evolve means missing opportunities. History teaches us that significant economic profits go to market innovators.

When discussing new markets, products or concepts, many business management consultants talk about "first movers," leaders versus followers, or retaining the right to play. While there is some uncertainty about the speed and ultimate market penetration of IRM techniques and products, there are enough signals to suggest that, at the very least, firms need to retain at least the right to play. Taking a wait-and-see attitude may be an appropriate strategy for purchasing a product; it clearly is not appropriate, however, when considering whether to integrate risk management. This implies an investment in the human capital, risk assessment and organizational structure to keep skills current.

THE CHIEF RISK OFFICER

An important development has been the emergence of the chief risk officer (CRO) within a number of firms, mostly in the finance industry. The CRO oversees both the identification and measurement of all risks faced by the firm, and the efficient use of risk capital. Today's CROs have learned mostly through on-the-job training. It is a new concept, and there is no systematic approach or academic program to train for the CRO position. This provides an opportunity for a progressive manager to design an approach suitable to the firm's particular situation. Firms interested in pursuing IRM processes and products would be well served by appointing a CRO. It is important that the person in this position be a senior member of management, preferably reporting directly to the CEO. This develops the necessary authority and sends the right message about the importance of firm-wide risk management. Much like independent auditors or accountants, the CRO should probably not have direct business or revenue responsibility, so as not to create any conflicts of interest. The CRO becomes the champion needed to promote IRM within the firm.

As we indicated throughout this book, risk is not all bad. It cannot be avoided—it must be managed. We have described several ways to do so. More than that, we have presented a framework to articulate the relationship between the variety of risks that a corporation faces and the capital resources it has at its disposal. We believe that the most successful firms and managers will embrace risk in all its dimensions, and manage it as part of their overall business strategy.

Notes

Introduction

1. Quote from N. Rose, *Mathematical Maxims and Minims* (Raleigh NC: Rome Press Inc., 1988).

Chapter 1: Everyone Is a Risk Manager

1. Swiss Re Economic Research & Consulting, "World Insurance in 1997: Booming Life Business, but Stagnating Non-life Business," *sigma 3* (1999): 30.
2. Risk & Insurance Management Society and Ernst & Young LLP, 1998 RIMS Benchmark Survey (New York: Risk & Insurance Management Society, 1999).
3. Firms prefer to finance internally. If external finance is required, they issue the safest security first, i.e. they start with debt, then hybrid securities and, ultimately, equity. See Richard A. Brealey and Stewart C. Myers, *Principles of Corporate Finance,* 5th ed. (New York: McGraw-Hill, 1996) chapter 18.
4. Of course, if the projects are particularly attractive, the firm might choose to borrow money or issue stock to fund them. In that event, it would incur funding costs due to its lack of internally-generated capital.
5. Peter Antunovich and David S. Laster, "Do Investors Mistake a Good Company for a Good Investment?" *Federal Reserve Bank of New York Staff Reports 60* (Jan. 1999).
6. PricewaterhouseCoopers, *Middle Market Barometer 9* (Summer 1998).
7. Steven D'Arcy, "Don't Focus on the Tail—Study the Whole Dog," Presidential Address, American Risk and Insurance Association, Boston, 18 Aug. 1998. D'Arcy mentions the elephant parable in the penultimate paragraph of his speech.

Chapter 3: Integrating Risk Management and Capital Management

1. In effect, Figure 3.1 is a representation of the function, $f\{$firm risk$\}$, since the simulation calculates the capital needed under various outcomes of the firm's risks.
2. The same function, $f\{$risk$\}$, is used for this discussion to denote that there is a functional relationship between a risk and the capital required to cover it. The actual functional relationship between any particular component of firm risk and the capital required to cover it may be different.
3. For example, Brealey and Myers, chapters 16 to 19, discusses dividend policy and capital structure.
4. Franco Modigliani and Merton Miller, "The Cost of Capital, Corporation Finance and the Theory of Investment," *American Economic Review 48* (1958): 261-97. See also Modigliani

and Miller, "Corporation Income Taxes and the Cost of Capital: A Correction," *American Economic Review 53* (1963): 433-43.

5. See any standard corporate finance text, such as Brealey and Myers, for a full treatment of the Modigliani and Miller propositions.

6. Such a premium is reasonable for a catastrophic loss event that has a low probability of occurrence.

7. Note that in standard finance texts, insurance costs are included in the operating expenses, in which case the gross income would be equal to the net operating income of $150. This would make the ROA = ROP = 15%. Replacing ROP with ROA in all the equations in this section would deliver the familiar equations seen in corporate finance textbooks.

8. If we assume that the firm is able to deduct its borrowing costs from its taxes, then that tax shield reduces its effective borrowing cost. See Brealey and Myers, chapter 18, for a full discussion.

9. When we refer to capital resources in this chapter, we use the convention that the "value" refers to the market value of that capital. For example, "equity value" is the market value of a firm's equity. We also use the term "cost" to refer to the percentage cost of a capital resource, based on its market value. For example, "cost of equity" is the cost of equity as a percentage of equity value.

10. Brealey and Myers, chapters 4 and 8, discusses these methods for determining cost of equity.

11. The insurer pays when losses exceed a minimum threshold. In insurance markets, that threshold is known as the attachment point.

12. Credit for this term goes to Judith Prager of Swiss Re New Markets, although, as a lawyer, she will be the first to confess that she did not have this theory in mind at the time.

Chapter 4: Risk Mapping

1. Empirical studies show that companies with high off-balance-sheet risks have to contend with significant discounts on the stock market because the future earnings potential carries a particularly high degree of uncertainty. See Deborah J. Pretty, "The Value Discount for Off-Balance-Sheet Risk," *The Oxford Executive Research Briefing* (Oxford: Templeton College, 1999).

Chapter 5: Converging Markets and Integrated Solutions

1. We use the term "insurance industry" to refer to both insurance and reinsurance companies, and the term "(re)insurer" as a shorthand for "insurers and reinsurers."

2. Excerpted from Swiss Re Economic Research & Consulting, "Alternative Risk Transfer (ART) for Corporations: A Passing Fashion or Risk Management for the 21st Century?" *sigma 2* (1999).

3. For further reading see, for example, Neil A. Doherty, "Financial Innovation in the Management of Catastrophe Risk," *Journal of Applied Corporate Finance 10.3* (Fall 1997) 84-95.

4. Shimpi, "Economics of Insuratives."

5. Swiss Re, *BETA: A Multiline, Multiyear Risk Transfer Product* (Zurich: Swiss Reinsurance Company, 1997).

6. In response to the liability crisis in the United States, the Federal Liability Risk Retention Act of 1986 introduced two alternative mechanisms designed to facilitate access to liability covers: risk-retention groups and purchasing groups. Risk-retention groups are specialized liability insurers with mutual liability. Membership is limited to companies within a certain business sector. Purchasing groups are groupings of companies within the same industry for the purpose of purchasing collective liability insurance cover. The number of risk-retention groups has stagnated at around 70 during the past few years, while the number of purchasing groups has steadily grown to reach 669 at year-end 1998. (Source: *The Risk Retention Reporter,* 12.12 (Dec. 1998).)

7. According to an estimate by Tillinghast-Towers Perrin.

8. In practice a minimum share of some 30% is assumed.

Chapter 6: Multi-Line and Multi-Trigger Products

1. The terms MMP and MTP were introduced in *sigma 2* (1999).

2. See John P. Mello, Jr., "Paradise, or Pipe Dream?" *CFO: The Magazine for Senior Financial Executives* Feb. 1997: 73-75.

3. See Willy Hersberger, *Corporate Risk Financing—The Emergence of a New Market* (Zurich: Swiss Re New Markets, 1998).

4. For example, the need for property and casualty coverage may vary greatly between the oil and petrochemical industry and the telecommunications industry.

5. He defined the oil hedge ratio, H, to be the percentage of the oil-related volatility (250) hedged, and the cat insurance ratio, C, to be the percentage of the cat loss (1000) insured. If EB is the earnings before hedging and insurance, and EA is the earnings after, then:

$$EA = EB + (H \times 250) \times [(-1) \text{ if oil rises, 1 if oil falls}] - (C \times 100)$$
$$+ (C \times 1000) \times [1 \text{ if cat, 0 if no cat}]$$

So for oil rise and cat scenario:

$$EA = 500 + (H \times 250) \times (-1) - (C \times 100) + (C \times 1000)$$

In Strategy 1 when H = 100% and C = 50%, EA = 500 − 250 − 50 + 500 = 700

In Strategy 2 when H = 40% and C = 100%, EA = 500 − 100 − 100 + 1000 = 1300

6. *sigma 2* (1999).

7. Sedgwick Europe Risk Services Limited, New Deals: Alternative Risk Transfer and Insurance in the Capital Markets (Oct. 1997) 10.

Chapter 7: Finite Risk Reinsurance

1. Finite re is already a standard tool for primary insurers. Increasingly, it is also being used by other corporations. In this chapter we refer directly to reinsurers and not (re)insurers, since a reinsurer is the ultimate source of capital for many of these transactions, even when the initial contract is written between a corporation and a primary insurer.

2. These features are not peculiar to finite risk reinsurance. For example, limited liability and profit sharing are also quite common in traditional reinsurance.

3. Of course, this is also true of long-term traditional reinsurance contracts.

4. In this connection, the liability crisis in the U.S. and the rapid increase in insured natural catastrophe losses (in the mid- to late-80s) are particularly noteworthy as precipitating events.

5. Swiss Re Economic Research & Consulting, "U.S.: Consolidation Accompanied by Weak Growth—A Business Challenge in Property and Casualty Insurance," *sigma 1* (1997).

6. A.M. Best Company is an insurance rating agency.

7. For example, liability claims which are reported only after a delay of several years or even decades.

8. See Appendix 7A.

9. In practice, the term "LPT" is understood in several different ways. For example, some providers always assume underwriting risks in LPTs, while some LPTs sold in the past (such as time and distance contracts) included neither underwriting nor timing risks.

10. Unless otherwise noted, the examples in this chapter ignore the reinsurer's margin and other transaction costs.

11. David J. Undis, Peter J. Gakos, Jr., and Timothy Kolojay, *Strategic Risk Financing Tools and Approaches,* Defining Moments in Risk Management: The 1997 RIMS Annual Conference Procedings (New York: Risk Management Society Publishing, Inc., 1997) 11–24.

Chapter 8: Run-Off Solutions

1. See Swiss Re, *The Run-off Phenomenon: Extracting Value from Discontinued Business* (Zurich: Swiss Reinsurance Company, 1998).

2. Kevin Cammack and Mark Hake, *Hanson: "Dirty Deeds Done Dirt Cheap,"* comment (London: Merrill Lynch & Co., 6 Aug. 1998): 2.

Chapter 9: Contingent Capital

1. Bank for International Settlements, "International Banking and Financial Market Developments," *BIS Quarterly Review* (Mar. 1999).

Chapter 10: Insurance-Linked Securities

1. ~~Bermuda allows reinsurance companies to apply for protected cell status that permits the seg-~~ regation of contracts.

2. Expected principal loss is defined as the average of all possible outcomes, weighted by their respective probabilities.

3. For a fuller treatment of this subject, see *Natural Hazard and Event Loss* (Zurich: Swiss Reinsurance Company, 1989).

4. More formally, if the investor earns a return of r* in the event of no catastrophe and (r* − 1) if a catastrophe does occur, then the security has an expected return of $E(r) = q\ (r^* - 1) + (1 - q)\ r^* = r^* - q$, where q is the probability of a catastrophe occurring. The security's

variance of returns, it can be shown, will equal Var(r) = q (1 − q) which, as noted, is an increasing function of q.

5. This calculation assumes that the portfolio of risky securities earns a risk premium of 5%. The results are very similar for other values of the risk premium.

Chapter 11: Weather Risk Management

1. *Business Wire*, June 16, 1999.
2. The *Washington Post* article by Sharon Walsh, "Vulnerable companies bet billions on weather," July 12, 1998.
3. Assuming that the risks are not correlated.
4. See Peter Gakos, "Fooling Mother Nature," *Weather Risk,* special report of Energy & Power Risk Management and Risk, 1999.
5. "Weather Derivatives at the Chicago Mercantile Exchange," *Alternative Insurance Capital 94* (June 1999): 4–6.

Chapter 12: Global Outlook

1. Figures are based on estimates by Sedgwick for 1997.
2. See Pretty (1999).
3. See 1998 RIMS Benchmark Survey.
4. Defined as the 500 biggest industrial and service companies, for example.

Chapter 14: Migrating to the New Environment

1. Scott Lange, "Going Full Bandwidth," *Corporate Risk,* Nov. 1996.
2. Peter Nakada, *New Directions in Risk Management* (Oliver, Wyman & Company).

Contributors

Prakash A. Shimpi, FSA, CFA
Managing Principal (U.S.)
Swiss Re New Markets

Prakash is Managing Principal (U.S.) for Swiss Re New Markets (SRNM). He is the founding president and CEO of Swiss Re Financial Products and Swiss Re Capital Markets, and president and CEO of Atlantic International Reinsurance Company.

Prakash joined Swiss Re in 1995 to build the company's structured finance and capital markets groups, which have since become part of SRNM's Financial Solutions unit. This unit has pioneered the development of insurance-linked securities, multi-trigger products, contingent capital and other products that reflect the convergence of the insurance and capital markets.

Prior to joining Swiss Re, Prakash was managing director in the Global Insurance Corporate Finance Division of Chase Manhattan Bank, with responsibility for providing asset and liability management advisory services, as well as for derivatives transactions. Prakash previously was vice president and manager of the Insurance Portfolio Strategies Group at Drexel Burnham Lambert.

Prakash earned a B.S. degree in economics and statistics and an M.S. in operational research from the London School of Economics and Political Science, as well as an M.B.A. in finance and international business from the University of Chicago. He is a Fellow of the Society of Actuaries, holds a certificate in Actuarial Techniques from the Institute of Actuaries (U.K.) and is a chartered financial analyst.

David Durbin, Ph.D.
Head of Cat Perils & Retrocession
Swiss Re

David is head of Swiss Re's cat perils and retrocession in Zurich. He previously led Swiss Re's North American economic research and consulting unit where he was responsible for directing a wide-ranging research program for understanding the relationships and interactions between the general economy, capital markets, and the insurance and reinsurance markets as well as strategic consulting in North America.

David holds a Ph.D. in economics from the City University of New York and has been involved in insurance-related research for 18 years. He has published extensively on economic factors affecting insurance markets and on optimal design of insurance programs, and has testified in more than 20 states on insurance issues including profitability and the cost of capital.

David S. Laster, Ph.D.
Senior Economist, Economic Research & Consulting
Swiss Re

David is a senior economist in Swiss Re's North American economic research and consulting unit. Specializing in capital market topics, he is engaged in a variety of strategic consulting projects for Swiss Re and its clients. His current areas of research include asset-liability management, the demutualization of insurers, integrated risk management, and the securitization of insurance risk.

David holds a B.A. in mathematics from Yale University and a Ph.D. in economics from Columbia University. Prior to joining Swiss Re, he was a financial economist at the Federal Reserve Bank of New York. His work has appeared in the *Financial Analysts Journal, the Journal of Investing,* and the *Quarterly Journal of Economics.*

Carolyn P. Helbling
Group Head of Market Communications
Swiss Re

Carolyn is Swiss Re Group's head of market communications. Previously she served as a director in corporate marketing at Swiss Re New Markets, where she addressed the risk financing needs of telecommunications and high-technology clients. During her career at Swiss Re, she has been involved in the development of a number of blended and alternative risk structures for Fortune 500 clients both in the U.S. and Europe. These include integrated programs ranging from broad risk transfer multi-line insurance covers to the application of capital markets techniques for corporate risk financing needs.

Prior to joining Swiss Re in 1989, Carolyn was a consultant to the retail petroleum industry, working in the United Kingdom, Germany and in the U.S. She graduated with honors in 1981 from London University and was awarded a scholarship to study for one year at the University of Freiburg-im-Breisgau in Germany. Carolyn is a frequent speaker and panelist at alternative risk financing conferences and was chief author of a recent Swiss Re publication, *Rethinking Risk Financing.*

Daniel Helbling
Associate Director, Risk Underwriting
Swiss Re New Markets

Daniel is responsible for property risk underwriting for chemical and pharmaceutical Fortune 500 clients. Previously he acted as Swiss Re New Markets' client relationship manager for a number of U.S. Fortune 500 oil and energy companies. He has worked on the forefront of ART since he joined Swiss Re in 1990 as a property underwriter, helping to structure coverage of on- and offshore energy risks for Shell, Chevron and British Gas, among others. He brought with him a practical background and understanding of the client's viewpoint when he began working for SRNM at its formation in 1997.

Daniel began his career with Shell Chemical in 1986, marketing performance plastics to European, U.S. and Asian clients. He holds a degree in chemical engineering from the Technical University in Winterthur, Switzerland.

Esther Baur
Senior Economist, Economic Research & Consulting
Swiss Re

Esther is a senior economist and deputy head at Swiss Re's economic research and consulting department in Zurich. She is the author of several *sigma* studies on trends in the worldwide insurance industries, covering a broad range of topics, including the emerging insurance markets of Latin America and Eastern Europe, worldwide solvency issues and, most recently, trends in the ART market.

Esther established Swiss Re's North American economic research and consulting unit in 1998, and has spent several months researching for Swiss Re in Latin America. She holds an M.A. in economics from the University of St. Gallen, Switzerland.

Gail Belonsky, Ph.D.

Gail formerly headed the insurance securitization group at Swiss Re New Markets, and pioneered the development of a number of proprietary insurance-related financial instruments. She has executed insurance securitizations and committed capital facilities in Japan, the U.S. and Europe, and had overall responsibility for SRNM's catastrophe trading book. Previously, Gail was a vice president in the mortgage-backed securities department at Drexel Burnham Lambert, where she structured, issued and traded collateralized mortgage obligations.

Gail, a registered securities representative in the U.S. and the U.K., earned a Ph.D. in finance from the University of California at Berkeley, an M.S. from the University of Guelph and a B.S. from Cornell University. She has been an economic consultant at the New York Stock Exchange, researching several isues related to market quality and order strategy.

David Colarossi, CPA
Associate Director
Swiss Re New Markets

David is an associate director in Swiss Re New Markets' financial solutions group. He has developed and marketed a variety of insurance-linked financial instruments, including catastrophe bonds, Swiss Re's TOPS™ (Triggered Optional Preferred Securities) and CLOCS™ (Committed Long-term Capital Securities) products, integrated risk products, and insurance-related swaps and options. David joined Swiss Re in 1996. Prior to that he worked in the Financial Instrument Strategies Group of Deloitte & Touche Consulting.

David holds a B.S. in industrial engineering from Cornell University, and an M.S. in accounting and M.B.A in finance from New York University. David is a Certified Public Accountant and a candidate for chartered financial analyst. He is also a registered securities representative in the U.S. and the U.K.

Diane Houghton, CPCU
Associate Director
Swiss Re New Markets

Diane joined Swiss Re in 1989, working as a supervising claims consultant for Swiss Re's North American Division until transferring to Swiss Re New Markets in 1998. She is presently an associate director in SRNM's financial solutions, where she concentrates on developing run-off business and managing the due diligence process for risky run-off and all other ART-oriented deals.

Diane managed a department of claims specialists as assistant vice president of claims at Walter Kaye Associates from 1984 to 1989. She has a B.A. from Rutgers University, and holds a CPCU and an ARe. She is presently serving as president of communications for the New York Chapter of CPCU, and is a member of the Reinsurance Committee for the National CPCU Society.

Kai-Uwe Schanz, Ph.D.
Head of Economic Research & Consulting, Asia
Swiss Re

Kai joined Swiss Re in 1995 as an economist. In 1997 he was promoted to senior economist, and in 1998 he established Swiss Re Economic Research & Consulting (Asia) in Hong Kong. Kai's areas of specialty are ART, Asia-Pacific insurance markets and issues related to the world trading system. He has edited various Swiss Re *sigma* studies, and composed several pieces for Swiss Re's executive board.

From 1992-1995 he worked as a project leader and lecturer at the Swiss Institute of International Economic Relations in St. Gallen, Switzerland. Kai earned his Ph.D. in economics at the Swiss University of St. Gallen and his M.A. at the German University of Konstanz. He has published in *National Underwriter, The Review, Asia Insurance Review, Asia Cover* and the *Geneva Papers on Risk and Insurance*.

J. Scott Turner
Associate Director
Swiss Re New Markets

Scott joined Swiss Re in April 1997. He is now primarily involved in new product development for Swiss Re New Markets' financial solutions group. He joined Swiss Re from AIG Risk Finance, where he designed and marketed finite risk products for Fortune 500 clients. Scott gained primary and excess insurance experience with American Home Assurance Company and AIG Risk Management. Prior to AIG, he worked as a financial analyst at Smith Barney.

Scott received his B.A. in international studies from Johns Hopkins University and holds an M.B.A. from George Washington University in international business and finance. He is a registered securities representative in the U.S.

Acknowledgments

The editors and authors have benefited from the support of Swiss Re Group, in particular Erwin Zimmermann, as well as the valuable contributions of many colleagues at Swiss Re. Each chapter credits the principal authors, but a number of people helped shape the content with their ideas, suggestions and, in some cases, text. For this we thank: Larry Berger, Tim Cuddihy, Ed Ford, Pete Gakos, Ben Lashkari, Bill Anderson, Levi Pearson and Oliver Horbelt of Swiss Re, as well as Dr. Michael Selby of the University of London. Just as important is the production effort. We would like to thank Brendan Greeley for his editorial support and Evelyn Moreno, who developed the graphic design, as well as Joy Stapleton, Patricia Anderson, Antoinette Breutel-O'Donoghue, Juan Pertuz, Rudolf Hitzler and Gary Sullivan for transforming these ideas into a finished work.

Index

Swiss Re New Markets

Swiss Re New Markets combines (re)insurance-based innovations with other elements of corporate finance to help clients enhance capital efficiency, stabilize earnings and add shareholder value. It is a division of Swiss Reinsurance Company, a leading reinsurer, and the world's largest life reinsurer. With more than 9000 employees, Swiss Re is represented at more than 70 offices in over 30 countries worldwide. Gross premiums in 1999 amounted to CHF 22.4 billion, and the ordinary result after tax to CHF 2.8 billion. Swiss Re is rated "Aaa" by Moody's and "AAA" by Standard & Poor's.

http://www.swissre.com/newmarkets